James A. Robertson

Concise Historical Proofs Respecting the Gael of Alban

Or, Highlanders of Scotland, as descended of the Caledonian Picts

James A. Robertson

Concise Historical Proofs Respecting the Gael of Alban

Or, Highlanders of Scotland, as descended of the Caledonian Picts

ISBN/EAN: 9783337331641

Printed in Europe, USA, Canada, Australia, Japan

Cover: Foto ©ninafisch / pixelio.de

More available books at **www.hansebooks.com**

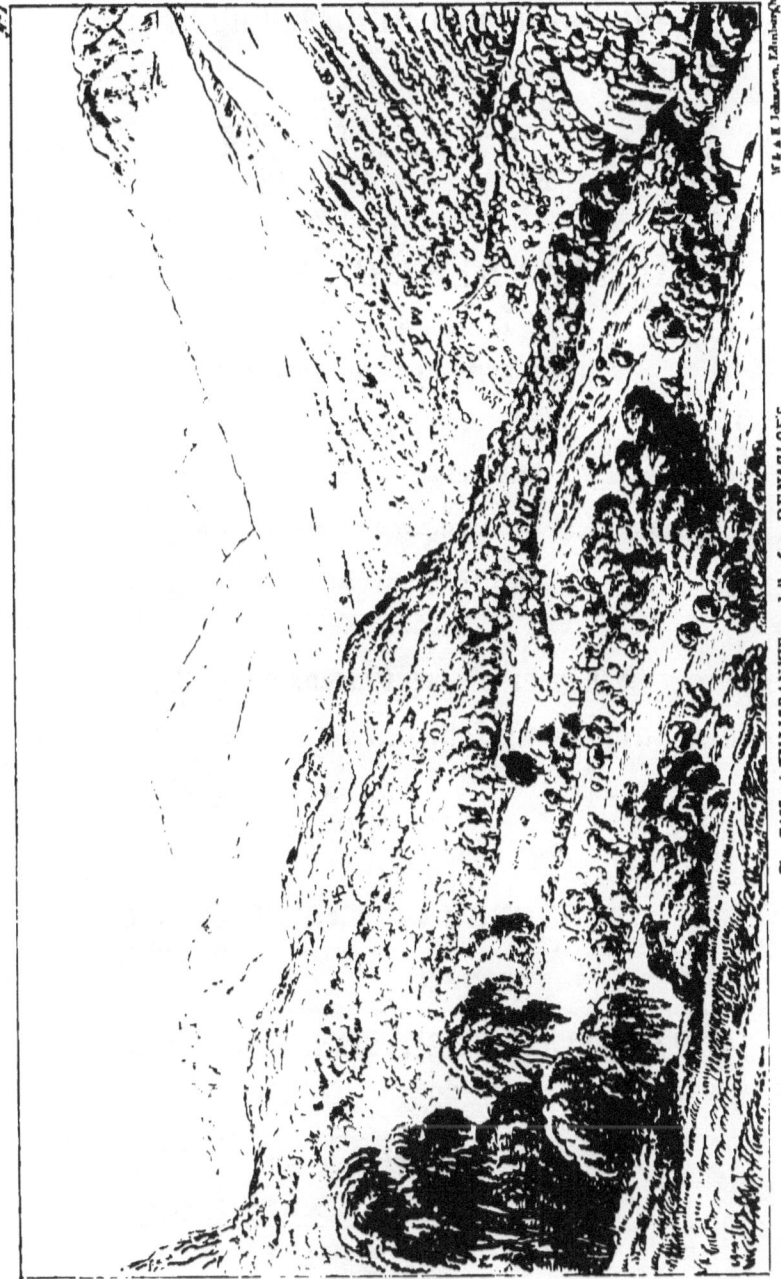
The PASS of KILLICRANKIE and the far BENAGLOE'S

CONCISE HISTORICAL PROOFS

RESPECTING

The Gael of Alban;

OR,

HIGHLANDERS OF SCOTLAND,

AS DESCENDED OF THE

CALEDONIAN PICTS,

WITH

THE ORIGIN OF THE IRISH SCOTS, OR DALRIADS, IN NORTH BRITAIN.

AND THEIR SUPPOSED CONQUEST OVER THE CALEDONIAN PICTS.

EXAMINED AND REFUTED.

ALSO THE

Language of the Caledonian Picts,

SHORT NOTICES REGARDING THE HIGHLAND CLANS.

*WITH EXPLANATORY NOTES, MAP, ILLUSTRATIONS,
AND DESCRIPTIONS,*

OF THE

COUNTRY OF THE GAEL.

BY

JAMES A. ROBERTSON, F.S.A., Scot.

EDINBURGH:
WILLIAM P. NIMMO, ST JAMES'S SQUARE.
SIMPKIN, MARSHALL, & CO., LONDON.

MDCCCLXV.

Crawford & M'Cabe, Printers, 7 George Street, Edinburgh.

Preface.

THE Highlanders of Scotland are unquestionably a most interesting race of people, the true descendants of the ancient Caledonians; and though their early history has been greatly obscured by some pretended historians, and continues to be so even to this day, whereby readers are misled, yet the true narration of ancient facts respecting them, is independent of all the vain prejudice of those who would represent them, and their language, to be merely derived from the insignificant colony of Irish Scots which came into Argyleshire in the sixth century, where still remain their descendants, properly the *only Scots* in Scotland. With this in view, the writer submits the present small work, which is not dictated with a desire merely to contradict others, but to point out and establish the truth, without any intention to depreciate previous writers. This he has endeavoured to do in a charitable spirit, when *obliged* to notice manifest errors (and for this the writer has always given the proofs and reasons), or when forced, in maintaining the liberty of opinion, to express decided opposite views to some who have not founded their assertions on proper evidence. The necessary researches on the ancient historical points herein treated of were commenced four years ago, and have been continued ever since, and originally were intended as a continuation of a small work the author wrote on the ancient Earldom of Atholl, which embraces the whole North Highlands of Perthshire. The investigations have led to the present volume, which has no pretensions to anything but a desire to place the true early history of the origin, etc., etc., of his countrymen, the Highlanders of Scotland, on an undeniable trustworthy foundation, supported by proofs and authorities, and to refute the unfounded claims of some grasping Irish writers, as also the false assertions of some Scottish ones.

Preface. vii

Much pains has been taken to make the proofs concise upon the subjects brought forward, at the same time, to be sufficiently comprehensive. A careful perusal will best enable the reader to judge on this point; and the explanatory notes being read along with the text is essential to the full understanding of what is wished to be known. There has been no attempt made otherwise than to convey to the reader as much strictly accurate, historical, and antiquarian information as possible, and thereby lead to the true understanding of the early history of the descendants of the noble race of the Caledonian Gael. Upon the subject of their language, it is hoped that some of the Highland clergymen, or others, may follow that subject in a similar manner, as the writer has endeavoured to do.

The descriptions of the illustrations of the country of the Gael of Alban will be found in a chapter together, though they are themselves placed in different parts of the work. This collection of proofs from the earliest times may, it is also hoped, prove useful to future writers who wish to go into greater detail, and that some interest may be felt in the Pictish Gael, who have been by many hitherto looked upon as quite an unknown people, and as the Rev. Isaac Taylor[1] says, '*disappear mysteriously*,' as also the supposed destruction of their language, the greatest marvel of its kind that ever passed for truth.

The writer had not the opportunity to notice, in the proper place (on the dress of the Caledonian Gael), the embellishment that appears on the binding. It is the most faithful representation of the ancient Highlanders' dress that can be given to the reader. It is derived from two different sculptured stones, namely, from that of Dull, Perthshire, which is described page 232, and it is a fac-simile of the countenance, bonnet, and shield of one of the figures thereon. The arrangement of the 'Breacan-an-fheilidh,' that is, 'the belted plaid,' or full dress of the ancient Gael or Highlanders, is a faithful copy from another ancient sculptured stone found at St Andrews. Both these sculptures are to be seen in the

[1] See the Rev. Isaac Taylor's 'Words and Places,' 2d edition, 1865, page 245.

Museum of the Antiquaries of Scotland, Edinburgh, open to the public, and wherewith the embellishment can be compared. The Map also, it is hoped, along with a most copious index, and very full table of contents, may prove useful to the reader.

The writer also expects hereafter to be enabled to bring out a short Supplement to this small work, containing further ancient historical and antiquarian information, interesting not only to the Highlanders, but also to all Scotchmen.

<small>118 Princes Street, Edinburgh,
5th July 1865.</small>

Contents.

CHAPTER I.

Introductory — Statement of the subjects to be treated of and proved 1

CHAPTER II.

Roman Invasion of Caledonia began in A.D. 78—Campaigns of Agricola to A.D. 85—Roman walls built—War carried on by the Romans under the Emperors Commodus and Severus—The Caledonian Gael nobly resist, and Severus retires and builds his Wall—A.D. 296, name of Picts given by Roman writers to the Caledonians—Picts and Caledonians proved to be identical—Events to A.D. 360 9

Contents.

CHAPTER III.

A.D. 360, the Scots first named, and appeared in North Britain, proved to be natives of Ireland—Proof that the Scots returned to their own country, Ireland—Roman war continued south of the Forth from A.D. 360 to A.D. 380—Proofs that the Scots belonged to Ireland alone, and that it was called Scotia from many ancient writers—A.D. 409, Roman Emperor Constantine slain—Departure of the Romans—Arrival of the Saxons . 19

CHAPTER IV.

True period of the first arrival of the Irish Scots Colony in Argyleshire proved to have been in A.D. 506—Proofs and Authorities given—Events up to A.D. 560 32

CHAPTER V.

The introduction of Christianity into North Britain, and its proper date—The error of a pretended mission of Palladius to Scots in North Britain A.D. 431 pointed out—Unsupported assertions as to the period of Christianity being in present Scotland shown—Arrival of Columba—His mission and success—Martyrdom in Kintyre, the country of the Irish Scots, of a Christian mission-

Contents.

PAGE

ary named Constantine, in or about A.D. 590—
Proof thereby of the majority of the inhabitants
being heathen, ... 46

CHAPTER VI.

Situation and extent of country of the various races in North Britain in the seventh century—Events to the end of that century—Early in the eighth century (A.D. 733) the Irish Scots Colony in Argyleshire attacked, defeated, and placed under subjection, by Angus M'Fergus, king of the Pictish Gael—King Angus placed a prince of his own family to rule the Dalriad country A.D. 749—Death of this great king of the Picts A.D. 761—Events to A.D. 794 when the Danes first appear—Events from A.D. 802 to 842, ... 59

CHAPTER VII.

The pretended conquest of the Caledonian Picts (the real ancestors of the Highlanders) in A.D. 843 by the Colony of Irish Scots of Argyleshire—Examined and Refuted by most numerous authorities both modern and ancient—Historical events from that period and other proofs to 1158 given, ... 76

CHAPTER VIII.

The Language of the Picts—Proved to be the same as the present Highlanders of Scotland—Numerous proofs from names of places in the Lothians or south of Scotland, whence the Picts had been wholly dispossessed by A.D. 547—Yet their language remains in these names they left behind them—Which also correspond with others in the Highlands—And also are identical with the language of the Highlanders of this day, . 118

CHAPTER IX.

The language of the Picts continued—Conclusive proofs against a new language or Gaelic brought in at the time of the fabulous conquest of Kenneth MacAlpin in A.D. 843—There being British names of places in Scotland, no proof they were given by the Picts—No British or Welsh names north of the Moray Firth or in the Islands of Skye, Lewis, Harris, etc., etc., yet all this territory was originally and for centuries Pictish—Proof also of the Picts' language being the same as the present Highlanders from Ossian's Poems—Numerous proofs of names of places given prior to Christianity—All in the Gaelic of the present day, ... 138

Contents.

xv

CHAPTER X.

PAGE

The Poetry of the Gael of Alban, with examples from Ossian and others—the National Dress of the Highlanders—Proved to be so from the most remote times, as also their Arms—and by a connected series of proofs brought down to the suppression of the Dress last century—The original Pipe Music of the Highlanders—With proofs, . 197

CHAPTER XI.

Short notices of the Highland Clans—Old Act of Parliament as to them, explanatory notes thereon—Information of the force and strength of the clans and their chiefs—The badges of the clans—War cries, etc., etc.—The historical origin of the chieftains of each clan, ... 258

CHAPTER XII.

Historical and antiquarian descriptions of the various illustrations given in the Work—Explanatory remarks on the Map, ... 328

CONCLUSION.

Showing the points which have been proved. . 353

APPENDIX.

List of the Sovereigns over the land of Alban from A.D. 554 to the present day—Ancient Gaelic poem composed in 1057, called the Alban Duan—Ancient documents illustrating the population of the Highlands—The power of the chiefs to raise men—A very ancient charter by a Bishop of Dunkeld, ... 357

ERRATA.

Page 89, marginal date, *for* '4 9,' *read* '849.'
.. 174, *for* 'Laithfail,' *read* 'Liathfail.'
.. 225, after the word 'bird's,' *insert* 'nest.'
.. 289, *for* 'Fitheah,' *read* 'Fitheach.'
.. 290, *for* 'Creag Allbh,' *read* 'Creig dubh.'

CONCISE HISTORICAL PROOFS

RESPECTING THE

HIGHLANDERS OF SCOTLAND.

CHAPTER I.

Subjects to be treated of and proved.

'Caledonia invicta.'

IT has always been held and said by the Gael of Alban, or Scotch Highlanders, that they are the representatives and descendants of the Caledonians; that noble race of men, who, with success, defended their country and maintained their freedom against all the attacks made on them by large Roman armies, under the command of celebrated generals and emperors, and which resulted in the defeat and withdrawing of the invaders.

To this claim the Highlanders of Scotland can have *no right whatever* unless they are the descendants of the Picts, who were the Caledonians under a new name, equally as at a subsequent period, the Caledonian Picts came to be called Scots. The identity of the Picts and Caledonians will be shown.

With regard to the people called 'Scots,' it ought to be remembered that they were the inhabitants of Hibernia, or Ireland—the name first appears towards the end of the fourth century, at and after which period, some stragling bands of Irish Scots, came over and fought along with the Caledonian Picts against the Romans, yet we have as clear evidence that they returned to their own country,[1] Ireland, as of their being in Caledonia.

The *first* permanent settlement of any Scots in present Scotland, cannot be authenticated till the beginning of the sixth century, or nearly if not quite, a hundred years after the Romans had left the country of the Caledonian Picts.

The Highlanders of present Scotland have ever called their native land Alban, and themselves the Gael Albanach, and do so to this hour; a concise historical narrative will be given of their ancestors the Caledonians and

---

[1] Ample proof will be given that Ireland was the country of the Scots—and also called 'Scotia.'

Subjects to be treated of and proved. 3

Picts, from the first century—as mentioned in the pages of Tacitus' Life of Agricola, and subsequent Roman writers; to the beginning of the fifth century—to these follow Gildas[1] the most ancient British writer,—Adomnan's[2] life of Columba, Bede's[3] history, and Nennius[4]—after this we have those valuable historical authorities 'The Irish Annals' for the succeeding events—as without these annalists, we should know nothing whatever of our early history.

The object, therefore, of this small work is by a short but comprehensive, historical sketch, to show that the Gael of Alban,—or Highlanders of present Scotland, are descended from the Picts, who were identical with the Caledonians—and the only exception to this is, those who derive from the Irish Scots, or Dalriads, who, as already mentioned, first settled in Argyleshire in the sixth century—but even among this branch of the Highland clans, the original native Caledonian Gael of Argyle, must have somewhat mingled with them, from the *very small* numbers[5] of the first settlers from Ireland,

[1] Written in about A.D. 550.
[2] Written in about A.D. 695.
[3] Written in about A.D. 731.
[4] Written in about A.D. 858.
[5] Only fifty men to each of the three leaders who came from Ireland, as will be shown hereafter.   A.D. 506.

and who themselves, it is possible, were also at some very remote period, descended of the same ancestors as the valiant Caledonians.

A most undue antiquity has long been attempted to be given to the settlement of the Scots in present Scotland—it is only to some writers of Irish history, and a few Scotchmen, that we owe the removal of the fables propounded by Fordun, Boece, and Buchanan, who appropriated to Scotland what belonged only to Ireland—for, as was concisely and well stated by the learned Pinkerton,[1] there is *no authority* for the name of present Scotland till the eleventh century.

To those three Scotch authors above mentioned, the obscurity of our national history is due—the first named (Fordun) had finished his Chronicle by the year 1400, and Buchanan his History by 1582—through them the supposed conquest of the Gael of Alban by the insignificant colony of Irish Scots in Argyleshire, has been related and believed; an examination of it will be submitted, as likewise a full and satisfactory refutation, drawn from authentic proofs, and fair deductions therefrom.

In support of the view here expressed of those fabulous writers, the following is from

[1] Pinkerton's Enquiry, Preface. Vol i., page 1. (50); and Vol. ii., page 158.

one of our best modern historical Scotch authors[1]:—

'*The true history* of the last half of the eighth, and first half of the ninth century, *has disappeared* from our annals. Upon this basis the *fabulous* historians reared the superstructure of their history, and through one channel or another it can be *traced to St Andrews.* Its germs are found in the end of the thirteenth and beginning of the fourteenth centuries. It received its first artistic development from John of Fordun, and the crowning capital was placed upon it by Hector Boece.' The important event of the introduction of Christianity among the Caledonian Gael, and *the true* period to be assigned to it, will be plainly stated. With regard to the point who were the first natives of present Scotland, the opinions of two of our historical writers (Innes[2] and Pinkerton) appear correct—namely, that the Cimbri, or Britons, were earliest—though of course very weak in numbers, and scattered along the coasts; whereby they became easily driven out, or absorbed, on the arrival of the far more

---

[1] See the Proceedings, Society of Antiquaries, Scotland, Vol. iv., Part 1, page 321, written by W. F. Skene, Esq , in 1863.

[2] See T. Innes's Critical Essay, Vol. i., pages 29 and 41, where he says—'*The first* place in order of time *is due to the Britons;*' and also of the Caledonian Picts, that they were '*the second* inhabitants of North Britain in order of time.'

numerous Alban Gael—and they (the Britons) disappear altogether from every section of present Scotland, at and after the Roman period, except the south-western parts.

Pinkerton,[1] speaking of them, says that they 'held Scotland *till the Piks came and expelled them.*' It is also, in a similar way, spoken of by an old Scotch writer, called John Mair or Major, who wrote a history of both the English and Scotch people in the year 1512. He rejected some of the fables of Fordun, and in his work (De gestibus Scotorum, lib. ii. cap. 2) says, that 'The Picts frequently possessed Lothian, and those parts beyond the Scottish Sea (that is the Firth of Forth), and the better and more fertile portion of what was north of it; both because they occupied the island before the Scots, and because, by their number and strength, they were superior to the Scots, which is shown by this, *that they* (the Picts) *occupied territory obtained from the Britons.*'

With regard to the period at which the Caledonian Picts first entered present Scotland, and then spread over the whole country, and lastly the islands, the opinion of Pinkerton may be justly considered as by no means too re-

---

[1] Pinkerton's Enquiry. Book 1, page 16.

Subjects to be treated of and proved. 7

mote, if indeed it is sufficiently so. He says, from the direct authority of Nennius—'The settlement of the Piks in the Hebud Isles' (that is, the Western Islands of Scotland) 'may be dated, with as great certainty as any event in the earliest Greek or Roman history, at 300 years *before* Christ.'[1]

Therefore, when it is considered that, in the year A.D. 78, the whole of Caledonia was found fully peopled, and their armies numbering many thousands of men, the inference seems clear, that the earliest settlers of the Alban Gael must have arrived in the country *at least* 500 years before the Christian era.

The language of the Caledonian Picts is a highly interesting point. Proofs, and reasons respecting it, will be fully adduced and submitted, showing, that as there was no conquest of the Picts by the Irish Scots, the former people remained, and of course their language with them; and that it must have been *the same* as that of the present Highlanders, or Gael of Alban, who are *the descendants of the Caledonian Picts.*

A short notice of the subjection of the Irish Scots, or Dalriads, by Angus M·Fergus, the King of the Picts, will be given. Also a short

---

[1] Pinkerton's Enquiry. Vol. i, page 207.

Subjects to be treated of and proved.

sketch of the early origin of the Clans; to those desirous of fuller detail, it will be found in Skene's Highlanders, and Gregory's Western Islands.

There will also be given very ancient proofs that everything accounted as national and peculiar to the Gael, or Highlanders of Scotland, was in no way whatever derived by them from the Irish Scots; but that their national dress, language, poetry, arms, and pipe music, etc. etc., were received from their ancestors, the Caledonian Gael.

Some illustrations and descriptions of their country will be given, which, with a fair consideration of the whole now submitted, it is hoped may interest some.

DUNKELD.

W & A K Johnston, Edinburgh

CHAPTER II.

From the Roman Invasion in A.D. 78 to A.D. 360.

> 'The waies through which my weary steps I guide,
> In this researche of old antiquitie
> Are so exceeding riche, and long, and wyde
> And sprinkled with such sweet varietie
> Of all that pleasant is, to eare and eye,
> That I, nigh ravisht with rare thoughts delight,
> My tedious travel quite forgot thereby
> And when I 'gin to feel *dreay of might*
> It strength to *me supplies* and *cheers* my dulled spright.'
> — SPENSER.

AS already mentioned, the earliest authentic information regarding present Scotland is given us by Tacitus, who recorded the campaigns of his father-in-law, Agricola; these began in the year A.D. 78 in the South of Scotland, and he took two campaigns to subdue what lies south of the Firths of Forth and Clyde.

We are next told by Tacitus (chapter 22)

A.D. 78–80.

A.D. 80.

that Agricola, in the third year of his campaigns, went farther north into the Caledonian territory, and laid waste the whole country to the river Tay. He erected also no less than three large camps, all in Perthshire (and for which see the Map), namely, one at Ardoch, called Lindum by the Romans; one also at Strageth, which they called Ierna, being on the river Earn; and another at Dalginross, near to Comrie, which they named Victoria.[1] These three spacious camps were all situated within the valley called Strathearn, in Perthshire.

A.D. 81.   The fourth summer was employed by Agricola in settling those parts he had overrun.

A.D. 82.   Was the fifth year, and the Roman General appears to have been in Galloway and Ayrshire, as Tacitus says it was that part of Britain which looked on Hibernia, that is, Ireland.

A.D. 83.   The sixth year, he again went north of the Forth, and began to move his army from his three stationary camps already named, whereby they were in three columns or divisions; and which movement, when the Caledonians discovered it, they by night attacked the ninth

---

[1] Tacitus. Chapters 22 to 25.

legion, which was at Victoria, that is Dalginross,[1] and severely assaulted them; and after that fight we hear no more of the exploits of the ninth legion.

The natives of Caledonia, we are told, then sent their wives and children into safe places, and armed every one they could, in defence of their liberty and country; and at this period Tacitus states, in his 27th chapter, that the people sanctioned their engagements *with sacrifices*.

This year the Roman fleet was sent north to plunder the country, and the army also proceeded there. The whole Caledonian forces then united under their king, called Galdi or Galgacus. Their arms[2] are described by Tacitus as huge swords and short targets. There were auxiliary Britons with Agricola's army at this time, and they amounted to no

A.D. 84.

---

[1] Almost directly opposite to where this attack took place, there is at the head of Glenturret, in Strathearn, the hill called in English Benahony, but properly in Gaelic ‘Beinn-na Coineadh’—‘the mountain of weeping.’ The Caledonian Gael likely had retired there after the battle, and the remembrance of those whom they had lost caused the name. The English pronunciation is very near the Gaelic, though the spelling looks so different; in English it is sometimes written Benhonzie—the Gaelic is Beinn'acoineadh.

[2] The very same continued to be the arms of their descendants, the Highlanders of Scotland, up to the middle of the last century.

less than 8000 men. The army of both sides, being assembled[1] opposite each other, prepared for the fight. A very eloquent speech is given by Tacitus, as that of Galcacus to the Caledonians; and if it is only the spirit of what he said, that people were well worthy of obtaining the liberty and independence of their country, for which they were fighting. This battle, called that of 'Mons Grampius,' is with good reason considered to have taken place near Stonehaven (see the Map): but with palpable exaggeration, Tacitus makes the loss of the Caledonians (or Britons as he calls them) to have been 10,000, and of the Romans only 340 men. This victory, however, gave no fruits to Rome, as Agricola, we are told, retired 'by a slow march' into winter quarters, no doubt to his permanent camps in Strathearn, Perthshire.

A.D. 85. This year the Emperor Domitian recalled Agricola. His successor was Trebellius, under whom the Romans lost all they had acquired in Caledonia.

A.D. 120. The Emperor Hadrian next came into Britain; but instead of being able to regain the former Roman territory within Caledonia, he built an extensive turf wall, from the Solway

---

[1] Tacitus. Chapter 28.

Firth to the river Tyne, eighty miles in length, and which then became the Caledonian boundary, and known as Hadrian's Wall; and it is marked in the Map.

Lollius Urbicus was the General of a succeeding Roman Emperor named Antonine, who, having gained some advantages about this time, built a wall[1] where Agricola had previously placed some forts. This wall was called the Wall of Antonine; it extended from the Firth of Forth to the Clyde, and it is shown on the Map. A. D. 140.

From another writer[2] we are told, that of all the wars carried on at this period by the Emperor Commodus, the war in Britain (that is, with the Caledonians) was the greatest; and that, therefore, he sent his general, Ulpius Marcellus, against them, who inflicted heavy losses on them. A.D. 182.

The same author (Dio) says,[3] that the Caledonians at this time did not keep their promises, but prepared to defend their fellow countrymen near the north and south of the Forth, called by the Roman writers the A.D. 197.

---

[1] This wall must undoubtedly have gone through the country of the southern Caledonian Gael, after this known as Meatæ, and who partly lay in the Lothians, etc. etc.

[2] Dio. Book 72, chapter 8.

[3] Book 75, chapter 5.

Meatæ[1]; and the Roman General had to obtain peace by a large sum of money.

A.D. 207. The Emperor Severus entered Caledonia this year, says Dio, to reduce and conquer it; but had much more to do than he expected—from the forests, marshes, and rivers—the native Caledonians also continually harassing the Roman soldiers, who fell into ambushes and snares, and they also suffered from the want of water. The losses of the Romans are put down by this writer at 50,000: and after having reached no further than the Moray Firth, the Emperor retired, having previously entered into a treaty with the Caledonians, by which they agreed to yield a part of their country — probably what lay south of the Forth—and this likely was done to get rid of the Romans.

A.D. 208. This year the Emperor Severus seems to have retired altogether from the hopeless effort to conquer the Caledonians, as he now built his immense wall, close to Hadrian's, going from

---

[1] This word is considered to be similar to the May in Invermay and Innermeath, Perthshire, and Meath in Ireland, being only the Latinised form of it. There is also the Gaelic word '*maith*' for '*good*,' which might have been applied to the Lothians, a part of the country of this portion of the Caledonian people. Innes calls the Meatæ, Britons; but this they could not be, as the Caledonians were ever their enemies.

the Solway to the Tyne. This was the greatest of all the walls of the Romans, and became known as the Wall of Severus; and again it formed the Caledonian southern boundary, and will be found laid down in the Map. It is most highly honourable to the Caledonian Gael the noble resistance they made to retain the liberty of their country; and the building of these walls was the greatest proof the Romans could give, that to conquer Caledonia was a hopeless task.

The next thing to be recorded, is the first intimation we have of the name of the 'Picti' or 'Picts'—this is by the orator Eumenius in the year A.D. 296; which was the date of his first oration, and delivered in the presence of the Roman Emperor Constantius, and he therein speaks of 'the Picts' and Irish as the only enemies the Britons had known prior to the Romans.

A.D. 296–309.

It is very material to be understood, that the Picts were identical, and in every way the same people as the Caledonians, only under a new name; precisely as, before said, at a still later period they came to be called Scots;— and this fact is proved by the same author (Eumenius) when he delivered a second oration —in 309—before the Emperor Constantine, son of the above Constantius, wherein he speaks of 'Caledonii et alii Picti,' that is, '*the Caledonians and other Picts.*'

Thus the same author who first speaks of them proves their identity.

The name undoubtedly came from the practice of self-painting—and which, Cæsar[1] says, was universal with the Britons—the writer Herodian also states[2] that in the time of the Emperor Servius, when he made his invasion to the north in A.D. 207, the Caledonians were all painted; also the Roman poet Claudian says, as if to justify the new name

'Nec falso nomine Pictos'

'Not wrongly named Picts (or painted).'

This same author is quoted by Robertson in his work on the early kings of Scotland[3] (vol. ii., page 225, in a note), and also by Kitson in his Annals of Caledonians, vol. i., pages 18, 19, showing the manner in which it was done, namely punctured or traced with iron, probably needles:

'ferroque notatas
Perlegit exangues Picto moriente figuras.'[4]

[1] Cæsar, lib. 5, cap. 14.
[2] Herodian, lib. 3.
[3] This book is the most authentic and valuable history ever written on ancient Scotland.
[4] Claudian de Bel. Get. 416.

'He discovers bloodless figures with iron marked,
Upon the dying Pict.'[1]

The earliest Scotch writer on the identity of the Picts, and Caledonians, is T. Innes,— he most clearly proves the impossibility of the Picts being a new people who had come into the Caledonian territory in the third century —(see his work, vol. 1., page 451). He is commonly called father Innes, from being a Roman Catholic Priest. His work is in two volumes, and called a 'Critical Essay,' etc.— many of the foregoing authorities have been derived from it—in his second volume some valuable documents were given for the first time to the public—the date of his work is 1729.

In the end of last century (1790) the learned antiquarian writer, Pinkerton, also declares that the Caledonians and Picts were unquestionably the same people, he says, 'it is unnecessary to dwell longer on a subject so universally known and allowed, as the identity of the Caledonians and Piks, and which, indeed, no one can deny, who does not prefer his own dreams to ancient authorities of the best note.'[2]

[1] The writer of the book called 'the Scottish Nation,' in defiance of authorities says, 'the word Pict does not mean painted;' this conjecture, he appears to have adopted from the one made by Chalmers without authority.—See Scot. Nation. p. 208, word 'Fife.'

[2] Pinkerton's Enquiry Book, *i.*, page 120.

The Roman Invasion.

Skene says, 'We may, therefore, hold it established as an incontrovertible fact, that the Picts and Caledonians were the same people, appearing at different times under different appellations.'[1] Chalmers, the historian, also testifies to the Picts and Caledonians being the same, he says,[2] '*the Picts were the old Caledonians under a new name.*'

A.D. 360. Up to this period we have never heard of the people called the Scots. The Caledonian Picts alone are mentioned in history, the manner in which this new people from Ireland first appear in North Britain, and afterwards came to form a settlement in Argyleshire, will be fully treated of in the next chapter.

[1] See Skene's Highlanders, vol. i., page 14. Edition 1837.
[2] Chalmer's Caledonia, vol. i., page 225.

CHAPTER III.

From A.D. 360 to departure of the Romans A.D. 410, and arrival of the Saxons in A.D. 449.

IT is at this date that we *first* hear of the people called 'the Scots;' but they were *not natives* of present Scotland. This is most clearly proved and made known by the Roman writer, Ammianus Marcellinus, the *first* author who mentions them. He says[1]—' Eo tempore Picti in duas gentes divisi, Dicaledones et Victuriones, itidemque Attacotti bellicosa hominum natio — *et Scoti per diversi vagantes* multa populabantur;' that is—' At that time the Picts divided into two nations, the Dicaledones and the Victuriones, likewise the Attacots, a warlike nation of men, *and the Scots wandering about various parts* ravaged many.'

Thus this author most distinctly makes

A.D. 360-364.

---

[1] Liber 27, cap. 8.

known that these '*Scoti vagantes*' or '*wandering Scots*' were *not* natives; and further, from the oldest British writer Gildas, we have clear proof from whence they came—namely, from Ireland—to plunder the Roman province in the south of present Scotland. He says[1]—'Revertuntur ergo *impudentes grassatores Hiberni domum*'—which is, 'The impudent *Hibernian robbers* therefore *return home*.' Those writers who attempt to make it believed that these Irish Scots were natives of present Scotland, or conceal what the Roman author Ammianus and Gildas say of them, suppress the truth and deceive their readers.[2]

The learned Dr Reeves, in his edition of the Life of Columba by Adomnan, has an excellent note on this subject, when remarking on what Bede says of these Irish

[1] Gildas, cap. 19.
[2] The writer of the recent work called 'The Early Scottish Church,' the Reverend Dr Thomas M'Lauchlan, in speaking (at page 23) of *the first* appearance of the Scots in A.D. 360, makes *no mention* of what Ammianus calls them, or what Gildas says of their return to Ireland *their home;* but in defiance of these authorities, asserts (at page 23)—'*every reliable testimony* that can be gathered from ancient writers on the subject goes to show, *that so early as* A.D. 360 the Picts inhabited the east and north of Scotland, while a people called *then for the first time Scots, inhabited the west.*' As there is *no other authority* for the name of Scots at A.D. 360 but Ammianus and Gildas as to their native country, we see how grossly in contradiction is the assertion of this writer *to their testimony*.

Scots coming into North Britain—'The occupation by these Scots was anterior to the Dalriadic settlement in 502.[1] They were more migratory, but to guard against mistake concerning *their origin*, he (Bede) calls *these same marauders Hiberni*;[2] lower down (chapter 14), the mention of Scoti in Britain no more proves that *it was Scotia*, than that of Romani does that it was Rome.'[3]

The Gaelic name given to the Scots is extremely applicable and highly descriptive—calling them 'Scuit,' or 'wanderers,' exactly corresponding with the Roman writer's designation of their being 'Scoti vagantes'—'Scotch wanderers;' in fact, the word Scoti seems to be but a Latinised form of the Gaelic Scuit.

The word in Irish is very similar—namely, Sceite, meaning scattered, as shown by Chalmers, in his Caledonia.[4] The Britons or Welsh call it almost the same—namely, Y-scut; and the old Saxon chronicle, Sceotas.

[1] This is a misprint for 506, as Dr Reeves accepts that as the correct date in his notice of the origin of the Dalriads in this same work, page 433.

[2] Here we have the express authority of Bede to refute the Reverend Dr Thomas M'Lauchlan's assertion, as quoted in the foregoing note, that these Scots were inhabitants of the west of present Scotland, as being in *direct opposition* to Bede's testimony, who declares them to be ' *Hiberni*,' or ' *Irishmen* '

[3] See Reeves's Edition of Adomnan, page 184, note

[4] See Chalmers's Caledonia, vol. i., page 271.

22 A.D. 360 to Roman departure A.D. 410.

In the extract from Ammianus, given at the beginning of this chapter, we are informed of the Picts forming into two divisions—one of which, it will be seen, is called the 'Dicaledones.' This has always been considered a strong proof of the identity of the Picts and Caledonians, and which it certainly is.

Of the other people named in the extract (the Attacoti), they are never mentioned after A.D. 368 till the early part of the fifth century, when, according to an extract from Orosius given by Skene,[1] they had joined the Roman army, and so become the enemies of the Caledonian Picts.

<small>A.D. 360-380.</small> Ammianus informs us of several attacks being made by the Picts and Irish Scots on the Roman province in the south of Scotland between these two periods, and on one occasion they are mentioned as having broken the truce; but it would be ludicrous to suppose that any Roman general or emperor ever entered into a truce with these 'Scoti vagantes,' mere Scotch wandering plunderers, or 'predatory bands,' as Skene calls them.[2] With the Pictish nation and people, no doubt, the Romans would do so; but as a very recent

---

[1] Skene's Highlanders, vol. i., page 14.
[2] Introduction to the Book of the Dean of Lismore, page xxiii., date 1862.

writer[1] obscures this point in such a manner as likely to lead readers into error, there was a necessity to notice it.

We are also informed by the same Roman writer,[2] that in the year A.D. 369 the Roman General Theodosius reasserted the power of the Roman arms over that part of the country of the Caledonian Picts that was south of the Forth, and recovered the province, and named it Valentia, after the Emperor Valens.

The Roman poet Claudian wrote at this period. A.D. 400. He states that it was from Ireland the Scots came into Britain, proving the former to be their proper native country. He (Claudian) thus introduces Britannia,[3] saying—

... 'Totam quum *Scotus* Iernen
Movit, et infesto spumavit remige Tethys.'

... 'When all Ierne *the Scot* in motion put,
And Tethy's foamed with the vexatious oar.'

---

[1] Namely, the Rev. Dr Thomas M'Lauchlan, in his book called 'The Early Scottish Church,' which, from its title, would imply it was devoted to what concerned the Church *alone*, instead of which, its contents are quite as much composed of conjectures and assertions on civil events, and as to *the Scots plunderers* from Ireland of this period, see this writer's book, page 17, where appears that the *Scots* broke the peace.

[2] Liber 27, cap. 9.

[3] Claudian, liber 2, v. 140. See Ritson's Caledonian Annals, vol. i., page 152.

The word here used for Ireland, Ierne, is the same as Hibernia; and Tethys is a poetical name for the sea, being in Roman mythology, wife of Oceanus—hence evidently arose the expression of the Tethycan valley of Gildas,[1] or sea[2] between Ireland and Scotland, but which some authors have vainly attempted to say should be either Scythicum, or Scoticum valley. Of such a reading, Ritson[3] proves no MS. has yet been found, and he gives several examples from Virgil and Claudian as to Tethys, meaning the sea.

Orosius[4] is the next author who mentions the Scots. He wrote in or about A.D. 430. He states that the Scots were the inhabitants of Ireland, and calls them 'Scotorum gentes.'

Here it is right to mention, that no ancient writer calls the Irish Scots, either Goths, or had come from Scythia. The assertion is shown to be absurd, as the Scots of Ireland *spoke Gaelic,* not Gothic.

Gildas, the oldest British author, in or

---

[1] Gildas, cap. 15, and Nennius, cap. 27.
[2] Dr Reeves gives two examples in Irish Gaelic of the sea being called, figuratively, a plain.—See Adomnan's Life of Columba, note, page 184.
[3] Annals Caledonian, vol. i., pages 165-166.
[4] Liber 1, cap. 2, as quoted in Maitland's History of Scotland, introduction, vol. i., page 19

about A.D. 550, as already quoted, says *the Scots* robbers returned home to Hibernia.

Isidore, who wrote A.D. 600, proves that the name of *Scotia* was identical with Ireland, and applied to it. From this author we also learn that the Irish Scots were Picti, or painted, as well as the Gael of Alban, he says,[1] . . . '*Scoti* propriâ linguâ nomen habent *a Picto corpore*, eo quod aculeis ferreis cum atramento variarum figurarum stigmata annotentur.'— that is, '*the Scots* in their own tongue have their name from *the painted body*, for that they are marked by sharp-pointed instruments of iron, in blackish stuff, with various figures.'

There can be *no mistake* about the people to whom he alludes, for elsewhere he says, '*Scotia, eadem et Hibernia* . . . quod a Scotorum gentibus, colitur, appellata,'— that is, '*Scotland is the same as Hibernia*, and called so from the Scots people.'

Here Ireland is clearly proved to be *Scotia*, or the country of the Scots; but there is another ancient writer who likewise proves the same thing, and one of the highest authority, namely, Adomnan (who wrote A.D. 695). His

---

[1] Liber 9, cap. 2, and Liber 14, cap. 6, as quoted by Robertson in his Scotland, under her early kings, vol. ii., pages 362 and 363—note, as here given.

work has very numerous instances of Ireland being *Scotia*, that is, Scotland—the following, however, is amply sufficient. Speaking of the country from whence Columba came, he says,[1] that it was '*de Scotia ad Britanniam*,' 'from Scotia to Britain,' which, with the other authorities already given, should exclude all doubt on this point. Yet some vain and prejudiced Scotch authors, though they have not *a writer*, or vestige of authority to show that north Britain was called Scotia at this period, *or for centuries afterwards*, they attempt to decry these historical evidences.

The next authority on the subject is Bede (he wrote A.D. 731), and to whom reference has already been made in the quotation from Dr Reeves. In another place he even more strongly speaks of the Scots being natives of Ireland. He says,[2] ' Hæc (Hibernia) autem proprie patria Scottorum est,' meaning, 'Ireland is properly the country of the Scots;' but in conclusion of this point there is a large and very numerous collection of authorities made by Cambden, quoted by Chalmers in his Caledonia,[3] wherein Ireland is clearly proved *to be Scotia*, and to place it beyond any cavil, it is

---

[1] Dr Reeves's edition of Adomnan, page 9.
[2] Bede, Lib. 1, cap. 1.
[3] See Caledonia, vol. i., page 272.

and arrival of the Saxons in A.D. 449. 27

also most distinctly shown by four ancient writers *to be an island*.

The narrative will be now continued from A.D. 400, the last date mentioned.

The Roman Emperor Constantine was in or about this year slain in Gaul, and the island of Britain then revolted. A.D. 409.

Gildas[1] tells us that this year the Romans sent a legion from Gaul to the aid of the Britons against the Caledonian Picts. A.D. 414.

This year (according to the Saxon chronicle) the Romans left south Britain; they had, of course, previously evacuated the country of the Caledonian Picts, probably eight or ten years sooner. A.D. 418.

Thus ended the Roman aggression in the land of the Gael, and which had lasted for the long period of at least 330 years, and the Highlanders of Scotland can say, that by the valour of their ancestors, Caledonia remained free and unconquered.

The southern Britons,[2] suffering greatly from the incursions of the Picts, the Saxon chronicle states under the above date, 'This year the Britons sent over sea to Rome, and prayed help against the Picts (called therein A.D. 443.

---

[1] Gildas, cap. 12.

[2] That means those Britons south of the wall of Severus, which went from the Solway firth to the river Tyne.

Peohtas), but they had none.' Here it is to be observed there is no mention of Scots, it was against their well known and most numerous enemies, the Caledonian Picts, they desired aid.

A.D. 449. This year Bede and the Saxon chronicle relate, that the Britons invited the Angles and Saxons over to their assistance against the Picts, yet there is reason to believe their first arrival was at an earlier period,[1] and it is now generally understood that this new race of people formed their settlements in Britain by a long course of predatory invasions. They did not become formidable enemies to the Caledonian Picts till about the middle of the next century, whereby a very considerable period of peace existed in the country of the Gael of Alban.

There is a very curious and highly ancient structure that still exists in the south of Scotland, which deserves to be here mentioned; it is called 'the Picts Work;' also 'the Catrail.' From its great extent (upwards of fifty miles) it must have been formed by a vast amount of labour. Almost every writer on it, Chalmers included, consider it to have been formed soon

---

[1] See a communication written by W. F. Skene, Esq., Proceedings, Society of Antiquaries, Scot., vol. iv., part 1, page 269.

and arrival of the Saxons in A.D. 419.

after the Romans left Caledonia, and that it was for protection; but this idea has been wholly disproved in an excellent account of this interesting piece of antiquity, communicated to the Society of Antiquaries of Scotland[1] by W. N. Kennedy, Esq., Hawick. This gentleman had very closely examined it, and the dimensions he gives are as follows:—At the bottom of the ditch four to five feet wide; at the top of the inner edge of it the width is twelve feet; on *both sides* of the ditch are mounds, formed by the earth excavated from it; the depth from the bottom of the ditch to the top of the mounds is four to five feet. The reasons are very conclusive which this writer gives, that it was merely a territorial division— namely, it is only made where no stream or natural boundary exists, and it is still in many places the only boundary between adjoining properties. But what most strongly proves it never could have been intended for a defensive work is, that it is *not* continuous, but often near streams and morasses stops altogether, whereby the flanks would be in constant danger of being turned: besides, the mounds or walls of earth are on *both* sides of the ditch, and of the *same* height, whereby one of them certainly

---

[1] See Proceedings, Society of Antiquaries, Scot., vol. iii., part 1, page 117, dated 1858.

would obstruct the defenders reaching whichever side was to be occupied. This ancient division also, from the direction it takes (being from north to south), wholly excludes the idea that it was formed as an obstacle and defence against the Angles of Northumberland, as if so, it would have gone from east to west. It begins on the Gala Water some miles north of where the Leader joins it, and thence goes south-west within the county of Roxburgh, and then goes south-east to the county of Northumberland, where it ends at the source of the Lid or Liddel, which passes Longtown in England. From its commencement to its termination, the Picts Work thus makes nearly a due *south course*, as can be seen in the Map, where it is represented. The communication of Mr Kennedy contains full particulars of different rivers and streams that this boundary approaches; and if going in its direction it disappears and then reappears again, keeping its direction, and that the alternation of these natural and artificial lines rendered it perfect and continuous. And he well says—'The only rational conclusion which can be arrived at, by an investigation of its remains as at present to be seen, is, that *it must have been* an innocent, peaceable boundary line.'

From the position this very ancient work

occupies in the south of Scotland, and having been proved to be a boundary, it does seem fair to conclude it was the frontier line between the territories of the Britons on the west, and of the Caledonian Picts to the east of it (as it makes a due north and south course); and that it had been raised by them (to prevent disputes) about or very shortly after the Romans had departed—that is, in or about A.D. 410. Besides, the name of 'the Picts Work,' which connects it with that people, it is also called 'the Cat rail,' which has been derived from the British ' Cud-rhail,' meaning, 'the ditch fence,' and which also connects it with that race. It becomes a valuable evidence, from the great probability of its being the frontier line, as before said, of the Picts and Britons; and as the Picts were dispossessed by the Angles of the Lothians, and that they also took Galloway from the Britons, seems very strongly to confirm it.

CHAPTER IV.

True period of Arrival of the Irish Scots Colony in North Britain proved to be A.D. 506, and events to A.D. 560.

A.D. 506. THE first permanent settlement and occupation by the Irish Scots in North Britain, for which there exists any evidence at all credible, took place in the year A.D. 506, under Fergus M'Erc; and, as the name of the district in Ireland from whence they came was Dalriada, they also received the appellation of Dalriads.

The usual date has, till very recently, been held to be A.D. 503,—the difference is exceedingly slight, yet the correct date, notwithstanding, ought to be adopted,—it was discovered by the learned Dr O'Donnovan, and made known in his edition of the Annals of the Four Masters,[1] where he proves from the Chronology of Pope Symmachus, that it could not have been earlier than A.D. 506; the date

[1] See his edition, vol. i., pages 160-161, note m.

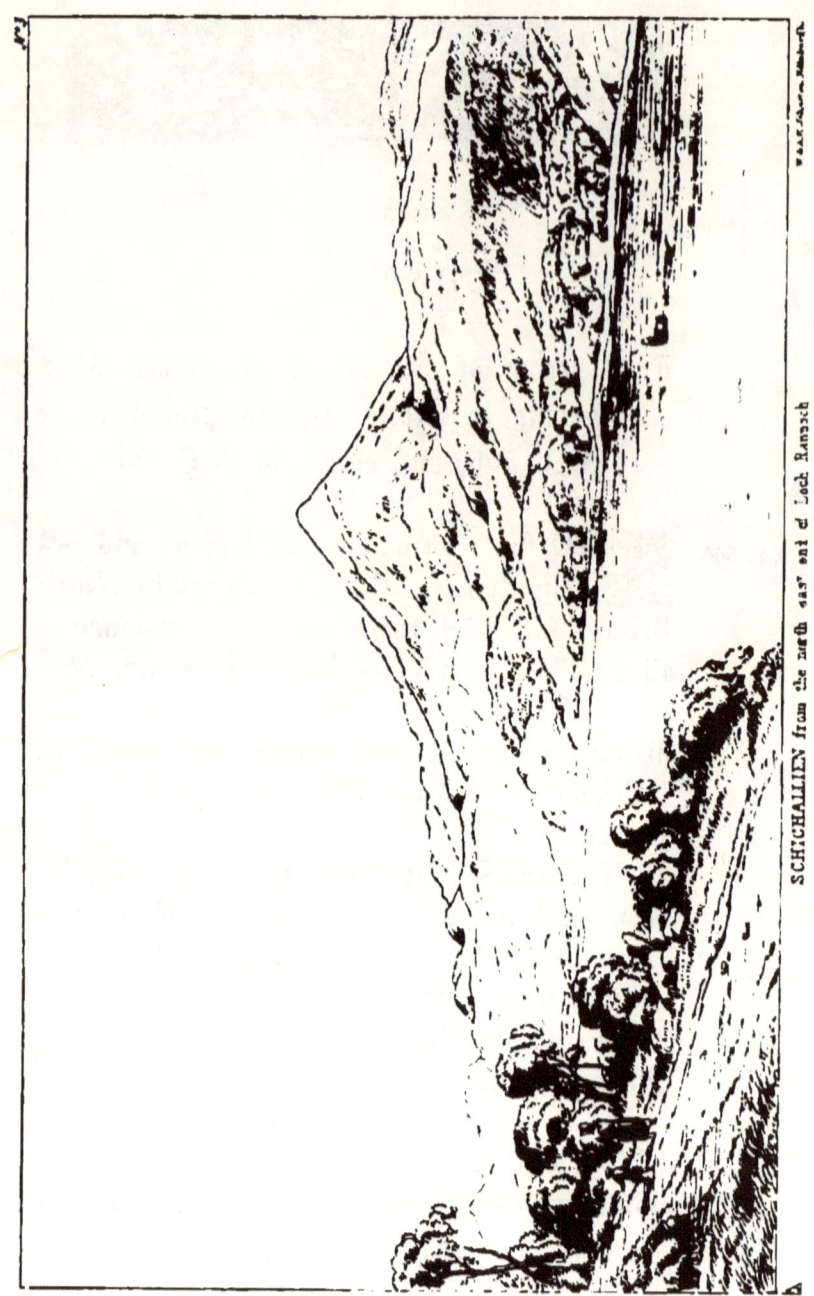

SCHICHALLIEN from the north east end of Loch Rannoch

formerly relied on, arose also from the mention, in the Ulster Annals, of the emigration having taken place twenty years after the battle of Ocha, the true date of which must now be received as having happened in A.D. 486, and not 483 as hitherto.

The learned Dr Reeves, in his edition of Adomnan, adopts A.D. 506 as the correct date, when stating his origin of the Dalriads [1] or Irish Scots in North Britain. That this (the beginning of the sixth century) was the period of *the earliest* settlement of this new people into present Scotland, is authenticated both by modern and ancient writers; as to any previous, they are now justly held as fabulous, and unworthy of any attention. It has already been proved by the authority of the ancient writers, Gildas and Bede, that the wandering Scots robbers, named up to the end of the fourth century, returned to their native country, Ireland; and as to the fifth century, the evidence first printed by Innes makes it clear, along with other testimony, modern and ancient, now to be given, that the arrival of the Irish Scots colony, under Fergus M'Erc and his brothers, took place, as already said, early in the sixth century.

Chalmers, a writer of great research, says.[2]

[1] See Dr Reeves's edition of Adomnan, page 433.
[2] Chalmers's Caledonia, vol. i., page 269, note.

'I do not concur with those writers who speak of permanent settlements of *Irish Scots* during Roman times;' and he adds, 'from all my enquiries it appears to me that no permanent colonization of North Britain by the Scots Irish people began till the recent period of the sixth century.'

A writer of an earlier period, namely, Archbishop Ussher, a very high and learned authority, in his works,[1] gives it as his opinion that the emigration in the sixth century, under Fergus, etc., was *the first* permanent settlement of the Scots from Ireland into Britain.

Both these writers, Chalmers and Ussher, were of course perfectly aware of the statement of Bede, that the Irish Scots came to Britain under a leader he calls 'Reuda,' but neither they or subsequent ones, to be hereafter quoted, *believed it to be true*.

The late Donald Gregory, Esq., an excellent antiquarian writer, says,[2] 'Historians seem now to have agreed that the Picts were, in fact, the Caledonians under a new name; that they were a Celtic race; and that *until the sixth century* they continued *to be the sole nation north of the Friths*.'

A.D. 506. To the south of the Clyde were the Britons

[1] Vol. vi, page 147.
[2] Gregory's Highlands and Isles of Scotland, page 2.

—south of the Firth of Forth and along its shores, the three counties of the Lothians. also Berwick and Roxburgh shires, the Caledonian Picts held at this period, and until dispossessed by the Angles.

This writer (Gregory), in the same work and page, says, 'In the beginning *of the sixth century, a new people* was added to the inhabitants of Scotland north of Forth and Clyde,—for, at *that period, the Irish Scots*, frequently called *the Dalriads*, effected a settlement in the western districts of the Highlands.'

Another good authority says, 'it is thus beyond a doubt that *the Scots had no permanent settlement* in Britain, as late as the early part *of the fifth century;* and that *Ireland* was the habitation of those Scots who joined the Picts in their attacks upon the provincial Britons.' Again, he adds further down, in the same page, adverting to Bedes mention of their arrival in Scotland, 'although, like all monkish traditions, an appellation *for the leader* of the colony, *has been formed out of their generic name of Dalriads*." [1]

It is well here to explain to the reader the error of Bede as to the colony of Irish Scots being under a person he calls 'Reuda,' and not, as is well authenticated, to have been

[1] See Skene's Highlanders of Scotland, vol. i., page 19.

Arrival of the Irish Scots Colony

under Fergus and his brothers. He says[1] that Britain, besides the Britons and Picts, received a third nation, '*the Scots*,' who migrated from Ireland under their leader Reuda, and occupied the settlements among the Picts which they held in his own time—that is, in A.D. 731. This statement, it will be shown, is wholly erroneous. There were *no such people* in existence as the Scots at the period when this Reuda or Riada lived, as the date assigned to his arrival is A.D. 250, which is also near 500 years before the period Bede had written his history, whereas the only true and historical emigration (that of Fergus, etc.) took place only 225 years before he wrote. Bede could not possibly know of the pretended ancient colony (of A.D. 250), and yet be ignorant of the one so much nearer his own time; besides, he speaks of only *one* emigration. The error of Bede (as to Reuda) appears to have arisen from the name of Dalriads being given to these Irish Scots, as they came from Dalriada, in Ireland; respecting which name he makes it to be from that of their leaders, stating that in their language 'Dal'[2] signifies

---

[1] Bede. Liber 1. cap. 1.
[2] Bede knew nothing of either the Irish or the Pictish Gaelic. In this case he might have been thinking of his own language, as it appears 'Dal,' in Anglo-Saxon, means 'a part,' or 'portion'—according to Bosworth's Anglo-Saxon Grammar.

a part, or portion, which, in Gaelic, it does not.

Dr Reeves, in his work already often quoted, mentions (at page 433) that Fergus M'Erc and his brothers, who came from Ireland in A.D. 506, were the senior representatives of Reuda or Riada.[1] This may likewise have contributed to mislead Bede. Lastly, not a single proper authority has ever been produced to support the fabulous story of an Irish colony under Reuda, when *no Scots existed*, should be received; and the authenticated one under Fergus, etc., when *Scots did exist*, should be rejected, and which would of necessity follow, as Bede knew only of *one emigration* of Irish Scots into Britain.

As mentioned by a very good authority, C. Innes, Esq., Professor of History, University of Edinburgh, it is necessary to be cautious in receiving Bede's statements of events remote from his own time. The Professor remarks[2]— 'Even the venerable Bede must be taken with a grain of reservation;' and again, 'it requires discrimination to turn his information to account for matters more remote.'

[1] This further shows Reuda's emigration cannot be believed, as he would thereby have left his children in A.D 250, behind him, and they never to have joined him, but remained in Ireland.

[2] Scotland in the Middle Ages; and Sketches of Early Scotch History—at notes on Maps, pages xii. and xiii.

Arrival of the Irish Scots Colony

The following is from a work written by the Reverend Dr Thomas M'Lauchlan, called 'Celtic Gleanings,' and which has been translated into Gaelic. It contains much authentic information, in a small compass, interesting to Highlanders. He says[1]—'Irish writers have maintained that there were two great migrations of the Scots from Ireland into Scotland; one about 250 years after Christ; and another, commonly called the Dalriadic settlement, in the year 503 A.C., when Lorn, Fergus, and Angus, the sons of Erc, led a colony across the Irish Channel, and settled with them in Argyleshire. For this latter emigration *the authorities are unquestionable. Bede is quite distinct;* nor could he have been mistaken regarding an event that took place less than 200 years before his own time. The Irish annalists *are equally distinct* with regard to it.' At the same page as the above it is also stated—'The first of these migrations is now very generally given up as an event for whose occurrence we have *no evidence of any value.*'

It is necessary to mention that this is the same author who has, within these few months,

---

[1] 'Celtic Gleanings; or Notices of the History and Literature of the Scottish Gael,' pages 53 and 54, by the Reverend Dr Thomas M'Lauchlan.

written another work, called 'The Early Scottish Church,' and already noticed. In it he gives an entirely different account of the origin and arrival of the Scots—though the evidence of Bede, the Irish Annalists, etc. etc., remains *precisely the same* as it was when the first work was written; a most erroneous assertion, that is in *the last,* has been noticed, and therein appears[1] also the fables of Fordun, even the most grotesque one, namely, that of *the total extermination of the Pictish people!* It does look strange such fictions should be repeated if they are not believed. The statements also of the two books are altogether so opposite, they cannot *both be correct.*

It has been already mentioned that Innes was the first to publish some ancient and valuable documents relative to Scotch history. One of them, which dates so far back as 1158, and was written by desire of Andrew, Bishop of Caithness,[2] known as 'de situ Albaniæ,' because it treats of the geography of Alban. By it Fergus M'Erc is proved to be *the first of his race* that had any rule in that country. This, therefore, still further excludes the story of his progenitor Reuda ever having brought over a colony to North Britain from Ireland. In the original,

[1] Pages 18 and 140.
[2] Innes states, vol. ii, page 602, that this Prelate was appointed to his See in or before 1150.

as printed by Innes,[1] there appears—'Fergus filius Erc *ipse fuit primus qui de semine* Chonare suscepit regnum Albaniæ.' The Chonare mentioned here is said to have been an Irish king in A.D. 212, and from whom Fergus descended. The very same words are also recorded in another chronicle printed by Innes[2] regarding Fergus Erc.

In the Irish Annals of Tigernach (as well as the Annals of Ulster) we are informed of the date of the arrival of Fergus in present Scotland. This annalist is the most ancient of them all. He probably wrote the whole of the earlier part between 1050 and 1060; he made no entry later than 1072, and died an aged abbot in 1088, and is a most trustworthy authority. He says,[3] A.D. 502—Fergus the great, the son of Erc, held a part of Britain with the Dalriadic nation, and died there.'

This further authenticates the date of the emigration not being till the beginning of the sixth century. Along with Fergus came also,

[1] Innes's Crit. Essay, vol. ii., page 778—Appendix No. 1.
[2] Innes, vol ii., page 789—Appendix No. 4.
[3] All the references from the Irish Annals are taken from the Iona Club Transactions, page 213, etc.; and this extract from Tigernach wholly contradicts the assertion of the Reverend Dr M'Lauchlan in his book, 'Early Scottish Church,' where, at page 143, he says—' Tighernac makes Fergus *the first King of Dalriada ;*' but we see he does *not call or make him king at all.*

according to most accounts, his brothers Lorn and Angus. As to the former, he is said, in the Annals of the four Masters,[1] to have been a brother of Erc, whereby he would be uncle to Fergus. The Annals of the four Masters are not to be judged by the date at which they were collected, but by the date of the various manuscripts from which it can be proved the facts were taken. Lorn has been, by tradition, called eldest brother of Fergus; but this notice goes to prove his seniority arose from being uncle.

From the foregoing evidence, both modern and ancient, it is believed no one can reasonably deny that the period of *the first* settlement of the Scots in present Scotland is most clearly proved and authenticated to have been in the sixth century.

With regard to some remarks that have been made on this entry of the Annals as to the manner in which the occupation or holding was acquired by Fergus, it is manifest, from the way it is described as a tenure, 'tenuit' in the original, that he had obtained it by consent and sufferance of the Pictish monarch and people; besides, the number of the emigrants

---

[1] Lorn was born in A.D. 434, and was son of Eochaidh Muinreumhar.—See the Annals four Masters, vol i., p. 133, edition of Dr O'Donnovan.

that came from Ireland was so *very small*, that it could not possibly be otherwise. The proof of this is given by *a very ancient tract*, called 'the men of Alba,' properly Alban (that is Scotland), and quoted by Dr Reeves in his work,[1] says, that three times fifty were the number of men '*that went forth with the sons of Erc*,'—this bears the mark of truth, as, had it said the numbers were 1500, or 15,000, it would have the aspect of an invasion, but the weakness of the numbers shows it was a peaceful occupation. Chalmers[2] says, 'the poetical notion of conquest *cannot possibly be true;*' and it is not improbable that these first Irish chieftains were invited by the Pictish king to take the rule in the western part of the county of Argyle, and act as leaders of the native Caledonian Picts therein against the Britons, and restrain them from spreading further into the Highlands; for fighting with the Britons seems to have been the constant employment of the Irish Scots.

Another remark has been made, that this entry of Tigernach would infer the death of Fergus to have happened the same year; but it does not state that it so happened; and even if it did, the Latin lists of the kings, and the

---

[1] See Dr Reeves's edition of Adomnan, page 433.
[2] See Chalmers's Caledonia, vol. i., page 275, note.

chronology of Malcolm Canmore's bard, must yield to the far superior authority of the Irish Annals.

The writer of 'The Early Scottish Church,' The Rev. Dr Thomas M'Lauchlan, in attempting to make out an undue antiquity for the arrival of the Irish Scots colony under Fergus M'Erc, brings forward for his authorities the fables of Fordun and Bœce,[1] and he even tries to support them by argument. The fiction these writers state (and repeated in the above named book) as to Fergus, is, that he was an exile 'in Scandinavia!' and that he ascended the throne about A.D. 404, that is, more than a hundred years before the true date of his arrival, and long before he could have been born. When the writer of 'The Early Scottish Church' can only support his assertions as to the period of the Irish Scots colony coming into Britain a century *before it happened*, by the fables of Fordun and Bœce, it proves how worthless the statement is; and, as Innes justly and truly remarks, on those who adopt or follow Fordun, as to Fergus M'Erc's arrival being *ante-dated by a whole century*, he and they, he says, 'build upon a crazy foundation, the building they erect must necessarily be tottering.'[2]

[1] See 'The Early Scottish Church,' page 140.
[2] See T. Innes's Essay, vol. ii., page 750.

44   Arrival of the Irish Scots Colony

The small districts in Argyleshire that came to belong to the descendants of these first leaders was, Kintyre the largest to that of Fergus, that of Lorn to his descendants, and which seems wrongly stated to have been so named after himself, it being almost certain the district of Lorn must have had the name long ere the sixth century—to Angus the youngest, belonged the island of Islay.

None of these chieftains of the Irish Scots held any higher title than Toisach, lord, or leader. Dr Reeve's clearly states this;[1] but they afterwards became dignified as petty princes of Dalriada, between A.D. 575 and A.D. 590, at a convention held at Drumceat[2] in Ireland, previous to which time they were dependent on the Irish Scotch monarchs.

A.D. 547.   This year brought an invasion into the southern possessions of the Caledonian Picts of Angles, under their great leader Ida, who bore the destructive title of 'the flame-bearer,'[3] he acquired the three counties of the Lothians, and Roxburgh, and which were never again held but for a short period by the Caledonian Picts.

[1] See Dr Reeves's edition of Adomnan, page 435. Yet the author of 'The Early Scottish Church' makes Fergus M'Erc to have been *a king* in 502—at page 143 of his book.

[2] The date by the Annals of Ulster would be A.D. 575, and O'Flaherty A.D. 590.

[3] See Robertson's Scotland's early kings, vol. i., page 3.

in North Britain proved to be A.D. 506. 45

This was the period of that new people (the Anglo-Saxons) coming into the south of present Scotland, and whose descendants still occupy the same district of country.

This year, we learn from the Irish Annals of Tigernach, that the Pictish king named Bruidhi, defeated the Dalriads, or Irish Scots; they had probably been encroaching on the territories of the Caledonian Picts, as Dr Reeves mentions[1] that the Annals of Ulster add the word 'expulsio' in addition to the mention of the death of Gabhran, the grandson of Fergus M'Erc, in connection with the flight of the Irish Scots from the above Pictish King Bruidhi.[2]

A.D. 560.

[1] Reeves's Adomnan, page 435.
[2] In the Irish Annals the spelling of this king's name appears thus, and in the original extract of a MS., quoted in the Highland Society's Report on Ossian, dated in the twelfth or thirteenth century, at latest, if not more ancient. In both the Gaelic and English the name is spelled 'Bruidhi.' See page 311 of Appendix of the Report on Ossian's poems. Dr T. M'Lauchlan spells it differently, both in the Gaelic and English,—he professes to give *from this same* MS. See 'The Early Scottish Church,' page 35.

CHAPTER V.

The introduction of Christianity into North Britain and its proper date.

THE introduction of Christianity among the Caledonian Picts, cannot be proved to have taken place earlier than the opening of the fifth century—that is immediately after the departure of the Romans.

Chalmers, the most industrious writer on ancient Scottish history, endeavoured, without success, to discover if any grounds existed to believe that during the Roman occupation Christianity existed, or was professed by either the Caledonians or the Picts: he has devoted considerable space[1] to the subject, and we learn that the preaching of Ninian to the southern Picts, is the earliest period we can

---

[1] See Chalmers's Caledonia, vol. i., pages 313 to 330 included on the introduction of Christianity into North Britain.

rely upon, connected with the Christian faith being made known to the Caledonian Picts—Adomnan and Bede are the two oldest writers who give any reliable information—the latter speaks of Ninian[1] as having preached to the Southern Picts, and *converted* them, 'as is reported'—which expression clearly conveys that Bede had some doubts of the latter being the fact—and there exists no proof to cause belief that one-half of the nation had become Christianised by Ninian, and whose success, whatever it may have been, was no doubt greatly exaggerated in later times—his period was also very remote being close upon the time of the Roman occupation, the date that has been given[2] is A.D. 414, at which time the Romans could not have left North Britain above five or six years—Chalmers considers that the diocese of Ninian was south of the wall of Antonine, which formed the province of Valentia—but the southern Picts lay mostly in the large counties of Perth, Fife, etc.; and had Ninian converted the population belonging to them, he would surely have built his church and fixed his residence among his converts—instead of which, he went as far off as he well could, and settled among his own countrymen,

[1] Bede, lib. 3, cap. 4.
[2] See Skene's Highlanders, vol. i., page 187.

48 The introduction of Christianity

A.D. 431.

the Britons, in the county of Galloway, as at this period (A.D. 414) the Irish Picts had not yet settled there. This year Pope Celestine sent Palladius to Ireland as bishop[1] of the Scots believing in Christ—'it would be unnecessary here to refute *the absurd idea* formerly held, that the Scots to whom Palladius was sent were the Scots of Britain, as there is no point which has been so clearly established as the fact that his mission was to Ireland'[2]—and to Ireland *alone*, though it is vainly attempted to have it believed it was to Scots also in North Britain, as is asserted by the Rev. Dr Thomas M'Lauchlan, in his 'Early Scottish Church,'[3] who gives a whole chapter respecting Palladius.[4]

The assertion of a Christian mission to any Scots in North Britain in A.D. 431 by Palladius is fully refuted by the fact that *no Scots were then settled there*—but were the inhabitants of Ireland *alone* until A.D. 506, as has been fully

[1] 'Primus Episcopus' as quoted by Robertson from Prosper ad an 431—Scot. Early Kings, vol. i., page 321.
[2] Skene's Highlanders, vol. i., page 186.
[3] See page 86.
[4] No Episcopalian could be more desirous of proving than this author, that the government of the newly formed church in North Britain had been placed under a bishop; as also it had been under a previous bishop, namely Ninian,—yet at page 169 this writer states, in the early Scottish Church there was 'no evidence of the existence of bishops.'

proved, and though the author of 'The Early Scottish Church' tries to make it believed that they were settled in North Britain in A.D. 431, has utterly failed, having been unable to produce any proper proof of it. The fables of Fordoun cannot be received, either as to the period of the origin of the Scots in North Britain, or as to when Christianity was introduced among them—he fabricated an account of a pretended Scotch king in A.D. 203, sending ambassadors to Pope Victor the first, and which, even the author of 'The Early Scottish Church' acknowledges (at page 52) to be an impossibility. Yet with all the fables that Fordoun abounds, none appear more extraordinary than the statement made at the same page[1] of that book, where we are told by the author, that notwithstanding the fact that in A.D. 203 the name Scot was then unknown,[2] yet, '*the people afterwards called Scots were at the period inhabitants of North Britain!*' —where or whence this was derived, *is not* mentioned. It certainly is quite unknown to all Irish historical writers hitherto, that in A.D. 203 the people afterwards called Scots, were not inhabitants of Ireland, but of North Britain—such an origin for either the Scots of

---

[1] 'The Early Scottish Church' page 52
[2] It is first mentioned in A.D. 360.

Ireland, or North Britain, is clearly imaginary, and cannot be received.[1]

Fordun, in 'The Early Scottish Church,' is also quoted,[2] as stating that there was a church in north Britain, *long before* the coming of Palladius into present Scotland, and the author further asserts,[3] that 'for Fordun's statement *we have ample vouchers in the words of Prosper and Bede.*' This is impossible, as Prosper knew nothing whatever of Palladius being in present Scotland, and therefore he could not vouch for Fordun's statement, that he ever was *there*, or could vouch as to any state the church of present Scotland was in previously, from this fact, that Prosper wholly ignores Palladius ever going to Scotland, which shows the whole story is a fable and must be rejected. For proof of this see the subject as

[1] The great error of the Rev. Dr Thomas M'Lauchlan asserting in opposition to historical writers that the people called Scots were settled in the west of North Britain has been already shown, but the extract from his book (page 52) above given, it will be seen he goes even beyond that, by asserting that the ancestors of the Scots were the settled inhabitants of North Britain in A.D. 203—and at page 81 of his book argues also for a fabulous antiquity for the Scots—all this is in defiance of the historical authority of Bede, who declares that when the colony of Irish Scots came over— *Britain received a new race of people.*

[2] Lib. 3, cap. 8, in 'The Early Scottish Church,' page 86.

[3] 'Early Scottish Church,' page 86.

noticed by Robertson in his work of 'Scotland under her Early Kings' (vol. i., page 323). where he has a note on it. Bede also *does not say* that Palladius came into north Britain, he only says[1] he was sent 'to the Scots that believed in Christ,' *that is to the Irish.*

It would undoubtedly be very pleasing to think that there was any foundation to believe in an earlier introduction into Scotland of Christianity than the beginning of the fifth century; but, as already said, when Chalmers, our most indefatigable writer on ancient historical facts, has failed to discover this, it must be concluded no satisfactory evidence exists. The first in North Britain[2] he tells us of who became Christians, were the inhabitants of the province of Valentia, and who, he says, were called the southern Picts by Bede and the contemporary writers of the middle ages, and that they 'were converted from their ancient superstitions at the commencement of *the fifth century,*' and that it was effected by Ninian. Another much more recent writer, and who, from scholarship and investigation, is entitled to attention, says, 'the *first advent* of Chris-

---

[1] Bede, lib. 1, cap. 13. Thus we see he does *not vouch* for Fordun's fables any more than Prosper does.

[2] Chalmers's Caledonia, vol. i., page 315.

tianity of which we have *any authentic account*, is the mission of S. Ninian."[1]

This being therefore the true period of the introduction of Christianity into present Scotland, how impossible is it to receive the assertion of the author of the work last alluded to when he says[2] 'the mission of Palladius took place about 350 *years after Christianity first entered Scotland*'!! The mission of Palladius to Ireland was in A.D. 431, therefore, instead of the fifth century being the period of the introduction of Christianity into present Scotland, this statement brings it to the year A.D. 81; for this the author gives not a single writer nor authority of *any* description. The title page speaks also of a Christian church existing in the first century—no proof is given of it, nothing but unsupported assertions. Those who are not ignorant of the early history of Scotland, are well aware, that for the first century there is nothing authentic existing, except what is made known to us in the few pages of Tacitus' Life of Agricola; and instead of there being a Christian Church in A.D. 81, that Roman writer tells us, in his 27th chapter,

[1] Preface by the Bishop of Brechin to 'Missale de Arbuthnot,' page iv.

[2] See 'The Early Scottish Church,' page 86. This writer also tries to include the notices by ancient writers as to Christianity in *Britain* as extending to Caledonia and its natives.

that the natives confirmed their engagements *with sacrifices.*

This was the year of the arrival of Columba, A.D. 563. from Ireland, among the Caledonian Picts, as is mentioned in all the Irish Annals; and that of Innisfallen adds, 'his first night in Alban was on Whitsunday.' He appears to have introduced Christianity throughout near two-thirds of present Scotland. His great success seems to have arisen from the blessing of God that attended his visit to the then Pictish monarch, named Bruidhi, who, by Bede, is called [1] 'Rex potentissimus,' a most powerful king—he was converted by Columba, and then followed that of the whole nation. Bede likewise tells us[2] that it was King Bruidhi that gave the island of Iona to Columba, and which, according to immemorial tradition, had previously belonged to the Druids (and this is further attested by Druidical remains), and who were the heathen priests of the Caledonian Picts. It is said by Tigernach, that Conall, the then petty ruler of the Irish Scots, or Dalriads, had given Iona to Columba. This consisted, in all probability, of a promise not to disturb him in his possession, by any of the piratical expeditions of the Irish Scots, and

---

[1] Bede, lib. 3, cap. 4.
[2] Bede, lib. 3, cap. 4.

one of which is recorded in the Irish Annals as having happened before Columba could well have built his monastery and got properly settled. The Annals of Ulster relate, under the year A.D. 568, of a piratical expedition by this Conall, in the western regions, that is, the Western Isles. This act discloses the very limited possessions of the Irish Scots, and a similar proceeding and attempted encroachment had most probably been the cause of the Pictish king Bruidhi, as already mentioned, in A.D. 560, having expelled and severely chastised the Irish Scots.[1]

Besides, it is nearly impossible that at the period of the arrival of Columba the Irish Scots could have had any rule or authority so far north from their original settlement of Kintyre[2] as Iona, situated close to the large and independent island of Mull, in which, even after more than 200 years from the arrival of the Irish Scots, they had but a *portion* of it. This is shown very clearly by both Skene[3] and Dr Reeves.

[1] The Annals of Ulster make known another case of a piratical expedition by one of these Irish Scots petty kings called ' Aidan,' in A.D 580.
[2] The Irish Annals and other authorities, connect all the earliest rulers of the Irish Scots with Kintyre, in Argyleshire.
[3] See introduction, Book Dean of Lismore, note, page xxiv. Dr Reeves has a note to the same effect.

It was the establishment at Iona, by Columba, of a body of sincere Christian men, who went forth from it all over the nation, that made known the blessings of the Gospel; and the numerous churches dedicated to him prove the gratitude of the Gael of Alban. The system introduced by Columba at Iona was carried on by his successors, as is shown by Adomnan; and though they are properly called Scots, they must not be supposed to have been natives of present Scotland—they were *all from Ireland*, the proper country of the Scots at that period. Dr Reeves gives the pedigree of almost every one of the Abbots of Iona, proving them to be Irish.

Under the date of this first named year we have an extract from the Annals of Ulster given by Dr Reeves in his edition of Adomnan (page 371), and on which he likewise has a note. By the extract from the Annals, it is proved that the 'conversio ad Dominum,' 'the conversion to the Lord,' of Constantine, king of Cornwall, took place A.D. 588: and in the note at the above page, Dr Reeves informs us this king became a monk under St Mochuda, at Rahen, in Ireland. He afterwards passed over to North Britain, and founded the church of Govan, near Glasgow. The work called the 'Origines Parochiales' of Scotland, likewise

A.D. 588-590.

mentions this King Constantine in connection with the parish church of Crawford, in Lanarkshire, and which was dedicated to him. The Origines add, that after his return from Ireland he joined S. Kentigern, the reputed founder of Christianity at Glasgow, and that he sent him to the heathens in Galloway, where he attained to the rank of abbot. After which, Dr Reeves, the Origines, and all the authorities,[1] prove he went to preach to and convert *the inhabitants of Kintyre, and where he suffered martyrdom.* This, therefore, must be the period at which Christianity was introduced among the heathen Caledonian Picts of Kintyre; because it is impossible to suppose there was *a population* of Christian Scots throughout the district, as surely they would not murder a Christian teacher; and though Kintyre was nominally, since A.D. 506, under the rule of Irish Scots leaders, their numbers must have been *very trifling,* as this event unquestionably proves; some further remarks on it are required

---

[1] The authorities are very sufficient, and incontestably prove all that is here mentioned. They are—The Annals of Ulster, as given by Dr Reeves in his edition of Adomnan, page 371; note by Dr Reeves at same page; Breviary of Aberdeen, folio 67; Fordun, lib. 3, cap. 26; Colgan, page 577; Kalend. Aber. Registrum, Aberdeen, Preface, page lxxxvi; Origines Parochiales, vol. i., pages 163, 164; Proceedings Antiquarian Society, Scotland, volume ii., part 2, page 262.

to prevent readers being misled. From the date at which the conversion of this Christian martyr took place, and the subsequent events, as has been stated, that he was engaged in prior to his last labours in converting the *whole of Kintyre*[1] in Argyleshire, there must have elapsed at least a couple of years, so that he could not have been put to death by the heathens of Kintyre sooner than A.D. 590. Therefore it is a fact, that prior to that date the native inhabitants of Kintyre were almost entirely heathens, which confirms the whole that has been stated in these pages as to the *true date* of the arrival of the Irish Scots in North Britain, and of the very small numbers that the emigration consisted of. This event likewise proves to demonstration that all the assertions[2] in 'The Early Scottish Church,' of *Christian Scots* inhabiting present Scotland so remote as the year A.D. 431, or that Palladius, a Christian bishop, was then sent to them by the Pope of Rome, is *altogether visionary and unfounded.*

It is also very remarkable that the author of 'The Early Scottish Church' takes no notice

[1] Fordun, and the other authorities above quoted along with him, prove this.
[2] See 'The Early Scottish Church,' page 86; and the whole chapter on Palladius.

whatsoever of this Christian martyr, or his successful labours in various parts, particularly as he seems to have deserved to be mentioned for what he did for the cause of Christ in Kintyre, etc,[1] far more than others that appear; besides, it is the only one martyrdom that can be authenticated to have taken place, connected with the introduction of Christianity, within the main land of present Scotland[2]—and that one took place in the country where it has been *pretended Christian Scots alone were the native inhabitants.*

[1] Dr Reeves, in his edition of Adomnan, says, at page 371, that the church of Kilchousland, in Kintyre, is named after this martyr.

[2] The only other is said to have happened at the remote island of Eigg.

BENAULI from the South West of Bridge of Tilt

CHAPTER VI.

Events to end of Seventh Century and Conquest of the Dalriads in the Eigth Century, with Events up to A.D. 842.

THE events known of the seventh century are very few; but, previously to mentioning them, it will be proper to consider the situation and extent of country belonging to the different races then inhabiting North Britain; and in this the Map will be found to give assistance.

According to Bede there were four—the Picts, Britons, Angles, and Scots. Of these the first, the Caledonian Picts, were the predominating race. They held and inhabited the whole extent of present Scotland north of the two firths of Forth and Clyde, the only exceptions being the very limited districts forming modern Argyleshire, which belonged to the Irish Scots, and the rock of Dumbarton and its near neighbourhood, to the Britons. Thus the far greater extent of territory and number of inhabitants rendered the Caledonian Picts vastly the most powerful and formidable of these different races. Of the islands situate along the west coast of Argyle, the Irish Scots had possession, and of them Islay being the largest; but it also, like the main land of Argyle, was *fully peopled* by the Caledonian Picts *before the arrival* of the Irish Scots. This is proved by the same ancient tract, already quoted, from Dr Reeves's edition of Adomnan, called 'The Men of Alba,' preserved in the book of Ballymote, which[1] gives the names of places and houses inhabited in Islay, number of families, etc. etc., of the island of Mull as already shown, the Scots had only a part of it. Of all the other islands, the Caledonian Picts were sole possessors. With regard to the Britons, except Dumbarton, with a portion of the Lennox, they were entirely to the south of the Clyde, and originally had held the whole of the south-west country from it, including Galloway. That country appears to have received a colony of Irish Picts, as we may understand from Isidore[2] (quoted by

---

[1] See Reeves's edition of Adomnan, page 123, note.

[2] Isidore Origines, lib. 9, cap. 2. The Cruithne, or Picts of Ireland, formed the original population of Ulster and the north part of Leinster, and they were subject to the Caledonian Pictish kings till about A.D. 608.—See Introduction, Book Dean of Lismore, pages xxiii-xxvi.

Logan in his Scottish Gael, vol. i., page 64, note), who calls the inhabitants 'Scoti'—that is, people from Ireland; and the number of churches dedicated in Galloway to Irish saints, strongly confirms this. The Picts of Galloway have often been confounded with the Caledonian Picts; but they were altogether distinct, as clearly shown by Bede,[1] who describes the latter as dwelling north of the Forth, and south of the rugged mountains that separated them from the rest of their fellow countrymen, thus proving they belonged to a very different part of North Britain than Galloway,[2] which, in remote times, must have belonged to the Britons, as Robertson, in his work 'Scotland under her Early Kings,' makes very clear in his Appendix on the subject of the Picts of Galloway.[3] The Irish Annals of Ulster, also under the year A.D. 823, call it 'Galloway *of the Britons*,' showing they still held some part of it.

The fourth race were the people called the Angles. Their country, in North Britain called Bernicia, was the territory they chiefly acquired from the Caledonian Picts, being the three Lothians, etc., on the south of the Forth; and

[1] Lib. 3, cap. 4.
[2] Chalmers, in mentioning the coming of the Irish Picts into Galloway, places it in the eighth century, which seems far too late.—Chalmers's Caledonia, vol. i., page 358.
[3] Robertson's Early Kings, vol. ii., pages 382, 383.

62 Events to end of Seventh Century.

Galloway, in Bede's time, also belonged to the Angles; and he states that, 'Candida Casa,'[1] therein was the church of S. Ninian, and also known as Whithern. These Angles had their original territory, however, in Northumberland, and it was thence called the Northumbrian kingdom.

A.D. 670. This year Egfrid became king[2] of Northumbria. He descended from Ida before named, and
A.D. 681. eleven years afterwards placed a bishop named Frumwin, at Abercarnig, now called Abercorn.

The king of the Caledonian Picts at this period was named Bruidhi, being the same as in Columba's time; but it is not thought they were of the same family. This monarch also, like his namesake and predecessor, extended his power over the Orcades, or the Orkneys (and which are marked in the Map).
A.D. 682. In the Irish Annals we find in this year 'the Orcades are wasted by Bruidhi.'

A.D. 686. Egfrid, king of Northumbria, invaded the territory of the Caledonian Picts with a large force, and penetrated even beyond the river Tay (and on crossing it burned Tullach-Alman),[3] till he was confronted by King Bruidhi in the

[1] Bede, lib. 3, cap. 4.
[2] Bede, lib. 4, cap. 5.
[3] This is mentioned in the Annals of Ulster, and was undoubtedly the Rath at the mouth of the Almond, where it joins the Tay, and where was also ancient Perth.

province of Angus. It was at Lin Garan, in the parish of Dunnichen, that the two armies fought a battle (which will be found marked in the Map), where the victory was triumphantly gained by the native Gael of Alban,[1] and which was of the highest consequence, as, had they been defeated, all that part of Scotland laying north of the Forth to the district of Angus would have been gained by the Anglo-Saxons. The Irish Annals, both of Ulster and Tigernach, call it the 'battle of Dunnichen,' and that it was fought on the 20th May, on the Sabbath-day, and in which Egfrid, the son of Oswy, was slain, with the whole of his large army, by King Bruidhi. The consequences of this victory were very great—all the country the Angles had acquired from the Caledonian Picts, south of the Forth, fell again (though not permanently) into their possession, and the Saxon bishop fled from Abercorn, and did not consider himself safe till he had reached Whitby, in Yorkshire. 'The Dalriads (the Irish Scots) also recovered their former liberty, and even the Britons enjoyed a momentary independence.'[2]

[1] The Irish Scots had nothing to do with gaining this important victory over the Saxons, though they benefited thereby.

[2] See Rolertson's Scotland, 'Early Kings,' vol. i., page 13. who adds, in a note, 'No Saxon tax-gatherer ever again took tribute from the Picts.

A.D. 693.

A considerable period of peace, of course, followed this great overthrow to the Angles, and which lasted during the reign of King Bruidhi, whose death is recorded in A.D. 693.

The notices of the Dalriads, or Irish Scots, at, and until some time after this period, are wholly devoid of the slightest interest; they were either engaged in continual fightings between the two tribes of Lorn and Kintyre for the rule of their petty kingdom, or with their neighbours the Britons of Strathclyde, and their numbers for carrying on such a continual strife and bloodshed would soon have been exhausted had they not probably often been recruited by fresh supplies of men from both Alban and Ireland—as also, that all the thieves and desperate characters of both these countries would likely flee for shelter to the Dalriad territory, and this would be a suitable riddance to one party, and a useful acquisition to the other.

A.D. 709

This year the Annals of Ulster mention the Orkneys again as having been attacked, and from the other similar entries previously, it would appear they must have been inhabited by a race of pirates, who, by their plundering habits on the inhabitants of the mainland, brought the power of the Pictish sovereigns upon them.

Twenty years after the last mentioned date arose the powerful Angus MacFergus, the greatest of all the ancient Pictish kings, he attacked and subdued all competitors. Among others he overcame the provincial king, or more properly the maormor of Atholl—and, indeed, all the petty provincial rulers seem to have been now brought into far greater subjection to the 'Ardrigh' or 'supreme king' of the nation than ever hitherto. It was evidently the great Angus MacFergus who laid the foundation of the future kingdom of present Scotland, whole pages of the Irish Annals are filled with the accounts of his triumphs. A.D. 729.

This year the Dalriads drew upon them the vengeance of the formidable Angus, and from which resulted their complete defeat and subjection. This arose from one of the Dalriad princes named Dungal, having desecrated a sanctuary in the island of Toraic (now Tory)[1] off the coast of Ireland, wherein a son of Angus, named Bruidhi, then was, and who the Annals state was seized by Dungal. A.D. 733.

This outrage caused Angus to invade the country of the Dalriads, and his vengeance first fell on the district of Lorn, as Dungal belonged to the petty princes of that Dalriad tribe—and at Dunolly, a strong-hold near Oban, he en- A.D. 734.

[1] Off the coast of the county of Donegal.

countered his former antagonist Talorgan, the maormar of Atholl, who, no doubt, had fled to the Dalriad territory for safety. The Annals of Ulster state Angus took him prisoner, and that he then attacked Dungal's fort on the river Leven, called Dunleven, which he took and destroyed. Dungal was wounded, and to escape the power of Angus fled to Ireland. The Annals of Tigernach add, that in the same year Angus further laid waste the Dalriad territories, and took Dunad, which is in North Knapdale, and parish of Glassary, Argyleshire, and was the head quarters of the tribe of Lorn.[1] He here found Dungal (who had returned from Ireland), and his brother Feredach, took them both prisoners and placed them in chains, and carried of much spoil. Soon after this event, Angus's son Bruidhi, died, most probably from the barbarous usage he had received from Dungal.

A.D. 734. The Annals of Ulster mention King Angus placed an army under command of his brother, Talorgan, to attack Muredach, the king of the
A.D. 736. Irish Scots, or Dalriads, he was completely defeated by Talorgan, in a battle on the shores of the Linne Loch, at a place called Knock Cairpre, Muredach was put to flight, and was pursued by the Pictish army[2]. This defeat

---

* See Dr Reeves's edition of Adomnan, page 377, note.
² Chalmers says that King Muredach was most probably

wholly ruined the tribe of Lorn, and this member of them appears to have been the last ruler of the race in Dalriada.

This year, the Annals of Ulster show that the subjection of the Dalriads was fully completed by the Pictish king, and is thus stated,[1]—'*the downfall of the Dalriads by Angus MacFergus.*'

A.D. 741.

The author of "The Early Scottish Church,"[2] endeavours to make it out to be only 'the smiting of Dalriada,' etc., but of that there had already been very much recorded, and it was something far stronger the annalist desired to make known, namely, the complete overthrow and '*downfall of the Dalriads.*'[3]

To follow up the conquest over the Dalriads, Angus, the king of the Picts, placed a prince of his own family over their territory, named Aidan, also called Aodh, who 'could not from the period of his reign, have been the same person with Edfin, as is generally supposed; and the fact that Aodh commenced his reign in the very year that the Pictish monarch, as we have seen, over-ran Dalriada, *and con-*

---

slain in his flight, as he certainly died that same year. Chalmers's Caledonia, vol. i., page 293.

[1] Iona Club Transactions, page 247.
[2] Page 263.
[3] It ought always to be remembered that 'the Dalriads' is but another name for the people who were the descendants of the colony of Irish Scots in Argyleshire.

quered *the whole district of Lorn*, affords a strong presumption that he must have been put there by the Pictish king, and that he ruled over the Pictish possessions in Dalriada. This presumption is placed almost beyond a doubt by the Annals of Ulster, where we find, in 749, 'the burning of Cillemoire of Aidan, *the son of Angus.*' Aodh could not have been of the line of Lorn,[1] for the first of the proper kings of Dalriada during this period, as given by the Latin lists, is Ewen, the son of Muredach, of that line. He could not have been of the line of Fergus, for Ewen is succeeded in the thirteenth year of Aodh's reign by Edfin of Fergus line; and, when during the reign of Aodh, we find Cillemoire, *a place in Lorn*, actually in possession of a person of the same name, and when that person is described as the son of *Angus,* shortly after the district of Lorn had been conquered by *Angus,* king of the Picts, we must hold it to establish beyond a doubt, that Aodh, or Aidan, was the son of Angus MacFergus, king of the Picts, and that he was the first of a line of Pictish princes, who ruled over the Pictish possessions in Dalriada."[2]

A.D. 761. In this year took place 'the death of Angus, king of Alban,' as mentioned by the Irish an-

[1] Pinkerton also fully confirms this.
[2] Skene's Highlanders, vol i., pages 52, 53.

nalist Tigernach, and others. As already said, he was by far the most formidable and powerful of the ancient kings of the Caledonian Picts. He it was who placed the Pictish kingdom (and which has ever since so continued) under[1] St Andrew as patron saint, and largely endowed churches in honour of him,[2] particularly Kilrymont, which subsequently became the seat of the primates of St Andrews. The legend that gives the particulars of this event respecting King Angus, states, that St Regulus or Rule came with the relics of St Andrew from Constantinople and arrived at a place in the county of Fife called Muckros; thence he proceeded to Forteviot, in Perthshire, one of the royal residences of the Pictish kings, where he found the three sons of Angus, namely, Owen, Nectan, and Finguien; but, he himself was absent on a great expedition in Argyleshire. They being anxious for their father's safety, gave a tenth part of Forteviot to God and St Andrew. They and St Regulus then proceeded over the mount, that is Drum Alban, and met their father returning, who prostrated himself before the relics. The place

[1] See the account of this by Skene in Proceedings Antiquaries Scot., vol. iv., Part 1, page 300.
[2] Nechtan, king of the Picts, had previously placed the kingdom, in A. D. 710, under St Peter.—Bede, Lib. v., cap. 21.

where this took place was then called Doldancha, but is now known as the Church of Kindrochet in Braemar, Aberdeenshire, which the king gave to God and St Andrew. They returned to Forteviot, and thence to Kilrymont, where a church was also built and endowed by King Angus.

A.D. 761. The successor to this great Pictish monarch was his brother Bruidhi. This was the invariable and fixed rule of the ancient Pictish kingdom that brothers should succeed in preference
A.D. 763. to sons. His reign, however, was very short—only two years.

Kenneth was the name of the next sovereign, and there is a single notice in his reign of a foray into the Pictish territory on the
A.D. 763. Forth by the Dalriads. Their proceedings now become wholly undeserving of any record, and ' which bear about as much upon the *general history of Scotland* as the early Annals of Sussex might do upon the *general history of England.*'[1] Kenneth did not reign long after the above date, as he appears to have
A.D. 775. been succeeded by his brother Alpin, and other successors, until the grand-son of Angus
A.D. 789. MacFergus, named Constantine, succeeded in expelling his competitor, Conal, and who, ac-

[1] See Robertson's 'Scotland under her Early Kings,' vol. i., page 15.

cording to the practice of Pictish rebels, etc., etc., took refuge within the Dalriad territory.

This year first appeared those marauding pirates, the Danes and Norwegians, as mentioned in the Annals of Ulster. thus—' The ravaging of all the islands of Britain by the Gentiles,'[1] and four years later the same thing as to the islands is mentioned, with the addition of Ulster in Ireland being laid waste, and plundering in Alban. A.D. 794.

The author of ' The Early Scottish Church '[2] remarks on these events, ' this new enemy must have borne heavily upon the Pictish territory, lying as it did more immediately exposed to their depredations;' for the word *Pictish* territory we ought to read *Dalriad*, as it is known to every one that the whole coast of Argyle (or Dalriad territory) lies *within sight*[3] of the islands that formed part of their possessions, and therefore it was sure to be attacked by these pirates ' *lying as it did more immediately exposed to their depredations* ' than the Pictish territory; and seeing that the Dalriads had been so lately completely crushed and vanquished by the Picts, this additional ravaging A.D. 798.

---

[1] So called by the annalist, as they were then heathens.
[2] Page 266.
[3] The largest of the islands that belonged to the Dalriads was Islay. It is in sight, and near the land of Kintyre.

A D.
802-806.

of their islands and country must have borne heavily, very heavily indeed upon them. Besides the ravaging by the Danes, as already mentioned upon Iona and the other western islands, we learn from the Annals of Ulster, under the date of these two years, that again in the first, Iona was burned, and in the last, no less than sixty-eight monks which formed the establishment there were killed by the Danes.

It was, no doubt, in consequence of these barbarous outrages on the religious teachers of the Picts that King Constantine founded Dunkeld as the seat of the primacy of the National Church; therefore, in or about A. D. 806 may be considered with reason as the date he did so. At Dunkeld there had of course long before that period been a Christian establishment, and which tradition assigns, as having been placed there by Columbia himself. The Register of St Andrews even admits the foundation of Dunkeld by King Constantine, which, coming from a quarter that was jealous of all other churches, is strong confirmation of its truth; and, as the district of Atholl and country near Dunkeld was then in the Crown, by the conquest of its provincial rulers, by Angus MacFergus, King Constantine had it in his power largely to endow his church and place it also where it must have been considered safe from the heathen plunderers. The first abbot of Dunkeld, of Constantine's foundation, would most probably be a relative of his own family, and those who succeeded to the dignity appear also to have held the primacy until removed to St Andrews. One of them is mentioned in the Annals of Ulster thus—' A. D. 865. Tuathal, son of Artguso, *primate* of Fortren[1] and *abbot of Dunkeld* died.' Eight years subsequently appears the death of Flaith-bertach who is designed *princeps Duncaillden*,' which may have been intended to signify the primate[2] or bishop (and the same word is used in the Ulster Annals, A.D. 725, for the principal ecclesiastical person), and not to be understood literally as ' prince of Dunkeld,' as no such princes ever existed.

The author of "The Early Scottish Church"[3] alters the translation of the Annals as to Tuathal being the primate,[4] into '*chief bishop*'—which is but trying to make a distinction where there is no difference.

[1] Fortren and Fortrem was the name of the Pictish territory or realm that bordered on the Forth.
[2] As an additional reason it ought to be read ' primate ' is, that in A.D. 707 the word ' principatum' is translated ' primacy' in the Annals of both Tigernach and Ulster.
[3] Page 297.
[4] The original words in the Annals design Tuathal as ' *Primus Episcopus*,' proving him to be primate, and any other translation wrong.

A.D. 807   Connal, the competitor of King Constantine, already mentioned, appears again in the Annals of Ulster, 'for we find him in 807 fighting in Dalriada, having attacked the possessions of the southern Picts in that territory, although unsuccessfully, as he was killed in Kintyre by Connal, the son of Aidan, the Pictish prince there.'[1]

King Constantine seems to have had a peaceful reign after he had gained the Pictish throne. Being the grandson of the celebrated Angus MacFergus, and his representative, would of course add to his popularity with the nation. He is called by the author of the Alban Duan as 'the daring hero Constantine.' He appears to have obtained the right of succession to the crown to remain in his own family, as after the death of himself, his brother, his own son, and nephew, who were all kings, the sovereignty came to the issue of his sisters.

A.D. 820.   Constantine, king of Alban, died this year, as stated in the Irish Annals of Ulster, and Innisfallen. He was succeeded according to the Pictish rule by his brother Angus. The writer of 'The Early Scottish Church' says,[2] 'Constantine was *succeeded by his son Drest*,' which is perfectly erroneous and must be a misprint.

This King Angus, bearing the name of

---

[1] Skene's Highlanders, vol. i., page 56.
[2] Page 280.

MacFergus, as well as his grandfather, it of course caused many events to be attributed to the wrong person. During his reign the relics, real or alleged, of St Columba, were brought into Alban by Dairmat, abbot of Iona, which is stated by the Annals of Ulster, they being thus first brought to Alban, and as it was not for two years afterwards that any part of them went to Ireland, there seems no reason to doubt a portion of them remained in Alban, and from the reverence towards Columba by the nation, this result is almost certain, and afterwards they were placed at Dunkeld. King Angus died this year, and was succeeded by his nephew, Drost, the son of Constantine, and after a short reign he was succeeded by Eoganan, or Ewen son of King Angus, but very soon afterwards he and his brother, named Bran, were both slain in battle opposing the Northmen, that is the Danes and Norwegians. Two brothers[1] then appear to have come to the throne, they were probably sons of the eldest sister of Kings Constantine and Angus—the first was named Fered, he only reigned three years. Bruidhi then succeeded, but his reign was even more brief, lasting but one year.

A.D. 829.

A.D. 834.

A.D. 837.

A.D. 839.

A.D. 842.

---

[1] They are both called MacBargoit—sons of Bargoit. See Robertson's 'Scotland under her Early Kings,' vol. ii., Appendix A, page 185.

CHAPTER VII.

The pretended Conquest of the Picts in A.D. 843. By the Irish Scots of Argyleshire, examined and refuted.

A.D. 843

WE have now arrived at the period of the succession to the Pictish throne, by Kenneth MacAlpin, and which it has been pretended he effected by a conquest over the Pictish nation and people, and has been termed the Dalriad or Scots conquest, Kenneth being a prince of that race.

That this was an utter impossibility to have been accomplished by the weakened and insignificant remnants of the Dalriads or Irish Scots, is proved by the subjection in which they had so recently been placed by the Pictish king, Angus MacFergus. The Dalriad territory, as we have seen, was laid waste, their forts and strongholds captured and destroyed, their princes taken prisoners and placed in chains, and as they never appear again, doubtless died when in captivity of the Picts, also their other principal men slain;[1] and

---

[1] The Annals of Ulster, A.D. 736, already quoted as to the Dalriad defeat on the shores of the Linne Loch, by the brother of King Angus, state, 'in which conflict many nobles were slain.'

further, their territory placed under a Pictish prince, with whom there must have been stationed a Pictish army, and whose descendant appears in the century now being treated of, and the notice of him shows he asserted the Pictish power and authority *in Kintyre*.[1] All these facts are historically attested by the Irish Annals, and prove, at this period, that a conquest by the Irish Scots over the Pictish nation, which was ten times more powerful and numerous than themselves, is *incredible*.

The writer will show this to be the case, by adducing both modern and ancient authorities that fully refute the fable that *a conquest* over the Pictish people and kingdom was achieved by Kenneth MacAlpin *in any way* or ever happened, but on the contrary, that all the existing evidence proves his was a *peaceable* succession, and a precisely similar case to the succession of King James I. to the throne of England.

The first Scottish historical writer who appears to have denied the pretended conquest over the Pictish kingdom, was T. Innes,—he states it to be '*incredible*,' that the Scots under Kenneth MacAlpin could have overcome the

---

[1] This fact is very significant of the Pictish power within the Dalriad territory, and how greatly the latter must have been reduced.

Pictish nation; and, he also adds, 'nothing less than a miracle could have effected such an overthrow,'[1] and he further devotes many following pages to enforce this fact. The next authority of last century is the learned Pinkerton, who, after his investigations into Scottish History, altogether denies any supposed conquest by the Dalriads over the Picts, and he says that the last part of the Dalriad history is the most obscure, and that this 'certainly shows a kingdom *declining* in power, and not increasing so as to conquer *the great Pikish*[2] *kingdom* as vulgarly dreamed. Had the latter been the case, the history of Dalriada would have been more and more important and notorious; while, in fact, after its conquest by Ungust (Angus MacFergus), *it sinks to nothing at once.* The Pikish affairs *on the contrary,* become more and more known. This is left to the cool consideration of the reader.'[3] This same writer says subsequently, in speaking of the weak and reduced state of the Dalriads, and that they should suddenly become conquerors *is impossible;* as also, that the fact is important to be noticed, that while the

---

[1] Innes's Critical Essay, vol. i., page 149.
[2] This historian always uses the words, Piks and Pikish, for Picts and Pictish.
[3] Pinkerton's Enquiry, vol. ii., page 137.

Dalriads have their islands and country ravaged and over-run by the Danes offering no resistance, the Pictish people nobly *oppose them with large armies*.[1]

Chalmers likewise remarking on the Dalriad weak and miserable condition, from the constant bloodshed and fighting among themselves, says—'These facts evince that this enfeebling polity continued to distract *and ruin* the Dalriadinian kingdom, till the final period *of its wretched existence.*'[2] These writers thus describe the true state of the Dalriads, and their total inability at this period to have accomplished what is attributed to them; and these views are also held by the most recent historical writers: thus we are told by Gregory, when speaking of the accession of Kenneth MacAlpin to the throne of the Pictish kingdom, that 'it seems perfectly clear that the Dicaledones, *or* Picts, who formed the bulk of *the Highland population* in these early times, were secured from any sweeping change by the rugged nature of the country they inhabited. In these Dicaledones, or Picts, therefore, *we see the ancestors of the great mass of the modern Highlanders*, excepting those of Argyleshire, among

A.D. 843.

---

[1] Pinkerton's Enquiry into Scottish History, vol. ii. page 161.
[2] Chalmers's Caledonia, vol. i., page 297.

whom, in all probability, the Dalriadic blood predominated.'[1]

These very few words in the above extract contain the real truth as to the bearing of any supposed conquest over the ancestors of the Highlanders at this period, and the further modern, along with the ancient evidence to be given in this chapter, will amply verify and establish the truth of the extract.

Another authority, when speaking of how the name of Scotland came to be in use in North Britain, says, 'The name of Scotland must have spread over the country, from the fact of its kings being derived *from that race*, and of their political pre-eminence, than from an *actual subjugation* of all the Pictish tribes, as *feigned by the Scottish historians*—a theory the absurdity of which it is impossible not to perceive, if we look at the state of Scotland in 731, and *the very great superiority of the Picts over the Scots in power, extent of territory, and in numbers.*'[2]

The present learned Professor of History in the University of Edinburgh is also an authority against any sort of conquest over the Pictish kingdom. Speaking of how Kenneth MacAlpin had attained the throne of the nation,

[1] Gregory's Highlands and Isles of Scotland, page 3.
[2] Skene's Highlanders, vol i, page 62.

he says it was by '*succession*.' He also says 'the Scots and Picts were united under Kenneth MacAlpin, and from thenceforward by a strange process the name of the Picts, as a nation, disappears from history. *The change, however, was only one of dynasty and national name.*' The Professor also adds that, notwithstanding the alteration of rulers he had mentioned, '*the inhabitants do not appear to have suffered a change.*'[1] Thus properly denying that the succession to the Pictish throne by Kenneth had been by bloodshed and violence. The following also clearly points out the impossibility of the Irish Scots making a conquest over the Pictish kingdom:—'Our earlier writers in general have attributed to Kenneth the complete *conquest* and *extermination* of *the whole Pictish nation;* but although many attempts were made by their followers to bring this account *within the bounds of probability,* an examination into the more genuine authorities for Scottish history, and the total silence of contemporary writers in other countries (a silence *unaccountable* upon the supposition of a revolution of *such magnitude having taken place*) soon showed the absurdity of this fable.'[2]

---

[1] See 'Scotland in the Middle Ages,' by Professor Innes, at pages 15 and 17 of notes on the Maps.

[2] Skene's Highlanders, vol. i., pages 21, 22.

Another writer on the subject says, 'is it by any means probable that a small band[1] of emigrants, landing in Scotland from Ireland in 503 A.C., would have been able in the year 843 A.C. *to overthrow a kingdom which had successfully resisted the Roman*[2] *armies?*'

The next historical writer to be quoted is the author of 'Scotland under her Early Kings'—the very best work on the ancient history of present Scotland—he throughout denies the possibility of any conquest of the Pictish people by the conquered and weakened Dalriad tribes. In the second volume of this work, the subject of a conquest by the Irish Scots is separately and most clearly discussed, from it the following few lines are taken:— 'It is utterly impossible that the Picts could have been exterminated *and their language eradicated* by the broken remnants of the insignificant tribe of Kintyre, and it is equally improbable that such a conquest, if it *ever* took place, should have escaped the notice of *every contemporary writer*. The *Pictish name disappeared, but the Pictish people and their language remained* as little influenced by the accession

---

[1] Which we have before seen was so small that it only gave a band of fifty men to each of the three leaders of the first settlers of the Irish Scots.

[2] Celtic Gleanings, page 55, by the Rev. Dr T. M'Lauchlan.

of Kenneth MacAlpin, apparently in right of his maternal ancestry, as they were at a later period by the *failure* of the male line of the *same family* in the person of Malcolm II., and by the similar accession, in right of his maternal ancestors, of a *prince of the Pictish house of Atholl*.'[1]

These modern authorities will be amply confirmed and supported by the ancient evidence to be given hereafter, and it ought to be well remembered that the whole of these authors knew the fables in the writings of Fordun, Bœce, and Buchanan, as to the Picts and Scots, but which, it will be perceived, are *wholly disregarded*.

It is proper also to point out that Kenneth MacAlpin's claim to the sovereignty arose from his descent from the Pictish kings—the mother of his father Alpin, was a Pictish princess, whose name is Latinsed as Urgusia. She was sister to two Pictish kings, namely, to Constantine,[2] who reigned from A.D. 789 to 820, and of King Angus, who reigned from that last date till 834. After the death of the sons

[1] See Robertson's 'Scotland under her Early Kings,' vol. ii., page 373.

[2] It has been already alluded to that King Constantine had been enabled to make the throne hereditary in his family,—a great change in Pictish customs—the whole of the monarchs that succeeded him being of his race, either by the male or female line.

of these two monarchs, there appears, as already said, two brothers to have come to the throne, and if the supposition of their being the issue of an elder sister of Urgusia be correct, as it appears highly probable, then the succession would of course open to the issue of Urgusia—her son was Alpin[1] (a name used by Pictish kings) the father of Kenneth—this female descent from the Pictish kings makes the case precisely to resemble that of King James I., and all writers, from even the earliest times, have testified to this marriage, and future events still better establish the truth of it. Innes quotes Fordun and all subsequent writers for it.[2] Chalmers, also, fully states as to this marriage[3] with the provincial prince of Kintyre, etc., called Eoganan M'Aodh (also Achaius in Latin) his son Alpin, has been said to have been killed in a foray he made into Galloway, to attack the Picts, as the fabulous writers have it; but Chalmers has most distinctly proved[4] he must have been fighting with the

---

[1] The name of Alpin was wholly unknown among the Dalriad princes, and 'from the name of Alpin, and those of his descendants, it is plain that the Dalriadic king must have been connected with the Picts by the female line.'—See Skene's Highlanders, vol. i., page 60.

[2] See Innes's Crit. Essay, vol. i., page 141.

[3] Chalmers's Caledonia, vol. i., page 299, and note.

[4] Chalmers's Caledonia, vol. i., page 303, note.

Irish Scots, examined and refuted. 85

Britons, as he was killed near to the town of Ayr—the burial place of Alpin, in the reign of King William the Lion was known; and in a charter by that monarch to the town of Ayr, dated in 1197, it is mentioned as one of the boundaries, and called 'Lacht Alpin'—the grave stone of Alpin. Near to it are cairns and tumuli, and also the tradition of a battle having taken place there.

The ancient evidence, fully supporting and proving the quotations from the modern writers, will now be given.

The first authority in point of antiquity is the work called 'Nennius,' the author of it himself declares it was written A.D. 858, he therefore was alive both *before* and *after* the date of the alleged conquest of the Picts; but when he writes and speaks of them *fifteen years after* it has been asserted a conquest had been achieved over them by the Scots, he says, 'ibi, tertiam partem Britanniæ tenuerunt, *et tenent usque nunc*,'[1] that is, 'there, the third part of Britain they held, *and hold until now*.' Here there is clear and positive proof that the Pictish people and kingdom existed and held the same portion of Britain as they ever had done, and this evidence completely refutes the possibility

[1] See Nennius, cap. 5.

of any sort of conquest or violence having been the means whereby Kenneth MacAlpin succeeded to the Pictish throne—this writer being a living witness, and giving his testimony against it.

The next evidence to be given is also contemporary, namely, that of Asser (Bishop of Sherborne) called also Asserius in Latin. He lived in the reign of Alfred the Great, and wrote his life, and who began his reign A.D. 871. In this history, Asser often mentions the Pictish nation, and declares they were an existing people. He also speaks of the ravages of the Danes in their country, and this he particularly alludes to under the year A.D. 875. The translation of Asser's history by Dr Giles (published by Bohn, London, at page 58) also shows this proof of the Pictish kingdom as still subsisting as heretofore.

Therefore, when we consider that Asser[1] was living during the reign of Kenneth MacAlpin —his testimony (written soon after A.D. 901), that the Picts were still the same nation as at that prior period, and that they were engaged as a nation in resisting their enemies the Danes, is such clear evidence, that it satisfactorily proves

---

[1] Asser has been supposed to have been made Bishop in A.D. 871. He died in A.D. 910.—See Saxon Chronicle for that year.

the Picts had been neither conquered or exterminated.

The next evidence is also contemporary, namely, 'The Saxon Chronicle,' which is considered the oldest national record that exists of the Anglo-Saxon tongue. One copy is as old as A. D. 891 for events to that date, and is still preserved in Corpus Christi College, Cambridge.[1] This chronicle has a great deal about the Picts in the early part of it: and under the year A. D. 875 states, that the Danish king called Halfdene, 'went with some of the army into Northumbria (that is Northumberland) and took up winter quarters by the river Tyne: and the army subdued the land, *and oft-times spoiled the Picts* and the Strathclyde Britons.' The writer of this record being alive at the date of this event we see that he adds his testimony to the previous ancient ones, that the Picts were still the inhabitants and possessors of their country as hitherto. This last notice likewise proves that it must have been what are sometimes called 'the southern Picts' that we are here told were often spoiled by the Danish king's army from Northumberland; and that in A. D. 875 they are still called 'Picts.'

---

[1] See page 31 of the preface to the Saxon Chronicle, Bohn's edition, London. This is a most valuable collection of all the most ancient writers we have, and highly useful for quotations.

The Welsh Annals or Triads are also of very remote antiquity. They designate the Picts as Gwddel[1] Ffichti, or Guthel Phichti, that is, *the Pictish Gael,* but make no mention of any conquest over them.

The next authority to be adduced that there was no such thing as a conquest over the Caledonian Picts, by the Irish Scots, or Dalriads, is the Irish Annals.

These ancient and valuable authorities have recorded (as has already appeared) the most minute events regarding the history and proceedings of the Irish Scots, or Dalriads, ever since their first arrival in A.D. 506 up to the period now under review; and as we have seen, during this long period of considerably more than *three hundred years,* the smallest of their forays or expeditions have been mentioned. Therefore in the Irish Annals we ought surely to find confirmation of the pretended Scots conquest over the Picts, if *it had ever happened,* or that Kenneth MacAlpin had succeeded to the throne by force or violence over the Picts, an event of such magnitude, it is impossible to believe they would not have made known. But these authorities, instead of proving any overthrow of the Pictish king-

---

[1] Robertson's 'Scotland under her Early Kings,' vol. ii, page 361, and note; also see Skene's Highlanders, vol. i, pages 69, 70.

dom, or extirpation of the Pictish people, prove the contrary. Thus the Annals of Ulster, fifteen years after the alleged conquest, call Kenneth MacAlpin *'King of the Picts,'* proving both the kingdom and people then existed, as hitherto, and giving a complete contradiction to the fable *of any kind* of conquest. The events of his reign strongly confirm his having succeeded to the Pictish throne in a peaceable manner. Within a few years of his accession, A.D. 489. Dunblane, a frontier town of the Picts was burned by the Strathclyde Britons, upon which the new king raised, and advanced with a large army to the south, across the Forth. He also attacked and ravaged the country of the Anglo-Saxons.[1] He penetrated as far as Dunbar, which he burned, and next destroyed Melrose. All this *must have been* effected by a *Pictish* army, and if Kenneth had not been a monarch of the Picts by legitimate right, he could not have dared thus to leave the country had he been a usurper of the crown by violence, as the people would at once have risen in his abscence. The Danes also were, during his reign, opposed by the Pictish people, and these marauding

---

[1] Kenneth invaded the country of the Saxons no less than six times, with Pictish armies. See Innes's Essay, vol. ii., pages 782, 783, where the ancient authorities for these facts is given.

pirates were unable to reach further into the interior than Cluny in the Stormont, and Dunkeld, which were both burned by them. The chronicle printed by Innes,[1] which records these facts, states both places were in the territory of the Picts, calling it their country by the term 'Pictavia.'

There is a point not alluded to by any writers on this subject, of a conquest by the Dalriads over the powerful Pictish kingdom, namely, that Kenneth is never said to have encountered, or conquered, any king of the Picts, and it is surely impossible to believe that there was no one among the whole nation who had any claim to the throne. This strongly confirms the other evidence of Kenneth's accession of his being himself heir, by descent from the sister of Kings Constantine and Angus, and with general consent of the nation.

There is another subject connected with his reign that deserves to be pointed out. Kenneth's son was named *Constantine*. This was such an unusual name, and had only been borne by one king of the Picts, and never known among the Irish Scots, that it certainly is very strong presumptive evidence that it was derived from Kenneth's connection with the royal Pictish family, King Constantine

---

[1] See T. Innes's Essay, vol. ii., pages 782, 783.

having been brother to Urgusia, Kenneth's grandmother.

There are some expressions used by the learned editor of Adomnan's Life of Columba, as to Kenneth, to which the descendants of the Caledonian Gael may justly take exception, he calls[1] him 'the annexer of Pictland,' and in another place[2] 'the Pictish nation yielded to Scotic rule, and Kenneth MacAlpin *transferred*[3] the seat of government to the eastern side of the kingdom.' If any Scotchman was to say that King James I. annexed England to Scotland, or that the English yielded to 'Scotic rule,' it would be deemed an unfounded and vain boast, so neither can Kenneth's pretensions ever be established by such assertions as these. As to the seat of government (the same sentiment being used by the author of 'The Early Scottish[4] Church'), the Pictish nation and kings possessed *that* many centuries ere Kenneth, the petty king of the insignificant Irish Scots in Argyle happened to succeed to the throne of the Pictish kingdom.

[1] Dr Reeves's edition of Adomnan's Life of Columba, page 437.

[2] Dr Reeves's edition of Adomnan's Life of Columba, page 207.

[3] From this phrase, it might be thought the Pictish nation and kingdom had been without any seat of government prior to the time of Kenneth MacAlpin!

[4] Page 284.

There is another event connected with this period which becomes a very strong piece of evidence to show that the succession of Kenneth was a peaceful one. Had he been a usurper, or in *any way* attained the throne by violence over the Pictish people, then, as a conqueror, he would, beyond dispute, have given the throne to *his own son;* but from history we find he could not do so, and that *his brother* succeeded him in preference to his son, according to *the invariable Pictish* custom. This surely must be viewed, in connection with all the other evidence, as a very strong proof that the succession was the same as in the case of all the other Pictish monarchs; and it establishes the fact, that however far this 'annexer' may have most naturally desired his successor to have been his son, yet we see the Scotic had *to yield to Pictish rule.*

A.D. 858. The Annals of Ulster state, that this year 'Kenneth MacAlpin, *King of the Picts*,[1] died. Here, as has been alluded to before, his title gives further proof against the alleged conquest. The place of his death, according to every writer, was at one of the royal Pictish

---

[1] Kenneth is also called *King of the Picts* by Nennius, see Innes's Essay, vol. i., page 153.

residences, now called Forteviot,[1] in Strathearn, Perthshire.

Donald MacAlpin, the brother of Kenneth, A.D. 858. next succeeded. This was so remarkable a yielding on the part of a new family to the national Pictish custom, that it was brought forward by Robert Bruce in his competition for the crown against Baliol. He stated in his third plea, that the ancient manner of succession supported his claim, namely, that the brother, *as being nearest in degree* (ratione proximitatis in gradu), was preferred to the son of the deceased monarch, and he stated, when Kenneth MacAlpin died, his brother Donald was preferred to his son Constantine. Bruce even added further instances of this national custom of succession, namely, that when the above King Constantine died (which was in A.D. 877) his brother Aodh was preferred to his son named Donald, and lastly, he stated that the brother[2] of Malcolm III. (called Ceanmor) reigned after him to the exclusion of the son of Malcolm.

During the reign of King Donald (called

[1] It is called Dun-Fothir, and Fothirtavait, anciently See 'Robertson's Early Kings,' vol. i., pages 41, 108, and 232. Innes likewise mentions it under the latter name, of which Forteviot is a corruption.

[2] He is known in Scotch history as Donald Bane, or Donald the Fair; his reign began 1093.

'ruddy faced' in the Alban duan), an event took place which gives clear and strong testimony against the pretended conquest, and which is recorded in the ancient Pictish chronicle (first printed by Innes),[1] and makes known that a national council was held at Forteviot, by '*the Highlanders*,' called in Gaelic '*gaidheil*,'[2] (and which last word is Latinised, 'gœdeli,' in the ancient chronicle), who, being assembled[3] with their king, enacted the laws of Aodh Fin (called also Eochy Fionn), one of the petty Dalriad kings, and therefore a predecessor of King Donald. The following is a short extract from the chronicle—'in hujus tempore jura ac leges regni Edi filii Ecdachi fecerunt *Gœdeli* cum rege suo in Fothuirtabait.' This transaction of enacting fresh laws in the Pictish kingdom, and which had previously prevailed among the Dalriads, shows the whole

[1] See T. Innes's Critical Essay, vol. ii., page 783. The date admitted for this ancient chronicle is the ninth century, the very period that the alleged conquest of the Picts (by fabulous writers) is stated to have happened.

[2] This word has exactly the same meaning as 'Gael,' and is the plural of the word 'Gaidheal,' a Highlander—the spelling of this word in the Annals of Ulster, under the year 1034, is *Gaedhel*.

[3] This national council, was, of course, held at the Moot hill (called Mód in Gaelic) of Forteviot, according to the remote customs of the Gael—the date was prior to A.D. 862, when King Donald's death took place.

proceeding to be that of a free and independent nation—had the fable of a conquest any foundation, the laws of the conquerors, would, of course, have been forced upon the conquered. It was a solemn compact between the people of the Pictish kingdom and the new race of kings, it is also to be remarked, that it was to *the second* of this new dynasty, and not to the alleged conqueror that this concession was made, no doubt, by the Maormors, chieftains, and people of Alban then assembled.[1]

King Donald died at Inver-Almond,[2] which place has been already mentioned, as a Rath, or fortified stronghold, on the river Tay, where the Almond falls into it. The Irish Annals also prove this king was, like his brother Kenneth, never designed king of the Scots; but under the above date (A.D. 862) there is stated in the Annals of Ulster, 'Donald MacAlpin, *King of the Picts died.*'   A.D. 862

Constantine, son of Kenneth MacAlpin, succeeded. The Irish Annals still called his dominions the country of the Picts, as, under this date, the Annals of Ulster state that Ceallach, the abbot of Iona, died 'in regione   A.D. 865

---

[1] This assembly is fully noticed in Robertson's 'Early Kings,' when these laws were passed, and involving the right of King Donald's family to the throne, vol. i., page 478.

[2] Innes's Critical Essay, vol. ii, page 801.

Pictorum,' in the kingdom or 'country *of the Picts.*'

A.D. 875. The Danes had been successful in most of their encounters. In this year, however, happened the greatest defeat that hitherto the Pictish people met with, namely, by the Danish leader Thorstein, and it is mentioned in all the English Chronicles as well as the Annals[1] of Ireland. Thorstein, however, was unexpectedly surprised and killed by the Gael of Alban the same year, and, in consequence, there did not follow the bad results that otherwise would have happened.

A.D. 876. King Constantine died in battle this year,[2] and the Irish Annals likewise prove he was called '*King of the Picts,*' his brother Aodh or Hugh succeeded, the Pictish rule again enforced though he had a son. His reign was very short, only two years, a usurper named Cyric or Grig, having defeated and made him prisoner in the battle for the crown, that took place in Strath-

---

[1] The Annals of Ulster expressly state that it was the Pictish people who fought this year with the black foreigners or Danes. The words are, 'A.D. 875. Conflict between *the Picts* and the Dugalls.'

[2] See Annals of Ulster, which is the best authority, though the writer of 'The Early Scottish Church' puts it most erroneously (at page 287), down to the year A.D. 881. See also as to the place where this king's death happened, in Fife, and *not* at Perth, in Robertson's 'Early Kings,' vol. i., page 48.

allan, Perthshire. Aodh's death followed from his wounds.[1] The Annals of Ulster likewise call this monarch '*King of the Picts*,' in mentioning his death in A.D. 878. The dates and names of the successive kings of Alban will be found in the Appendix, and the intermediate ones, to another King Constantine, now to be spoken of, can there be seen.

This year this new monarch, properly Constantine III., ascended the throne of Alban. He was the son of the last Aodh mentioned. He avenged the former attacks by the Danes, who four years after his accession invaded Fortreim (the territory bordering on the Forth as already explained), under command of their great leader Ivor, who, as the Annals of Ulster state,[2] was slain 'and great slaughter of his followers.' This battle took place in Strathearn, which is one of the finest and most extensive valleys in Scotland, and it was always one of the principal strongholds of the Pictish kingdom, and where was one of the royal residences. Peaceful times followed for fifteen years, when the Annals state at great length an engagement between a large army of the Gael, who under King Constantine responded

A.D. 900.

A.D. 904.

A.D. 918.

[1] See Robertson's 'Scotland under her Early Kings.' vol. i., pages 49, 50.

[2] 'Annals Ulster.' A.D. 904, also Robertson's 'Early Kings,' vol i., page 53.

to an appeal made to them by the Lords of the Northumbrian Angles, to give them aid against their common enemy, the Danes, who had landed from Ireland in great force, and laid waste the whole of England, north from York inclusive. The Annals of Ulster[1] mention, A.D. 918, that the Danes 'afterwards invade the people of Alban. The men of Alban, however, prepared and opposed themselves to them, and gave them battle with the assistance of the Northern Saxons.' The Danish commander (named Reginald) made a skilful disposition of his troops, keeping one division concealed. The battle-field was at Corbridge-on-Tyne. The Annals say 'the men of Alban were victorious over the three battalions which they saw, and made a great slaughter of the Gentiles;' but the division of the Danes in ambush coming on the rear of the Gael and Saxons completely routed them, the heaviest losses falling on the Saxons, whose leader Edred was killed with many of his followers. The Annals state that though there were many of the men of Alban killed, 'but neither their king nor any of the maormors[2] were slain.' The Danes did

[1] See 'Annals of Ulster,' A.D. 918, also Robertson's 'Early Kings,' vol. i., pages 57, 58, 59.

[2] This was the title of the provincial kings of the Gael of Alban, to whom it was peculiar, and unknown to the Irish Gael.

not go north, which is a clear proof that Constantine and his army had retired in good order.

It is quite evident from the numerous armies of the Pictish nation that had now constantly opposed the Danes for more than a hundred years, how populous and powerful the Pictish people must have been, and thereby this fact becomes *certain proof* that such incessant warfare and resistance could not have been carried on by a conquered, but by *a free, valiant, and independent nation.*

This year the Picts are expressly stated as having fought under King Constantine at a battle in England named Brunanburgh,[1] near the banks of the Humber, and which was against the Saxon King Athelstane, who was victorious. A son of Constantine was killed there.

A.D. 937.

In the end of King Constantine's reign the inroads of the Danes ceased to be formidable, and no longer on the great scale as hitherto,[2] brought about by the powerful and constant resistance of *the Pictish* people *alone*, in accordance with the evidence and proofs already given, and the following is further authority for this fact, ' the people who opposed the in-

---

[1] See Ingulph's Ancient Chronicle, and page 75, edition by H. T. Riley, published by Bohn, London; also Robertson's Early Kings, vol. i., pages 64, 65.

[2] See Robertson's Early Kings, vol. i., page 68.

vasions of the Norwegians *at this period* (the tenth century) were unquestionably the descendants *of the very same people who fought with the Romans* many ages before, and who then exhibit the same division into tribes of a similar extent.'[1] It is to be observed that here is no mention of the Scots, they remaining within their own petty territory,[2] and even that they could not defend from being conquered by the Northmen, their whole islands and mainland of Argyleshire, became part of a dependency of that people for centuries, and from which they never could have freed themselves; but they were ultimately freed by the valour of their countrymen, by the true descendants of the noble Caledonian Gael, along with that of the southern Anglo-Saxon race of Scotland.

A.D. 943. This year King Constantine III. resigned his crown, and retired to the monastery of St Andrews, of which he became abbot. He was succeeded by King Malcolm, grandson of Constantine II., the son of Kenneth MacAlpin.

A.D. 949. Six years after taking this step the aged

---

[1] See Skene's Highlanders, vol. i., page 97, and for date see same vol., pages 106 and 96.

[2] This freedom from the power of the Northmen by the Caledonian Picts is, in 'the Early Scottish Church,' of course, attributed to '*the Scot,*' and not to the courage and skill of the Pictish people *who accomplished it.*—See page 303 of 'The Early Scottish Church.'

Irish Scots, examined and refuted.

king reappeared and took command of a large army which he led into England, even as far as the river Tees, and returned in triumph, again retiring to his monastery, where he died in A.D. 952, as mentioned in the 'Annals of Ulster,' and is called 'King of Alban,' as all the subsequent monarchs are. A.D. 952.

A very important piece of evidence will now be given, still further proving the *impossibility* of any sort of conquest over the Pictish nation by the Dalriads or Irish Scots, and which evidence likewise completely establishes the fact that, ' not a trace either of extermination *or of gradual colonization can be detected during this*[1] *period.'* There are two entries in the Irish Annals which make it known, namely, in those of Tigernach and Ulster. The former say,— 'A.D. 989, Gofraig[2] son of Aralt, king of Innsegall,[3] *slain by the Dalriads.*' The Ulster Annals A.D. 989.

---

[1] See Robertson's Scotland under her Early Kings, vol. ii., page 374.

[2] This name is Godfrey, and is so translated elsewhere, but the exact entry is given.

[3] Always afterwards called Inchgall. The death of this Gofraig, king of the Isles, is noticed by Gregory in his work on the Highlands and Isles of Scotland, page 5, and from what he mentions, it appears his father Aralt was son of Sitric, king of Northumberland, and that Aralt had been a younger brother to Aulaf (or Olave) king of the Isles, also a son of Sitric, and who Gregory also mentions fought at the battle of Brunanburg.

give the same words, with the addition that this king was 'slain in *Dalriada*.' The importance of this testimony will be evident, when it is considered that it distinctly proves that the Dalriads or Irish Scots had *never left their own country*, whereby it is beyond cavil *certain* they had neither conquered or colonised the Pictish nation. This evidence is as clear proof of the Dalriads being at this period *the inhabitants* of their country in Argyleshire, as of any event that the Irish Annals make known to us respecting them; and when we consider that Tigernach must have been alive within from twenty to thirty years, or even less, of the occurrence, whereby he must have met many who were living when it happened, and as the Dalriads were still remaining within the same territory as they ever had done, and that Tigernach continued his Annals till the year 1072,[1] and yet makes no mention of the Dalriads having ever left their country, which, from the importance of such an event during his own lifetime he would not have failed to have mentioned, had it happened, therefore, upon this undeniable authority, we are entitled to declare it is proved, that the Dalriads or Irish Scots of Argyle *never left* their original

---

[1] He died a very aged abbot in 1088.—See the Iona Club Transactions, page 210.

place of settlement, and likewise this evidence proves the pretended conquest *impossible*, and that Kenneth MacAlpin ascended the throne of the Pictish nation in a peaceable manner, precisely as did King James I. of England.

There are also two further proofs that fully confirm this fact, that the Dalriads remained within their circumscribed country—the first is, that any of the Western Clans who claim descent from the Irish Scots, are still situated within what was the *Dalriad territory*—a very clear and certain proof there never had been any removal by their forefathers into the territories of the original Caledonian Gael of Alban. It would have favoured the theory of a conquest by the Irish Scots if their descendants had occupied the highlands of Perthshire, Inverness-shire, Ross, Sutherland, or Caithness; but when they are found confined *to the Dalriad territory of Argyleshire*, the truth is apparent, and refutes in the clearest manner the pretended conquest. To anticipate objections, it may be well to mention that there is a very ancient clan—the Grants—whose chiefs, in their descent, are said to be from the same source as the M'Gregors, and therefore of the Irish[1] Scots; but this clan (the Grants) is as

[1] The descent of the M'Gregors from the Irish Scots or Dalriads is by no means proved, and is denied by very good authority.

pure in descent from the noble Caledonian Gael as any in Scotland—they are descendants of the ancient tribes inhabiting Strathspey,[1] and cannot be claimed as coming of the Irish, nor can any other of the supposed descendants of the Dalriads be so, who, perhaps, four to five hundred years *after* the date of the fabulous conquest, may have got a grant[2] of lands which had been Pictish territory, the inhabitants thereon naturally taking the surname of the owner, when surnames began in Scotland; but the clan descent was purely *Caledonian* Gael, and *not Scots.*

But besides this, there is another proof which further confirms the fact that the Dalriads or Irish Scots never quitted the Dalriad country, namely, *their language*—it being notorious that of all the Gaelic now spoken in Scotland, that in Argyleshire, formerly the Dalriad or Scots country, is the most *corrupted* with Irish Gaelic, and from which the Gaelic language spoken by the rest of the Highlanders *is free;* for this fact, those who wish to see written proof, will find it clearly established in the introduction to

---

[1] Strathspey was a part of that large province which belonged to the powerful and ancient maormors of Moray.

[2] Although the M'Gregors claim Irish Scotch descent, it is doubtful. They got lands in Perthshire, but after great research (by that excellent antiquary D. Gregory) their earliest connection with the lands go no further back than 1290 or 450 years after the Scots conquest.

the 'Book of the Dean of Lismore'[1] *throughout*, also in the Report of the Highland Society on Ossian's Poems;[2] therefore we find the result of the Irish Scots colony was, that their descendants *long after* Kenneth MacAlpin's time, are proved by the Irish Annals still to be remaining within their place of original settlement, and their descendants are also there to this day, and of course their peculiar Irish corrupt Gaelic language is also remaining with them; these facts are among the strongest proofs yet given of the absurdity of any conquest over the Pictish nation by the paltry insignificant colony of the Irish Scots.

The Dalriads having thus been most clearly proved to *have remained* within their original country (notwithstanding Kenneth MacAlpin's succession to the Pictish throne) quite as much, as in a precisely similar manner, the Scots also remained in their own country, when King James I. ascended the English throne, therefore this testimony most completely refutes the asser-

[1] By W. F. Skene, Esq., already often referred to.

[2] Besides the instances already noticed from this report, of the corrupt Irish spoken Gaelic of Argyleshire, there is another mention of it at pages 21 and 22 of the Appendix, where it is stated that in the southern part of the Island of Mull (the only portion of it ever belonging to the Irish Scots), though the poems of Ossian were known, they were only *Irish imitations*, and of that kind that M'Pherson had rejected from their corruptions.

tion of the author of 'The Early Scottish Church,' when he speaks[1] of the union of the Pictish nation and the Scots thus, 'their (the Picts) union with *the latter seems to have been the means of their preservation!!*' How the Irish Scots could have *preserved*[2] the Pictish people and nation when they never left their own barren country, will be a hard task for any one to prove, and the statement can only be looked upon as a boastful assumption, destitute of any foundation from history or fact; indeed, the object of this whole book is evidently an attempt to unduly exalt the colony of Irish Scots, particularly as to their antiquity, whereby many errors are made, as has been fully proved. The union of the Dalriad country to the Pictish kingdom is also spoken of by the author in two places,[3] as that of *the two great kingdoms* of the Scots and Picts. To prevent readers being misled by such exaggeration as to the Scots and the greatness of their country, it becomes necessary to make them aware, that what is here called '*the great*

---

[1] See page 290.

[2] If the Pictish people had only to look to, or depend on the insignificant Scots colony for '*their preservation*,' instead of their own valour, their situation *would indeed have been hopeless*.

[3] 'Early Scottish Church,' pages 229, 290.

Scots kingdom' was *the poorest* and *most insignificant* that perhaps ever existed under such a name.¹ Certainly the most so in Britain. Even the small kingdom of the Strathclyde Britons far surpassed the Scots in richness² and fertility, as likewise in extent, prior to the later acquisitions of the Angles (at the close of the eighth century), the territory of the Britons till then, comprehending a part of the Lennox, with that great stronghold Dumbarton,³ and stretching thence through the fine southwest country to Galloway. It formed in ancient times part of what was known as the kingdom of Cumbria, which extended 'from Dumbartonshire to North Wales.'⁴

At an interval of thirty years after the date last given from the Annals, both the Pictish people and country had come to be called

1020.

---

¹ A very strong proof, disclosing the poverty of the lands that formed the country of the Scots is contained in the rental of the bishoprick of the Isles, etc., in the Iona Club Transactions, where, instead of merk lands and pound lands, like the rest of the Highlands, it dwindles down *to penny, and even to halfpenny lands!*

² The whole of the banks of the Clyde from Dumbarton to Glasgow, and thence up the valley of the Clyde, is of the richest description of country.

³ Dumbarton was anciently called Alclyde—it withstood a siege by two kings of the Northmen for four months, as mentioned in the Annals of Ulster, A.D. 870.

⁴ Robertson's Scotland under her Early Kings, vol. i, page 70.

Scots and Scotland,¹ but this new name will be fully adverted to hereafter.

The male descendants of Kenneth MacAlpin ended in King Malcolm II., who came to the throne in 1005, and died in 1034. His daughter Bethoc, or Beatrice, married Crinan, abbot of Dunkeld, and Abthane, of Dull,² their son became king of the Scots, as Duncan I., from 1034 to 1040. This family has been designed 'the Atholl family,' and from them sprung the last and greatest of Scotland's race of pure Celtic kings, who ended in the death of King Alexander III. in 1285. The throne then came by female descent to King Robert Bruce, and next similarly through the Stewart's, kings of Scotland, it has descended to her present gracious Majesty.

Although Crinan, the father of King Duncan I. was an abbot, it must not be thought that at this time there was anything irregular for an ecclesiastic to be married; it prevailed from very remote ages, and continued for a period of two centuries afterwards, and the Rev. Dr Thomas M'Lauchlan, on the subject of the clergy of

---

¹ The name of Scotia, or Scotland, as elsewhere observed, was never attributed to the country now so called before *the eleventh century.*—See Ritson's Caledonia, vol. ii., page 16.

² Crinan's descent, it is possible, may have been from the hereditary abbots of Dunkeld, descended of the founder, the Pictish King Constantine. The Lordship of Dull, in Atholl, has likewise been considered as his family possessions.

the ancient church being married, has well and truly said, that this fact, '*so far from being an evidence of corruption, it is the very opposite.*'[1] Why should the clergymen of that period[2] be denied the blessings of marriage, and yet granted to those of the present day? Besides, the 'forbidding to marry' is one of the great marks of the apostacy predicted by St Paul.

Although it may now be thought that an abundance of testimony has been produced to refute and disprove the possibility of the pretended conquest by the Scots over the Pictish nation, there are some further proofs which should not be passed over.

There is still preserved, and has been printed by the Iona Club, page 70, at full length, a correct copy of the most ancient Gaelic genealogy of the kings of Alban (Scotland) that exists—it is called the Alban duan,[3] and is herein given in the Appendix. It was the composition of the court bard, or poet of King Malcolm Ceanmore, and its date would

[1] The Early Scottish Church, page 335.
[2] Robertson in his 'Early Kings,' vol. i., page 149, note—speaking of Queen Margaret's reforms, has a very interesting note, by which it appears she never proposed to separate the Culdees from their wives, and that numbers of her countrymen, the Saxon clergy, were married, probably her views were not propounded long before the death of King Malcolm in 1098.
[3] The word duan is nearly synonymous with the word canto.

be coincident with his coming to the throne. As to its historical merit there are errors, from the bard introducing Pictish kings into the list instead of Scots. He likewise makes two kings named Conall to succeed each other, that, also, is an error, likely from tradition having informed him, that 250 years before, a king Conall was killed *in Kintyre* by a prince also called Conall; as it was so common an occurrence for the petty princes of the Scots to kill each other, he put them both down as Dalriad kings; but with regard to its value as a clear testimony against Kenneth MacAlpin's pretended conquest, it is an undoubted genuine proof. The purpose of the poet is to extol and magnify the deeds of all the predecessors of King Malcolm, therefore, in this piece of evidence, we should have heard of the great achievement of Kenneth MacAlpin as a conqueror, or annexer, of the Pictish kingdom, if it had ever happened; but the account given of him is, that Kenneth was then unknown to have accomplished an undertaking of such magnitude with his paltry bands of Irish Scots from Argyleshire, *the only means belonging to him*. He is simply called Kenneth 'the hardy.' This evidence demonstrates, therefore, that in 1057 the fable of a conquest had not been heard of, and was *an invention* of later times.

There was an ancient Scotch historical writer who lived during this period named Marianus of Ratisbon, and called a Scotchman. He wrote of events of Scotch history so remote as A.D. 632.[1] He was born in the year 1028 (as mentioned in Robertson's Scotland under her Early Kings),[2] and that author also says he was junior to Tigernach, and adds 'their authority, therefore, at this period, *as contemporaries is very great.*' This ancient writer was also contemporary with Macbeth; and, as already mentioned, he wrote respecting very remote events of Scotch history down to his own time; yet he never once alludes to, or gives the slightest intimation of the pretended conquest; therefore this becomes another additional proof and evidence against it. Marianus was alive in 1085, as a MS. of his writing of that date exists. He died at Mentz[3] 1088. He was undoubtedly the first native writer of present Scotland that was acknowledged as such, both at home and in foreign countries, in contradistinction to the Scots of Ireland, who, prior to the opening of this century, had been ever held as solely belonging to that country.

[1] See Maitland's History of Scotland, introduction, vol. i, page 22.
[2] Vol. i., page 116, note.
[3] Maitland's History of Scotland, preface, vol. i., page 4

The whole of the most ancient chronicles of England mention nothing, or give the slightest intimation, of a conquest by the Irish Colony of Scots over the Pictish nation. The writers Æthelward, or Ingulph, the most ancient, have not a trace of such an event.

1158. In the twelfth century there was written, as already mentioned, under the authority of Andrew, Bishop of Caithness, a treatise called 'de situ Albaniæ' (and printed by Innes)[1] which has these words '*Albania quæ nunc corrupte Scotia appellatur*' is '*Albania* (or the land of Alban), *which is now corruptly called Scotland,*' very distinctly proves that at this period one of the most learned men of the kingdom declared it to be *a corruption* to call either the people or country of Alban *Scotch*, and that Alban[2] was the true name. This

---

[1] See Innes's Critical Essay, vol. ii., page 768, Appendix No. 1.

[2] It was called Albania or Alban still later than the period of the Bishop of Caithness' Tract. In 1160 an English chronicle writer called Roger Hoveden speaks of 'Albania,' and another English writer of nearly the same period, named Gervase of Tilbury, says, 'ab aquilone est Albania quæ nunc Scotia dicitur,' that is, 'on the North is Alban—*now* called Scotland,' proving that last name was of recent origin; and how completely does this evidence, dated after the middle of the twelfth century, refute the claims of present Scotland to be called 'Scotia' in the seventh, as has been very strangely put forward by the author of 'The Early Scottish Church,' and for which he has not *given any proof*.

becomes a very convincing proof that at that date (1158) any conquest by the Scots over the Gael of Alban *was unknown*. Had such been the case, it would have been impossible to have used such language with truth; and that the change of name must have arisen from other causes than by conquest, namely, from a new dynasty of kings who were of *Scotch race;* yet the name was, as has been proved, very long of being transferred from Ireland (the original Scotia) to North Britain; and even when given by the writers of chronicles and legends, at or about 1020, it was never adopted by the inhabitants the Gael of Alban, nor at this very hour do the Highlanders of Scotland own their name or designation to be Scots, or their language Scotch, they invariably call themselves ' the Gael of Alban,' and their language ' Gaelic ;' they disown the name *of Scots*,[1] they

[1] The proof under the year A.D. 989 is conclusive, that the descendants of the Irish Colony of Scots *remained* in Argyleshire. All the rest of Scotland are the descendants of a pure Caledonian Gaelic race in the interior Highlands, who defended their country against the Romans, and the remainder of Saxon origin, thus still exhibiting *the paltry numbers* of those who are properly of Scotch descent, and situated in Argyleshire only; in most of the islands and coast of Caithness, etc., etc., there probably are descendants of the Norsemen. Even the Rev. Dr T. M'Lauchlan, in a note in Book of the Dean of Lismore, admits that the Perthshire Highlanders are a pure descended Gaelic race, and fully verify what Tacitus wrote of the Caledonian Gael.

know nothing of it, and never so designed themselves, or have ever acknowledged that *foreign Irish extraction,* which all confirm the truth, that calling their country *Scotia,* was a corruption; and the only Highlanders who claim any descent of the Irish Scots colony that came to Argyleshire, are *still there,* and they are properly the *only* Scots that belong to present Scotland; the remainder of the inhabitants being the descendants of the Caledonian Gael and the Anglo-Saxons, the latter now greatly predominating in numbers.

We also learn from this last evidence that if it was a corruption in the twelfth century to call Alban, or North Britain, *Scotia,* how much greater is the error of those who pretend to say it ought so to be called in the seventh century, in preference to Ireland, the then true and original Scotia, for which we have the authorities already given. Adomnan being one of the most clear and distinct of them, respecting whom it deserves notice the manner his testimony is spoken of by the writer of 'The Early Scottish Church,' when Adomnan is speaking of a half constituted church, having no bishops, then Adomnan's testimony '*is the most valuable we possess.*'[1] But when he proves that Ireland was called *Scotia,* then he is de-

[1] See 'The Early Scottish Church,' page 169.

preciated, and that he had done so '*with the usual nationality of his countrymen;*'[1] and when saying the learned Archbishop Ussher had stated that Ireland alone was Scotia till the tenth century, then this can only be received, '*if Adomnan and writers of the same school alone be referred to as authorities.*'[2]

There has, in this chapter, now been presented to the reader, a continuous and genuine chain of evidence for upwards of *three centuries* from the date of the pretended conquest, which amply refutes it. The ground on which it rests, as well as the time when it was invented, will next be mentioned.

The fabrication of a conquest and extermination, by the Scots, of the Pictish nation, by the monkish writers of St Andrews during the darkest period of the dark ages, was inserted into the Register of that See in 1251,[3] which is upwards of four hundred years *after* the pretended event; and it was, as has been proved, wholly *unknown* to any writer previously. This monkish fable states that Alpin, the father of Kenneth, subdued all Galloway, and was killed there[4] (this has been al-

1251.

[1] See 'The Early Scottish Church,' page 83.
[2] See 'The Early Scottish Church,' page 84.
[3] See Innes's Essay, vol. ii., pages 606, 607, and the Extract itself, also vol. ii., page 797.
[4] Innes's Essay, vol. ii, page 798.

ready disproved). And next we are told that Kenneth did far more, namely, that he *destroyed the Picts!!*[1] This monkish cheat and fraud was not however promulgated till a hundred and fifty years after its invention, namely, by the writer called Fordun, who put it into his chronicle, with many other fables and exaggerations, respecting the colony of Irish Scots, as to their origin and antiquity in North Britain, etc., etc. This chronicle was finished about the year 1400, and many copies were made of it by monks of different monasteries. Fordun's chronicle was added to by Bower, abbot of Inchcolm down to the year 1436. Then followed a greater Scotch fiction writer, called Hector Boece, who increased the fabulous tales of Fordun. The writings of these two afterwards came of course to be printed, and though their inventions were evident, yet Buchanan adopted many of them; and notwithstanding that the fictions of these three writers have over and over again been disproved, yet they constantly re-appear in the pages of *some would-be historian,* as if they were genuine and had never been denied. Indeed the assertion of this pretended conquest by the insignificant body of Scots in Argyleshire over the Pictish kingdom, makes good the aphorism,

[1] Innes's Essay, vol. ii., page 801.

when falsehood is received as truth, the truth passes for falsehood.

It is therefore a fact which has been proved beyond contradiction, when the whole of the evidence furnished in this chapter has been maturely weighed and considered, that the truth is, that the succession of Kenneth Mac-Alpin to the Pictish kingdom *must have been a peaceable one;* that the ancient proofs most clearly and strongly support and confirm the modern; that the Pictish people, their language and nation remained, and they underwent no change but in name, receiving *that of Scots;* and the whole case of the union of the Picts and Scots bears an exact resemblance to the succession of King James I. to the throne of England; for, as the Scots in that case remained in Scotland, so also did the Dalriads, or descendants of the Irish colony of Scots *remain* within their section of country in Argyleshire when Kenneth MacAlpin succeeded. The Scotch Highlanders are therefore truly and undoubtedly descended of the noble and ancient Caledonians and Picts, who fought so valiantly with the Romans, and being so derived, their language (the Gaelic) also descended with their descendants, and remains among them to this day, a free and independent race of men, *the true representatives* of the ancient Gael of Alban.

CHAPTER VIII.

The Language of the Picts proved to be the same as the Highlanders.

IN the last chapter it has been proved past all doubt, that the whole population of the ancient Caledonian Pictish kingdom remained and continued the sole inhabitants of present Scotland, north of the Firths of Forth and Clyde, excepting the small country of the Irish Scots, therefore this fact established, it follows of necessity that the language of the people remained with them, wherefore evidence respecting the language of the Picts might almost be deemed needless, but the change of name from Picts to Scots having caused many fables to be believed, full and conclusive proof will be given to show that the Caledonian Picts spoke *the same language* as do their descendants, the present Scotch or Highlanders.

One of the most marvellous things, by some believed, regarding the language of the

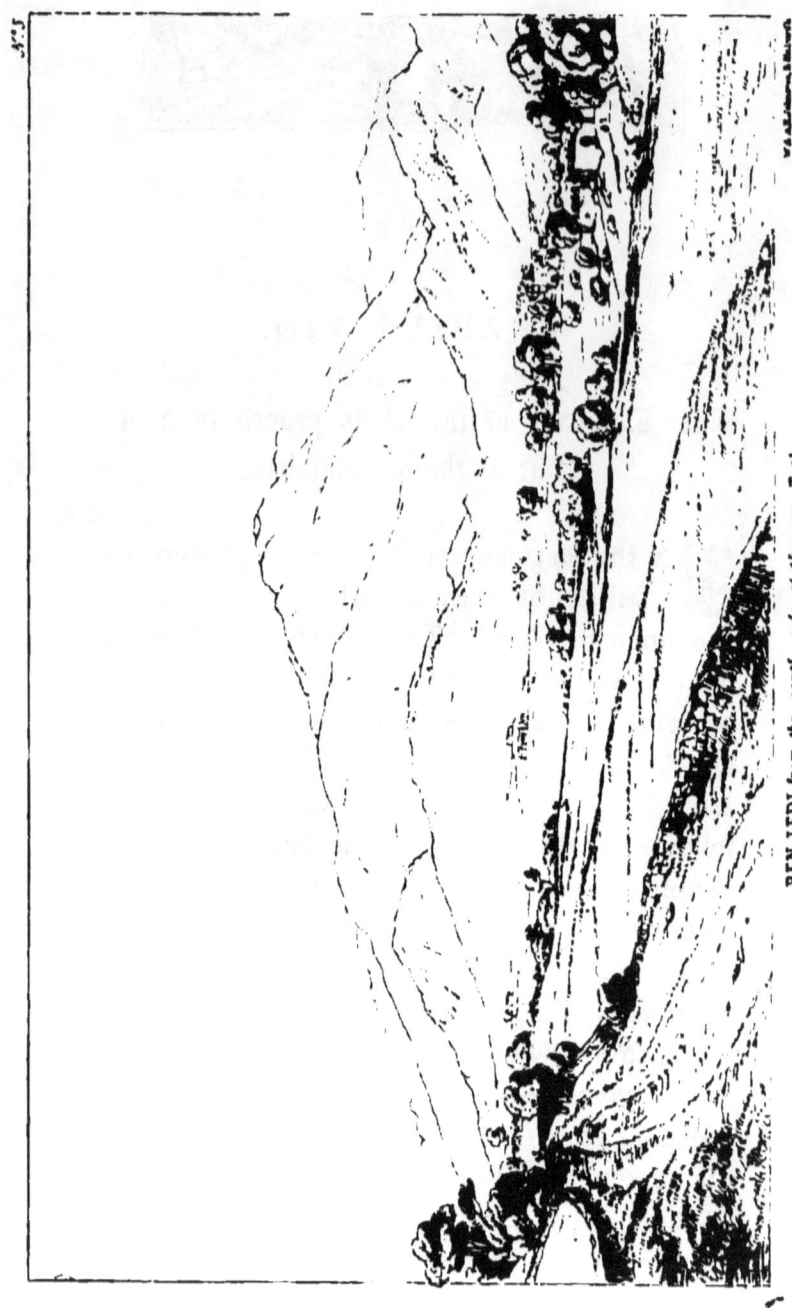

BEN LEDI from the south side of the river Teith.

The Pictish and Highland Languages.

Picts is, that it has been *altogether* lost and eradicated, and that only *one* word remained of the language of this powerful and numerous nation; but within the period of the present generation it is now said that there are *five* words; for this alleged story there is not to be found a parallel in the history of any nation since the world began, so it may be considered even a greater marvel that it should have been believed.

The wonderful endurance of the Gaelic language will be shown by the examples first to be submitted to the reader,—they are all derived from different counties of Scotland *south* the Firth of Forth, and wherein the Caledonians and Picts (who have been proved identical) have ceased to be the inhabitants, or their language to prevail for upwards of *one thousand three hundred years*, namely, since A.D. 547, when Ida, the Anglo-Saxon king dispossessed the Picts of this part of their country, and within which the Irish Scots *never* were the settled inhabitants, the names of many places and whole parishes will be given, showing them to be in the Gaelic language as *now spoken;* also, that in many instances these names will be proved precisely similar to those in other parts which were the territories of the Picts, and where they were the sole inhabitants, as also that their descendants, the Highlanders, are there now; and still further, that these examples will be confirmed by being proved to be in the language of the present Gael of Scotland, and the same in meaning at this day with those names of numerous places where their race has not been (as said) for upwards of thirteen centuries, which facts, when fairly and duly considered, will, beyond dispute prove, that the language of the Picts and the Highlanders of the present day must be considered as *identical;* and that though the Highlanders are now called Scots,[1] they are the descendants of the Picts and Caledonian Gael. The first name to be given in proof of what is above-mentioned, is the parish called *Garvald,* in the county of Haddington. This name is almost the exact pronunciation of the Gaelic language, from whence it is derived, namely, 'Garbh-alit,' or, 'the rough stream,' there is no letter V in Gaelic, but bh in this and all other words has the same sound, and is used instead of it. The Old Statistical Account of this parish[2] says, the name is derived from the stream so called in Gaelic, and that it is most descriptive,

---

[1] This new name, calling the Picts Scots, when they *were not so,* and their language also called Scotch, has been the chief cause of all the fables.

[2] See Old Statistical Account of Scotland, vol. xiii., page 353.

and the writer in the New Statistical Account [1] says, it is a most exact etymology of the local situation of Garvald. In the highlands of Aberdeenshire, near to Castletown of Braemar, there is a well known stream also called Garbh-allt,[2] this district was within the Pictish territory, and this identity of name proves that the people who gave the name in *both* places spoke the same language, and must have been the same people, namely, the Picts; and further, what confirms the truth of the present Highlanders being their descendants is, that in their language at this hour, 'Garbh-allt' is the Gaelic for 'a rough stream.'

The next name to be given is the parish of Innerwick, in the county of Haddington. There is a precisely similar name in the highlands of Perthshire, in Glenlyon—the Established Church of that district is at Innerwick—both these places are derived from the Gaelic. The whole of the Inners in Scotland are from the word 'Inbhir' (pronounced Inver), meaning 'a confluence' where a stream or river falls into another, or into the sea. The writer on the name of this parish in the New Statistical Account [3] very strangely says, it is derived from

---

[1] New Statistical Account, vol. ii., page 95.
[2] Pronounced as if it was spelled garv.
[3] Vol. ii., page 233.

the Saxon; but the ancestors of the Pictish Gael must have possessed the country and given the name at least seven to eight hundred years before the Saxon race ever occupied it; and his derivation that it is an inner hamlet cannot be correct, and with regard to the other part of the name 'Wick,' being from the Scandinavian word 'wic,' a bay, is altogether an error, as the Innerwick of Glenlyon is not less than 50 miles from the sea; both places are from the Gaelic 'Inbhir-bhuic,'[1] corrupted into Inner-vuic, which last word easily becomes wick.[2] The meaning of the Gaelic words are 'the confluence of the stream of the buck,' either of the roe or red deer. The names of these two places in the counties of Perth and Haddington are the same, and therefore the language of the same people, and the Gaelic now spoken by all Highlanders corresponds in meaning with the etymology here given.

The next instance to be mentioned is the town and parish of Dunbar, also in the county of Haddington,—the word Dun, is common all over Scotland, and most numerous in the Highlands. Dun means a fort, castle, or

---

[1] The bh has here, as before mentioned, the same sound and pronunciation as the letter v in English.

[2] The letters v and w, and also f, are kindred consonants, and often used instead of each other.

stronghold; barr, a point,—thus the words, 'Dun-barr,' is, 'the fort on the point,' which is most applicable and descriptive of the castle of Dunbar.[1] For an example of an ancient Dun or fort (that can be traced very far back), there is one in Kintyre, in Argyleshire, called Dunaverty, situated on a romantic rock overhanging the sea, in a small bay to which it gives the same name. This Dun was a fortress which came into possession of the Scots of Kintyre, and was besieged by Selvac, a petty prince of the tribe of Lorn (in one of their many miserable fightings with each other), and was taken by him early in the eighth century, as mentioned in the Irish Annals. It was at this Dun also, that Angus, Lord of the Isles, gave shelter to King Robert Bruce in his adversity. Here likewise, in more recent times, took place a cruel massacre of the Macdonalds by the Campbells, *after* they had surrendered to them. For an ex-

[1] This name affords a very strong proof indeed of the Pictish language, because the word is perhaps as near as any other that exists in Scotland, as an example of the pure present Gaelic language of the Gael Albanach, both as to spelling and pronunciation; it also completely refutes the assertion of Chalmers, that not one 'Dun' bears an appellation from the Pictish or British languages. Besides this one, there are two very strong 'Duns' situated at the head of Glentilt, in Atholl, guarding the entrance: they are called Dunmòr and Dunbeag, and a vast number besides could be brought forward to contradict Chalmers's assertion.—Caledonia. vol. i., page 343.

ample of the word 'barr' or point, we have it an island off Campbeltown, in Argyleshire, called 'Eilean-da-barr,' or 'the island of the two *points*; thus the identity of language and people who used the words Dun and barr in the county of Haddington and all the rest of Scotland, is manifest; and that as the Picts were the natives and original possessors of all these places,—and that from them the Saxon race acquired Dunbar,—and further, as the Gaelic words among the Highlanders at this hour for a 'fort on the point' is 'Dunbar,' it cannot be reasonably denied that the language of the Picts and that of the present Gael is the same, and therefore they must be the *same people*.

Within half-a-mile of Edinburgh there is a place named Dalry—there are several others of the same name in Scotland, and one parish bears it—but that which has the most interest attached to it, is situated in the Highlands of Perthshire, as there King Robert Bruce met with a defeat from M'Dougall, lord of Lorn. The corrupted word is the same in both places, namely Dalry, and is from the Gaelic, Dail (pronounced Dà'l), a field, haugh, or small level plain; and the word Ri (anciently so spelled) now Righ, 'a king,'—therefore Dailri, or Dailrigh,[1] means the king's field, or haugh,

[1] The word is corrupted in the maps, and in speaking English, into *Dalry*, in every place it occurs.

and thus the people who gave this name in the Highlands of Perthshire, the centre of the ancient Caledonian Picts territory, must have spoken the same language as those who gave the Gaelic name of Dalrigh (pronounced Dalree) to the similar named place close to Edinburgh,—which fact, combined with the *present* Gaelic for the words the 'king's field,' being *identical* with Dailrigh, proves the Highlanders now speak the same language as the Picts did. With regard to the question whether this name arose in the North-West Highlands of Perthshire, from its being given in king Robert Bruce's time, or not, is wholly immaterial, as whether it was given in 1306 (the first year of his reign), or a thousand years before that, still the identity of the language of the Picts, and that of the present existing Gael of Alban, is equally proved by its precisely corresponding with the name of a place in the Lothians, the former territory of the Picts, but where it is necessary to remember they have not been the native possessors for one thousand three hundred years.

In Linlithgowshire or West Lothian, there is a parish called Borrowstonness, but that is only recent.[1] The former and original name is Kinneil. All the words in Scotland which

[1] See Statistical Account of Scotland, vol. ii., page 120.

abound in its topography beginning with 'kin,' are universally admitted to be derived from the Gaelic 'Ceann,' meaning 'head,' or 'end.' The word Kinneil therefore comes from the Gaelic Ceann[1] and 'fal,' this last word meaning 'turf,' or 'wall,' or 'fence.' The possessive case of 'fall' is '*fhail*,' wherein the *fh* is mute. The word thereby formed is 'Ceannail,' signifying the head or end of the wall, and it was given originally from the line of Agricola's forts, and afterwards to the wall of Antonine or Grim's dike (built on that line) passing through the parish, and giving to it the English corrupted name of Kinneil. There are traces of this Roman work at two places near Kinneil house,— the situation of which is very commanding and suitable for the termination either of Agricola's line of forts or the wall of Antonine, constructed by his General, Lollius Urbicus. Nennius mentions this termination of the Roman wall by the true name, calling it Ceannail; but Bede, also speaking of it, calls it by a wrong name, that is '*Peanfahel*,' and that word, he says,[2] is in the Pictish language where the wall begins, but in the English tongue it is 'Penneltun,' two miles distant from the monastery of Aber-

---

[1] There is no letter k in Gaelic, c being always used instead.
[2] Bede liber. i., cap. xii.

curnig (now Abercorn), and that running to the westward ends near the city of Alcluith or Alclyde, now Dumbarton.

The above word given by Bede as *Pictish*, is the celebrated *single* word that is pretended to be left of the language of that nation, and on this fiction (nothing equal to it having ever happened to any people since the deluge) is built the theory that the language of the Picts must have been a Welsh or British dialect. Bede, it is likely, never spoke to, or ever saw any of the Pictish race. His life was passed at the two monasteries of Wearmouth and Jarrow,[1] on the Tyne, but the Gael of Alban were all north of the Forth. This word he evidently must have received from a Briton, as it is admitted it *is not Gaelic*. But we see the author of Nennius, in his history (chapter xxiii.), gives the true word[2] *Ceannail*, which is confirmed by the present Gaelic language of the descendants and the Picts, and further established by the name of the place itself, which has come down to the present day, and is thus identified by an ancient writer and authority of the ninth[3] century, who does not mention

---

[1] Preface to Bede's History by Dr Giles, page vii., etc., etc.
[2] See also Dr Giles's edition, published by Bohn, London, page 393.
[3] It is to be remembered that Bede only wrote his work the preceding century, before the work of Nennius, namely the eighth.

Abercorn or Carriden the adjoining parish, where at another period there may have been a different termination, and that *there* was the one spoken of by Bede. The case therefore clearly appears to be this, that the *Ceannail*[1] of Nennius and the Gaelic now spoken, is the present *Kinneil*, and at one time the head or termination of the wall, and where a village would naturally arise and retain its name, though the wall was afterwards extended to near Abercorn, which would become the 'peneltun' or 'wall town' of Bede, and which is *now* represented by the place called 'Weltun'[2] (properly Walltown), near Abercorn, to which the wall at last was extended, and a fresh hamlet would of course arise there.

For the whole of the above information respecting Kinneil and the wall of Antonine, and the authorities given, it has been taken from the clear and convincing statement of the Rev. Kenneth M'Kenzie in the New Statistical Account[3] of Scotland, which also

[1] It ought not to be forgotten that the signification of 'Ceann-ail' is, as before proved, 'the head of the wall' in the language of the present Highlanders, as it also was in that of the Picts.

[2] It cannot be considered strange that in such a prodigious space of time, names have become corrupted and abbreviated and that Peneltun became Weltun or Walltown.

[3] Vol. ii. New Statistical Account of Scotland, County Linlithgow, vol. ii.; Account of Borrowstonness Parish, pages 127, 128; also the notes.

shows his perfect knowledge of the Gaelic language.

It ought to cast suspicion on Bede's ever having got any Gaelic name correctly either of the Scotch or Irish dialects, when, in addition to the one last spoken of, so erroneously called 'Pictish,' we find that though he brings forward several words as Irish or Scotch Gaelic, he is in error in *every one of the significations* he gives to them. Thus in speaking of the colony of Scots from Ireland, being called Dalriads,[1] he says it was from 'Dal,' which, 'in their language, signifies a part;' but this it does not in either the Irish or Scotch Gaelic. Some writers have supposed that Bede conjectured the word 'Dal' to be the part or portion of a tribe. This, however, would only make his blunder greater. Another example of his errors is in the name he calls 'Alcluith' (now Dumbarton). He says[2] it signifies *the rock* of Clyde, but no such word as 'Al,' in either the Welsh, Scotch, or Irish Gaelic signifies '*a rock*.' Dumbarton belonged to the Britons when Bede wrote. Again, he says,[3] of Columba, that before he left Ireland he built a monastery at a place which, in the language of the Scots (that is the

---

[1] Bede, lib. i., cap. i.; also Dr Giles's translation, page 7.
[2] Bede, lib. i., cap. xii.
[3] Bede, lib. iii., cap iv.

Irish) is called 'Dearm-ach,' and he states, these words mean 'the field of oaks.' 'Dearm' does not signify an oak or oak trees in the Irish Gaelic, though ach, a field. These different words, and his pretended Pictish one, are the whole of the Gaelic ones he gives, and they *are all wrong;* therefore the conclusion is, he was wholly misinformed in *every* instance, and cannot be received as of the slightest authority to form any opinion of what the Pictish language was.

The origin of the name of Edinburgh,[1] also is another interesting example to prove the Pictish people spoke the same Gaelic as the Highlanders now do. The name they know it by is 'Dunedin,' meaning 'Edwin's Castle' or 'fort.' There was a primitive native Gaelic name, long ere it had got that last Pictish designation, as will be mentioned hereafter. It will be remembered that in A.D. 547 the Northumbrian King Ida dispossessed the Caledonian Picts of their territory south of the Forth. The second successor to him, as king of Northumbria, was the above named Edwin,

---

[1] There were two letters appeared not long since in an Edinburgh newspaper 'The Scotsman,' in which both of the writers tried to show it was derived from the Gaelic, but most unaccountably neither of them mentioned the name by which it is called by the Highlanders—'Dunedin.'

the same as the Highlanders.

who came to the throne in A.D. 617, and he was slain by Cadwalla, king of the West Britons, and Penda, king of Mercia, in the year A.D. 633.[1] Therefore some years between this last date and the former, King Edwin rebuilt the Pictish Dun, or castle, and which, in his language, was called a 'burg.' Hence in all the most ancient charters it was called 'Edwynsburg,' and now contracted into Edinburgh, but it is chiefly to show that the language of the Picts was identical with that of the present Highlanders the name is mentioned, though it is also of interest to any Scotchman. We learn, therefore, that not later than the year A.D. 633, the Picts used the same Gaelic word 'Dun,' to signify a castle, as do their descendants, the Highlanders of the present day; and slightly contracting the name of the king from Edwyn or Edwin, into Edin, whereby the word becomes 'Dunedin,'[2] and it is a most reasonable conclusion that this name must have been given *during Edwin's reign ;* also no Highlander could properly in his own language call

---

[1] See the Saxon Chronicle, under the years A.D. 617 and A.D. 633.

[2] If there had been delay on the part of the Picts in giving the name 'Dunedin,' it is evident they never likely could have known what Saxon king had built the castle, the intercourse between the two races being almost solely confined to invasions of each others territories.

it Edinburgh. This example proves to satisfaction that the word 'Dun' was a Pictish word, and in use among that people at that remote period.

The original Pictish Gaelic name of present Edinburgh, prior to the arrival of the Saxons, was '*Dunmonadh*,'[1] meaning 'the castle, or fort, on the hill,' hence we see that from the very earliest periods of time that we can trace the name of the locality of Edinburgh, in whatever language, it has always been derived from its castle. The proof of this primitive Gaelic name is clearly and satisfactorily made out by the testimony of Bishop Carswell, who, in writing and printing 300 years ago his Gaelic translation of the Protestant Liturgy, Administration of the Sacraments, Catechism, etc., etc., as used in the Reformed Church of Scotland for the Highlanders, dates from 'Dunedin' (or Edinburgh), otherwise '*Dunmonadh*,' his was the earliest Gaelic book printed for the Gael

---

[1] The Gaelic spelling here used for 'a hill,' is as laid down in the fourth edition, printed in the year 1863, and of the second or English part (by a most competent Gaelic scholar, Mr J. M'Kenzie) of MacAlpine's Gaelic Dictionary, the word is spelled 'Monaidh,' according to Dr Reeves, in mentioning Bishop Carswell; but the spelling of the well-known hills in Inverness-shire is '*Monadh-liath*,' in the latest maps, and also in Taylor's very recent second edition of 'Words and Places,' page 478.

of Alban or Scots Highlanders, the first edition was printed so far back as the year 1564, and another three years afterwards.[1]

This aboriginal Gaelic name of Dumonadh, for present Edinburgh and its castle, must have been given by the ancestors of the Caledonian Gael at a very remote period,[2] probably by the earliest settlers of the race, long before the invasion of the Romans in A.D. 78, at which period this part of present Scotland was so fully peopled (as we have seen before mentioned) that the Roman General Agricola took two years to subdue the country south of the Forth; therefore this is another additional example of the great endurance of the Gaelic language, that the same word (Dunmonadh) which must have been in use by the ancestors of the Caledonian race considerably above two thousand years ago, is still in use *at this day* in the spoken language of the Scotch Highlanders, as their word for ' the castle on the hill.'

There is near Edinburgh a barony, of which

---

[1] See additional notes by W. F. Skene, Esq., Book Dean of Lismore, page 137, and Highland Society's Report on Ossian's Poems, page 17.

[2] The rock, or hill, on which the castle of Edinburgh stands must have been to the first settlers of the Gaelic race a most conspicuous object; no natural feature in the whole south of Scotland would more attract their attention, and induce them to build a ' dun,' or ' castle,' there.

the name of the lands is 'Drum,'[1]—this is a pure Gaelic word used in the topography of the whole Highlands of Scotland, and is therefore very numerous—it signifies 'a ridge,' and is applied both to any rising ground, or even to a ridge of mountains. Of the former we have an example in 'Drummor,' or 'the large ridge,' in Strathbran, Perthshire, and also of the latter in Drum Alban, or the great ridge of the mountains of Alban. This very common name in the Gaelic topography and language of the present day we see was applied, in a corresponding manner, to describe the same thing in the Lothians, once forming another part of the territories of the Picts.

All the islands off the coast of the Lothians bear the name of Inch, *a corruption* (from the great similarity of pronunciation) of the Gaelic 'Innis,' an 'island,' and which is still the common word in the Highlander's language of this day for it—thus one of them in the Firth of Forth is called Inchgarvie—almost the identical pronunciation of the name in the Gaelic language for it, namely, 'Innis-Garbh (Inchgarv) or the 'rough island,' the name given by the Picts, his ancestors, as can be proved at this

---

[1] This name is not to be mistaken for 'Drem,' which is in a different locality, though it also is from the Gaelic, as will be pointed out hereafter.

hour by any one asking a Highlander for the Gaelic words that signify 'a rough island.'

Besides the islands off the Lothian coasts, we have in the confluences the pure Gaelic 'Inbhir,' pronounced Inver,[1] and Inner, and which names attached to rivers and streams in the Scotch Highlands are, of course, excessively numerous. In the Lothians there is Innerwick, Inveresk, Inverleith, and Inveravon, etc., the first has been already treated of. Esk is a common name for a river or water, as the rivers are very often called in Scotland; it is derived from the Gaelic word 'uisge,'[2] which signifies 'water,' and is in daily use in the Highlands, and the Inver joined with it makes it impossible the name was given by the Britons. The name Avon, mentioned above in conjunction with its term for a confluence, is from another Gaelic word 'Abhuinn,'[3] 'a river,' the pronunciation being very near as it is in English. "On the east coast we have Dunbar and Duntallon (Tantallon) between Scandinavian Berwick and North Berwick. We

[1] Of course the vowel I is E in Gaelic, and all the Gaelic vowels are pronounced as on the continent of Europe.

[2] From this word the south country Scot has his word 'whusky,' that is, whisky.

[3] Abhuinn is from '*abh*,' water, now obsolete, and '*inne*,' a channel. —See Gaelic Dictionaries, also spelled sometimes, but erroneously, 'amhain,' the same in meaning and pronunciation.

have Drem ('Druim,' a 'ridge') Tranent ('*Traigh,* '*the coast,*' *being quite manifest in the word*); Dalkeith ('Dalché,' 'the creamy dale'); 'Roslin¹ ('Rosslinne,' 'the projection in the stream,') and *innumerable other* instances of names *purely Gaelic.*²

From the whole of the foregoing evidence it is most clearly established that in the counties already named south of the Forth, which was part of the territory of the ancient Caledonian Picts (and whose descendants are now called Scots) there abounds a great number of places and even parishes bearing *pure Gaelic names*, which have been proved precisely similar to other names within the country inhabited, now as ever, by the Highlanders of Scotland alone, and that though their language has ceased to be the spoken tongue for the extremely long period of upwards of one thousand three hundred years in these districts (the Picts were deprived of them in A.D. 547) that still the whole of the names given are the same language with *the Gaelic now spoken* by the Highlanders, which testimony, combined with the facts stated in the last chapter, and that the Irish Scots *never* were *the settled* inha-

¹ Where the beautiful chapel is, and near to Edinburgh.
² See Celtic Gleanings by the Rev. Dr Thomas M'Lauchlan, page 45.

bitants of this part of the country, affords clear and undeniable proof, when duly weighed and considered, that beyond dispute the language of the Picts was *identical* with the Gaelic language of the Highlanders of Scotland of the present hour.

In conclusion of this branch of the subject of the language of the Picts, and which will be continued in the next chapter, the following names of places (all derived from pure Gaelic) are given from the county of Linlithgow, from which hitherto only one has been adduced, and they still further confirm and support the fact of the identity of the Highlanders and the Picts.

Names in Linlithgowshire :—Auchenbard,[1] Balbardie,[1] Avon river, Briech water, Ballen-Crieff, Craigengall, Dalmeny,[2] Drumbeg, Drumbowie, Drumlossie, Drumduff, Drummillie, Duntarvie, etc., etc.

---

[1] Both these names refer to the field and town of 'the bard,' in Gaelic 'Bailebard.' In Glenfarg, Perthshire, it is called 'Bailebhard,' and has been supposed to be the origin of the name of 'Balvaird.'

[2] Considered to be a corruption of 'Dalminn,' or 'the field of the kids.'

CHAPTER IX.

The Language of the Picts proved to be the same as the Highlanders.

IN the two last chapters having, it is hoped, proved to all readers, by clear and most satisfactory evidence, that the Pictish nation and people were not conquered, or that they and their language suddenly vanished, but, on the contrary, that it will be considered established, by the proofs in the last chapter, that the Gaelic language of the Highlanders of this day *exactly corresponds* with the names of places in the Lothians of Scotland, and which names must have been given some centuries before the arrival of the Romans in North Britain—that is, considerably more than two thousand years ago. Bearing this fact in mind, we see how completely it refutes the assertion of the Rev. Dr Thomas M'Lauchlan, that, at the period of the succession of Kenneth MacAlpin to the Pictish throne, in A.D. 843, a *new Gaelic language* had been brought in—that is, we must believe in what would have been as great a marvel as a conquest, and for which this writer gives *no authority*, and not one *single proof*, placing the date of the arrival of this new Gaelic also three hundred years *after* the Picts had left their country south of the Forth, and at least a thousand years after their Caledonian ancestors *had given* the Gaelic names therein, which have *been proved* to be *identical* with the Gaelic language of the Scotch Highlanders at this hour, as *now spoken by them*.

The assertion as to this new Gaelic being brought in is as follows :—' *The Scottish conquest*,[1] as it is called, in the ninth century gave complete predominance, *in large sections* of the country, to the Gaelic language.'[2] We see from this extract, that the bringing in of this new Gaelic rests entirely upon readers believing in the *monkish fable* of Fordun, of a conquest by Kenneth MacAlpin in the ninth century, which, with this assertion of a fresh language besides, certainly enhances the fiction, and

[1] The fable of the pretended conquest has, as we have seen, been assigned to the year A.D. 843.

[2] ' Early Scottish Church,' page 31, by this phrase also, readers are supposed to believe that, prior to Kenneth MacAlpin's time, the Gaelic language was unknown '*in large sections of the country*.' The Gaelic topography of the whole Highlands of Scotland fully contradicts this fable of a *new* Gaelic.

readers must indeed be considered to be highly credulous, that they should be expected to receive such an unproved statement as *an historical fact.*[1]

It may be well to notice what kind of Gaelic could have been brought in by Kenneth MacAlpin, the petty king of the Irish Scots colony in Argyleshire. It could only have been the most impure, and corrupted with Irish, that was then spoken, and which still remains in Argyleshire, and *no where else*, at this hour, among the Highlanders, which is a very clear proof what kind of Gaelic the Irish Scots of the ninth century would have propagated from Argyle; and where else was the corrupted Irish Gaelic to be looked for than in the country of the colony of the Irish Scots. The authority of the Highland Society Report on Ossian[2] is most distinct in speaking of the

[1] The date of the work called 'The Early Scottish Church,' is October 1884, and it shows that the fictions of Fordun, etc., though they have often been refuted, are *still* brought forward as if they were to be received as historical truths.

[2] The Highland Society of Scotland in their Report, among many instances of the Irish corruptions in the Gaelic MSS. sent them collected in Argyleshire, speak of them at pages 90 and 91. Even one of the most inland parts of that county, and furthest off from Irish Gaelic, namely, the village of Dalmally, is mentioned as having, from Gaelic poems collected there been found very impure, as said in another part of the Report, at page 50.

corruptions of the Gaelic in the islands and county of Argyle, which has also herein been already stated; as likewise has the same been shown in the introduction to the Book of the Dean of Lismore;[1] and if it abounds in that country *now*, how much more it must have done so in the ninth century, Kenneth MacAlpin's time, who no more introduced the impure Irish Gaelic of his paltry and insignificant district among the population of the Pictish kingdom, than did King James I. introduce the broad Scotch, spoken by himself and many of his people, into England.

'Not a fragment of Gaelic writing in *the Irish* character and orthography (with the exception of the recently discovered Book of Deer, a remnant of Culdee scholarship) has been discovered, as having been written previous to last century, in *any portion* of the central or eastern Highlands; while *abundant* remains of that description have been found as written in the Hebrides, and *on the west coast of Argyllshire*. And the *only* remains we have, so far as yet discovered, are of a different description, being either in the modern Roman

---

[1] See as to the corrupted Gaelic spoken in Argyleshire, introduction to the Book of the Dean of Lismore, pages xv., xvi.

or Saxon character, and in an orthography purely phonetic. Does not this fact suggest some historical inferences of importance? Does it not suggest, *very manifestly*, the inference, that while *Irish* influence was very powerfully felt on the *west* coast of Scotland, *the large body of the people in the central and eastern Highlands were strangers to that influence;* and with regard to their literature, as well as their history, followed a course of their own; and may it not also shed some light on the question as to whether the Scottish Highlanders are, as *an entire people, simply an Irish colony.*'[1]

The reply to this question must be obvious to every one, namely, that it is *impossible* the Highlanders of Scotland could have derived their language from the impure Irishised Gaelic of the descendants of the colony of Irish Scots in Argyleshire, where *alone* it still exists. Nothing can be stronger than this statement, by the Rev. Dr Thomas M'Lauchlan, to prove *such a new Gaelic* never was introduced among the ancient Pictish Gael. It is impossible to conceive anything could be more repugnant to their feelings of attachment to their own primitive

[1] Communication on 'an old Gaelic poem, found among the papers of the family of Fassiefern, by the Rev. Dr Thomas M'Lauchlan, Proceedings, Society of Antiquaries, Scotland, vol. iii., part 3, page 373, date 1860.

tongue,[1] so that, even on that view alone, we should be justified in rejecting the supposition; but when the direct and positive testimony of the last chapter is remembered, it can only be considered a fable. The original native Gaelic language of the Caledonian Picts resisted also all the efforts of their Irish clerical teachers, who brought in a more cultivated dialect with them when the introduction of Christianity took place, and they became established at Iona, by the gift of the Pictish king, Brudhi. It was a continued series of Irish ecclesiastics at that island, who, for two centuries after Columba's time, were almost entirely the clergy of the ancient Picts: but, in opposition to this clerical dialect, as it may be called, there was the ancient national Gaelic of Alban, which (W. F. Skene, Esq.) one of the best authorities on the subject says, was '*indigenous and antagonistic to it,*' and he adds, that '*its influence prevailed in the central and north Highlands where the best and purest type of the Scotch Gaelic is to be found.*'[2] This writer is thus an

[1] The following extract from Chalmers is highly applicable to any change of language being possible to have been received by the Pictish Gael,—' the Celts enjoyed from their earliest progenitors *an invincible attachment* to their own language, which naturally produced *a strong antipathy* to *innovations* in their *ancient tongue.*'—See Chalmers's Caledonia, vol. i., page 220.

[2] Introduction, Book Dean of Lismore, page xlii., date 1862.

undoubted authority, that the Picts spoke the Gaelic language, and were *the real ancestors* of the modern Highlanders,[1] *excepting* those in Argyleshire descended of the Irish Scots.

The author of 'The Early Scottish Church' *now* follows Chalmers in his conjecture as to the language of the Caledonian Picts having been Welsh (that is British), with only a mixture of Gaelic, or what he calls Gallocymbric.[2] Chalmers's British names are partly repeated by him, and a most useless labour to do so; because, that there should be British names found in what became afterwards the territories of the Caledonian Picts, was of course *a necessity*, seeing as already proved by our best historical writers, the Britons were the *first*[3] inhabitants of present Scotland, and *preceded* the Caledonian Gael. The quoting a number of Welsh or British names, therefore, that may exist within what became the Pictish territory, does not prove in *the slightest degree* the language of the Picts; for, among many other

[1] See Skene's Highlanders, vol. i., pages 69 to 79 inclusive.

[2] 'Early Scottish Church,' page 30.

[3] In proof of the very remote period to which the Britons were in present Scotland, Chalmers declares there were tribes of them inhabiting the country of North Britain '*a thousand years before the Scots came into that country from Ireland*.' See Chalmers's Caledonia, vol. i., page 215, note, and A.D. 506 is the true date of the first settlement of the Scots.

reasons, it obliges it to be believed, that *the Britons did not* give these British names, which, if the author of 'The Early Scottish Church' could prove, or that there never were Britons in Scotland, and therefore that the Picts must have given the British names, he would *then* have proved something as to the Pictish nation having spoken Welsh or British; but, as the facts from history prove that there were Britons in present Scotland, who *must* have given a British topography, therefore it is merely confusing readers to give a long list of British names as if *that* could in itself at all be received as a proof that the Caledonian Gael, who, in the earliest dawn of history (in A.D. 78) are proved the vastly dominant people, spoke the language of the scattered inhabitants[1] of the country they had conquered. Quite in a precisely similar manner, and upon quite the same grounds, a treatise might be written asserting that the race now inhabiting the Lothians of Scotland, were an English *Gaelic* speaking

---

[1] The British names are on the east side of Scotland, confined to a mere strip of the coast—few in the interior of Fifeshire, Perthshire, and Inverness-shire,—proving the Britons must have been a widely scattered race, and that country thinly inhabited by them; but in Strathclyde and the south-west of Scotland, where they seem to have been driven by the ancient Caledonian Gael of Alban, British names appear very numerously; and to the north of the Moray Firth they appear *never to have been*, or in any of the islands.

people, from the *innumerable instances* of '*names
purely Gaelic* '¹ which this *same writer* declares
abound within the Lothians, their country,
thus giving his testimony, that instead of any
British or Welsh, the Picts and their forefathers
spoke *pure Gaelic*. There is further proof from
topography, that the Picts did *not* speak as
asserted, a British and Gaelic mixed language,
namely, that the whole of those very large
counties, Ross, Sutherland, Caithness, along
with Cromarty, being all to the north of the
Moray and Beauly Firths, have no British
names of places,² they are *all Gaelic*, excepting
the vastly more modern Norse names; so likewise the very same is the case in all the islands,
namely, Skye, Lewis, Harris, etc., etc., that belonged, as well as the above named very extensive counties, to the Picts *alone*, the Irish Scots
never being the inhabitants thereof. This fact
as to British names is even admitted by the
writer of 'The Early Scottish Church' as to
the whole of the northern counties, though *of the
topography of the isles he takes no notice*, ' There
are few names *that can with any confidence be*

[1] Celtic Gleanings, page 45, by the Rev. Dr Thomas M'Lauchlan.
[2] Innes well remarks that all the names of places within what was the dominions of the Picts that cannot be proved British *must be Pictish*. Innes's Crit. Essay, vol. i., page 76.

called British to the north of the Moray Firth.[1] Therefore here is clear proof that the Britons never could have been the inhabitants of the above named large counties north of the Moray Firth and islands; and that, as it was the Caledonian Gael, the ancestors of the Picts *alone*, to whom the country belonged, and could have given the *Gaelic* names,[2] so their descendants' language must have also been *Gaelic*. This fact likewise, as to the absence of British names north of the Moray Firth, deserves some slight further notice, to point out that if the Picts' language, as the writer of 'The Early Scottish Church' would try and make his readers believe, was a *mixture* of British (or Welsh) and Gaelic, how does it arise that they (the Picts) forgot all their British language on their going past, or over the Moray Firth? Those who believe, or try to make others believe, that it was the *Pictish people*, gave the *British* names throughout Scotland, and *not the Britons*, must

---

[1] See 'The Early Scottish Church,' page 27.

[2] The Gaelic topography which exists in so very large a portion of present Scotland, as that which extends north of the Moray Firth, and thence west also, being free of Welsh names, is a most *positive proof* of the language of the Caledonians having been *pure Gaelic*, and that it was only where they had found the thinly scattered Britons, and then by their superior numbers absorbed them, that the British names could have remained and afterwards appear mixed with the Gaelic ones of the Caledonians.

give some substantial proofs of it, and not *mere assertions*, which involve the greatest absurdities. All readers, it is believed, who have attentively weighed and considered the proofs and evidence contained in the last chapter, have, it is hoped, found therein satisfactory assurance to conclude that the Scotch Highlanders of the present day speak the *same language as did the Picts*.

Another very convincing proof of the language of the Picts being the same that is now spoken by the Scotch Highlanders is the poems of Ossian.[1] They were composed in the third century, but the fable of a conquest by the descendants of the Irish Scots colony is (by any who have tried to make it believed) put down as having been effected in the ninth century; therefore, for a period extending to nearly six hundred years the poems were known and handed down from one generation to another prior to the fabulous conquest; and if the Picts spoke any different language than the present Gaelic, or if in particular they spoke a mixture of Welsh and Gaelic, as has been asserted and noticed already, it amounts to a perfect certainty that these ancient poems in the original must have been corrupted with

[1] Reasons will be given hereafter to show that the poems of Ossian are genuine.

the British or Welsh language of the Picts; but in disproof of this, not a sentence, or single line, appears among them in the British language. There is *no mixture*,— and in the Highland Society Report on the poems,[1] and respecting all the ancient MSS. that belonged to them they declare that with the exception of the Irish corruptions of *Argyleshire*, and some obsolete words which could still be understood from the context, the poems of Ossian had been composed in the *same language* as the present Highlanders. A testimony so clear from a committee of gentlemen and good Gaelic scholars, becomes another very strong proof of the language of the Picts from a very remote period. There is also topographical proofs, all in pure Gaelic as now spoken, throughout the Highlands as to Ossian; and all the Fingalian heroes he names, and which must have been given *centuries* before the date of the arrival of the Irish Scots, or of the pretended new language being brought in.[2]

There are throughout the Highlands of Scotland a great number of places that bear names in pure Gaelic of the present day that must have been given anterior to Christianity.

[1] See the Highland Society Report on Ossian's poems, throughout.
[2] See the Introduction, Book Dean of Lismore, page lxxxi.

The latest date to which we can affix the whole Pictish people becoming converted from heathenism is towards the end of the sixth century, therefore any examples that may be given of names that are clearly heathen, must unquestionably have been given *prior* to that last named date at the least, and may indeed reach back even prior to the Christian era, when the whole Gaelic population of ancient Alban were all heathens; therefore, if these names are in *the same* language as the Highlanders *now speak*, it proves that the Pictish Gael and their forefathers, who gave these heathen names, spoke *the same* language as *the present* Highlanders of Scotland. To illustrate this, there is situated in the highlands of Perthshire, and half way between the parish church of Blair Atholl and Strowan, a large stone block, the principal one left of a circle or Druidical temple, it is known and called by the Highlanders the ' *clach-n' iobairt,*' that is, ' *the stone of sacrifice,*' it is mentioned in both the Old and New Statistical Accounts of Scotland.[1] It is indisputable that this stone was never erected by Christians, and that they never could have given such a name, it was therefore placed and named by heathens; the part of the country,

[1] See New Statistical Account, vol. x., page 568; also Old Statistical Account, vol. ii., Parish of Blair Atholl.

the same as the Highlanders. 151

also, is nearly the centre of what was ever the dominions of the Picts, by them or their forefathers, the Caledonian Gael, the name 'clach-n' iobairt,' or 'the stone of sacrifice,' must have been given. No other people than the Caledonian Picts and their descendants (now called Scotch Highlanders) ever were the inhabitants of Atholl, Perthshire; and among *the first* things *the earliest* settlers of the Gael of Alban would of course do, was to raise a place of worship, and thus here we have it in this '*stone of sacrifice.*'

Perhaps, therefore, there does not exist in Scotland anything done by the hand of man of higher antiquity than this heathen stone of sacrifice, and which clearly by name shows it to be of the very remotest ages, and how very applicable to it are the words of Ossian,—

'We raised the stone and bade it speak to other years.'

Therefore when the above facts are considered, it becomes clear and manifest that the people who raised this stone[1] and gave the name were

---

[1] The writer showed this very ancient stone to a gentleman well acquainted with the sculptured stones of Scotland and their symbols, and he stated that he could discover faint traces of a bird on the side which faces the sun, it looking due south, thus also connecting it with the Druidical sun worship, and the bird perhaps indicating the nature of the sacrifices, possibly borrowed by the heathen Celts from the Jews, who had sacrifices of birds. See Luke chap. ii., verse 24.

heathens, and spoke the *same* Gaelic language as the Atholl, and all other Highlanders now do, and these three words, *clach-na-iobairt*, are unquestionably Pictish. And lastly, it is to be remembered that the Irish Scots never were in this part of Alban, and that the name must have been given *at least* three hundred years before the time the pretended new Gaelic language came in.

In the parish of Strath, in the Isle of Skye, and close in front of the parish clergyman's house, there stands a very interesting monument also relating to and connected with the heathen religion of the Gael of Alban in very remote times, it is described as 'a rude obelisk of granite about *ten feet* high, perfectly erect.' It is known by the appellation of '*clach na h' Annait,*' that is '*the stone of Annat*'—a goddess mentioned by mythologists.[1] This goddess, called by the ancient Caledonian Gael 'Annat,' was the goddess 'of victory,' and the name is known to classical writers who mention the fact, calling her very slightly different, as 'Andat,' or 'Andate;' and according to the custom of the Gael of contracting proper names, they called it 'Annat.' This heathen goddess and another called 'Andraste,' or 'the god of justice,' are

[1] See New Statistical Account in the vol. of County of Inverness, p. 315.

both mentioned by the ancient author[1] Dio,' (who wrote in A.D. 230), as deities worshipped at that period by the Celtic nations. Annat (or Andate) it appears had a temple dedicated to her at a place called Camalodunum.[2] There would unquestionably be a great veneration paid to her on the invasion of the Romans (in A.D. 78) by the ancient Gael. There is another place of worship also named after her close to the Castle of Dunvegan, in Skye, and there is a place near Perth called Annat; also on the north side of Loch Rannoch, Perthshire, there is a very large farm called Annat.[3] At both these places there had no doubt been stones or heathen places of worship dedicated to propitiate her, they may without doubt be assigned with fair probability in date, to the first or second centuries, nay, it is not impossible they might all have been given prior to the Christian era.[4] In the Statistical Account of the

[1] See the Report in the Appendix of Highland Society on Ossian, page 35; and Logan's Scottish Gael, vol. ii., page 332.

[2] See the Report in the Appendix of Highland Society on Ossian, page 35.

[3] In that locality sometimes it is also called Annaty, or Annate, which is nearer the classical writers' spelling.

[4] In the Iona Club Transactions there is printed an old bond of friendship dated at '*Annat*' in the year 1673, between Lord MacDonell (formerly of Glengarry) and M'Pherson of Cluny, page 207.

parish of Strath, already quoted, there is mentioned that close along side of the obelisk there is a well which is by the native Highlanders called by the Gaelic name of '*Tobar na h' Annat,*' or '*the well of Annat.*' This well would be used no doubt by the heathen worshippers for purification, when assembled there to pay divine honours to this deity, and the situation for placing the stone monument was most probably chosen on account of the well. We are acquainted by the works of the learned Archbishop Ussher,[1] that another very ancient author, namely, Origen, who wrote so far back as the year A.D. 230, likewise mentions this Annat or Andate as a heathen goddess of the Celts, and it is a very remarkable thing to consider that at the very time these two extremely ancient authors were writing (in A.D. 230) respecting this Celtic heathen goddess Annat, there was, without doubt, this and other monuments *then* existing among the Caledonian Gael dedicated to her, one even in the remote Isle of Sye, and which also exists to the present day.

Every thing that has been said respecting the clach n' iobairt, or stone of sacrifice, in the parish of Blair Atholl, applies equally to this heathen monument, and also the well, as proof beyond question that the name was given by

[1] Ussher in his Primordia, page 2.

the Picts or their forefathers, and is therefore (most clear evidence that their language as it is the *same* Gaelic as now spoken) was identical with the present Highlanders. How is it possible to conceive that the name of this stone, and well, could have come down through the immense space of time since it was first given, and through so many generations, unless the people were a Gaelic-speaking race? and so thereby passed from one age to another, and this fact shows what a fable it is to speak of *a new* language being brought in. The writer of the Statistical Account of the Parish of Strath already referred to (where stands Annat's obelisk), mentions one of those highly curious Druidical remains, called 'rocking stones' in English, but very different in Gaelic, he says,[1] 'there is *an immense* block of granite on the glebe weighing at *least six tons*, which is so nicely balanced on a level lime rock that it moves by the slightest pressure of the finger. It has been evidently placed there by the ingenuity of man, but in what manner or by what mechanical power, is a subject for the antiquarian to discover.'

These extremely curious Druidical stones are known in the Gaelic language as the

[1] New Statistical Account, vol. for County of Inverness, page 316.

'Clach na brath,' or 'Clach-bhrath,' meaning 'the stone of information or knowledge,'[1] the name thus bestowed in very remote heathen Pictish times being identical in meaning with the Gaelic language *now* spoken. These stones of information are numerous in other parts of Scotland,[2] and the name becomes another proof the language of the Gael of this day being identical with that of the Picts of the heathen ages.

In considering the deductions that may be made from the names of these stone monuments that have been mentioned above, and as illustrating the religion of the heathen Caledonian Picts, there will now be given an expression which is in constant use by the present Highlanders, and to which attention is particularly requested, as it bears very strongly in proving that the language of the present Highlanders is *the same* as that of the Picts. This consists in a corresponding expression employed by them at this day, when going to a place of

---

[1] This name, given by the heathen Picts, was likely, with reference to the vibrations the stone would make after the pressure had been applied to it, and which their superstition would cause them to look upon as an answer.

[2] There is a very large one at Kirkmichael, county of Perth.—See Old Statistical Account, vol. xv., page 517; also Chalmers's Caledonia, vol. i., page 76. Another in the parish of Abernethy, one on the stream called the Farg, near Balvaird (Bailie bhard) or the bard's town.

worship, the question commonly used is, '*am bheil thu 'dol do 'n clachan,*' the meaning being, '*are you going to the stones,*' no reference to a church, but 'to the stones.' From whence is it possible for this expression to have arisen, but from the practice of the Pictish ancestors of the Highlanders, in heathen times, going to their stone circles, stones of sacrifice, and those dedicated to their deities. The above question, therefore, must have been in constant use by the Picts prior to Christianity, meaning also, of course, are you going to the worship to be held at the stones of sacrifice, etc., etc. That the expression is still in constant use, every clergyman within the Highlands, and the whole Gaelic people, can testify that it is employed in making the inquiry. The mature consideration of this Gaelic expression will surely prove to conviction, that it is impossible a new language could have been brought in, as is pretended, *three hundred years after* the Picts had become Christians, or could have brought with it such a heathen expression; and still further, it could not have been imported by the Irish Scots of Argyleshire into the Highlander's language (which involves many absurdities), because they were Christians before their arrival from Ireland in A.D. 506; those therefore who assert the fiction of a new language so late,

The Pictish Language

A.D. 843, being brought in by Irish Scots 300 years *after* the Picts were Christians, are bound to explain how the Gaelic language of the Highlanders contains names and subjects wholly heathen. To those who hold that the Picts are the real ancestors of the Scotch Highlanders, the explanation is plain and simple, *and accords* with historical truth, namely, that from the Picts, their forefathers the Highlanders, received their language, which of course contained much relating to the period when heathenism prevailed among them, and *thereby* came down to them, and thus was continued. Another remark worthy of attention is, What could have been the reply to this Gaelic question in heathen times? at which period it could *only have originated;* it would, if in the affirmative, be, ' *Tha mi' dol do' n clachan,*' or ' *Yes, I am going to the stones.*' This would be the answer to the question in Pictish times, quite as much as it is at this moment in Christian times;[1] and it is hoped this will be considered a very clear and perfect illustration in proof of the identity of the language of the Gael of the present day, and those of the remote heathen times.

[1] Therefore the whole of the present Gaelic language can thus be very justly considered to have existed among the Picts, and precisely the same language that now does among the Highlanders.

The native Gael of Alban (now Scotland) must, at even the earliest period of their settlement in their present native land, have had a government of some kind, as also that justice among the different tribes must have been maintained somehow; and though as to kings or other rulers we have no positive evidence prior to the arrival of the Romans in the first century, yet it seems fair to conclude they brought with them, at their earliest settlement, customs relating to justice among each other. The Gaelic term for the places where they held their courts or councils is 'mòd' in the Gaelic of this day; they are artificial mounds, and in English are called 'moot-hills.' There was one at the Pictish Dun Fothir, or Forteviot; another very large one (though unfortunately much obscured by the number of trees on it), at Scone Palace, a residence of the ancient kings. A small village in Strathearn, Perthshire, derives its name from what must have been the ancient moothill of that district, and is corrupted into Muthil. In Strathord, Perthshire (close to where Nairne House stood), there is a very perfect moot-hill, all artificial, with terraces going round it, denoting most probably where the assembled people stood according to their rank. This one is now called 'The Hangman's Hill,' it being the place where, in far later times, the feudal proprietors[1] of Strathord had their 'Furca et Fossa,' or 'Pit and Gallows,' as it is also often called in crown charters. This ditch or pit is supplied with water from the small stream that passes near, called the Crdie. There is also a very large moothill at Inverury,[2] Aberdeenshire; but besides this enumeration of places where the 'mòd' existed in very ancient times, it abounds also in the Highlands, and is in general called '*Tomamhōd*,' or 'the knoll of the *Mòd*.' In very remote ages, therefore, the assembly of the Gael of Alban tribes, and larger national councils were held, and justice dispensed, at the 'Mòd;' and this word becomes a singularly strong proof of the high antiquity of the *present* spoken Gaelic, when we find in that language '*Mod*,' at this hour, is the word for '*a court of justice*,' and which must have been in use from a period prior even to the name of Picts, but descended *through them* to the present Highlanders, it

---

[1] The Earls of Fife were proprietors of the Barony of Strathord in the early part of the reign of King David II., as shown by a charter contained in the book of Original Charters, No. 57 of Sir James Balfour's Collection, and of the Advocates' Library, No. of MSS., No. 15—1-18.

[2] The moothill at Inverury is situated close to the old site of the church, and it is generally called 'The Bas,' from the Gaelic signifying the place of death or judgment.

being *impossible* to have come into their language from the Irish Scots in 843, *centuries after* its use among the Picts. If a Highlander is going, in the present day, to a district or county court, or any other place of justice, he would say he was '*a' dol do 'n mhod ;*' that literally is, '*going to the mòd*' or court of justice. This expression surely it cannot but be allowed, *must* have been in use in, and before even (as already said) the time of the Picts (A.D. 296), when we consider the Caledonians must *also* have had their courts, and whenever they attended a 'Mòd' in those very remote ages, would use the same words; and it becomes a very strong proof indeed of the identity of the Caledonian, Pictish, and Scotch Highlanders' language.

The topography of the Highlands also contains most numerous examples of names derived in heathen times and connected with their worship, etc. Thus, on the north side of Loch Tummel, Perthshire, there is situated the lands called Grenach or Grenich, where there is the remains of what had been a heathen stone-circle or temple, and all round it, as is also mentioned by the writer of the Statistical Account of the parish, '*there are cairns innumerable.*'[1]

[1] See Old Statistical Account, vol. ii., and parish of Blair Atholl.

The above name is derived from the Gaelic — 'Grian-achadh,' or '*The field of the sun.*' In the last word for field the dh is not sounded, and the word is therefore pronounced very near the English corruption of the Gaelic—namely, Greeanach.[1] Thus this heathen name of the Pictish place of worship we see gave also the name to the lands, and even to Loch Tummel itself, as is mentioned in the Crown charter[2] for the barony of Strowan in 1451. The numerous graves (or cairns) alongside of this Druidical work also proves that the heathen Gael buried near their places of worship, as is also done now in Christian times, and the Druids or magicians buried within their circles. There is a very remarkable expression in use at this day among the Highlanders connected with this remote heathen manner of burying the dead, namely, '*Cuiridh mise clach ad charn,*' that is, '*I will place a stone on your cairn.*' How very strongly does this show that the practice of the heathen Gael was that method of interment, and the expression also signifies that they would not forget their friends even after their death. This mode of speech, coming from such remote

[1] In the large island of Lewis, 'ach' is the Gaelic for a field or meadow.—See MacAlpine's Gaelic Dictionary.
[2] See the Record of the Great Seal, Book iv., No. 227.

the same as the Highlanders. 163

times, it will surely be allowed to be a most undoubted evidence that the language of the Picts was the present Highlanders' Gaelic, and who use the *same words now* as a term of endearment, namely, '*I will befriend you.*' Evidently the Highlanders must have inherited the expression from their heathen ancestors the Picts. The name '*Grianachadh*,' also, most distinctly connects this Druidical work with the sun worship of the heathen Celts, or of the god Bel,[1] who they represented by fire. This name 'Grian' for the sun, bestowed at that remote period by the Picts, is still the present word of the language of the Highlanders for it, as also the other for the field, and is therefore a further illustration and proof that the language of the Picts and Highlanders of this day is identical.

In the parish of Blair Atholl there is further examples relating to the ancient heathen religion of the Caledonians and Picts. About a mile to the eastward of Blair there is a strath, called in English Strathgroy,[2] which is

[1] This heathen god is often mentioned in the Scriptures, and considered the same as Baal.—See Jeremiah, chap. li., verse 44; Isaiah xlvi. 1, etc., etc.

[2] In an old charter, dated 1343, it is written 'Strathgroye.' This charter was printed lately from the Atholl charter-chest. It was granted by King Robert II., when he was Earl of Atholl.

a corruption from the Gaelic Strath-dhrui, or Sradhrui, which is pronounced Srăgrui, and corrupted when speaking or writing in English, Sragrúóé, or Strathgroy—the meaning of the Gaelic words is, 'the Druid's strath,'[1] and the lands are of considerable extent. The writer in the Old Statistical Account of this parish was the Rev. Mr M'Laggan, a superior Gaelic scholar, and who furnished the Highland Society of Scotland, and also Macpherson, with many poems of Ossian, collected in Atholl; and in the account he derives the name of these lands in the same way from the Gaelic, and signifying the Druid's strath.[2] Adjoining to these lands of the Druid's strath are those of *Balnagrew*, corrupted from the Gaelic (but not so much as in the former case), namely, 'Baile-na-dhrui,' or, 'the Druid's town,' which Gaelic words are pronounced nearly as Balnagru-e, or Balnagrew—it is situated higher up, looking down on the Druid's strath; the name Balnagrew has been changed, but only very recently,[3] into that of Lude, which original name gave the designation to that ancient

[1] This derivation of this place was given to the writer by a friend, who is a very competent Gaelic scholar.

[2] See the account of the parish of Blair Atholl in Old Statistical Account, vol. ii.

[3] Namely, by John Robertson of Lude, the writer's great-grandfather, in 1731.

barony. Lude proper is three miles distant from Balnagrew.[1] Here, then, are two topographical names of undoubted remote Pictish times come down to the present day, and are in the same Gaelic as now, because it must be remembered the corruptions of these names are *not* used by the Highlanders when speaking their own language, they being pronounced by them the same as when the names were given ages ago, as is the whole Gaelic topography, and not as it is written in English.

In other parts of the Highlands there is evidence of the Druids being the occupiers of land. Thus, in the parish of Applecross, in Ross-shire, there is mentioned in the Old Statistical Account[2] of a shealing (that is, the summer pasture of the higher grounds), called in Gaelic, 'aridh na Dhrui,' or, 'the Druid's shealing,' proving the immense antiquity of

[1] In a straight line due east from Balnadhrui (now Lude), 'the Druid's town' (and on part of Strathgroy lands), there is a place called '*Dochanlelas*,' it is marked and can be seen in Stobie's map of Perthshire—it seems undoubtedly connected with the Druidical heathenism, and to be a derivation from the Gaelic words, 'Dochann-le-las,' or, 'the agony belonging to the flame of fire,' alluding to the ordeal by fire of the Druids, and that it was at this spot it was inflicted. The whole topography hereabouts is connected with the Druids; this place, and the Druid's town, are within sight of '*Clach n'iobairt*,' or, '*the stone of sacrifice*,' which has been before mentioned.

[2] See the Old Statistical Account of the parish of Applecross, Ross-shire, page 381.

these summer shealings, as well as the present
Gaelic corresponding exactly with the ancient
Picts language for a shealing. When we consider this evidence of the situation where these
names of the Druidical period exist, we learn
that the Irish Scots could *never* have brought
into the language of the Highlanders of Scotland anything about Druids, as, how could
they (the Irish Scots) know where the Druid's
straths, towns, or shealings were situated?
They (the Irish Scots) never were located in
Atholl, or in Applecross, Ross-shire.

There is also to be remembered the name by
which Iona is known to the native Highlanders,
namely, 'Innis nan Dhruithnach,' 'the island
of the Druids.' This has been the designation
both in modern and ancient times, and that
notwithstanding the veneration the Highlanders
properly entertain towards the great apostle of
their nation, Columba; yet this name still sur-
vives, as the *original* name of Iona. It is given
in the Old Statistical Account of Scotland of
the last century, and again in that of the present,[1] as the name that it had formerly, and
as such is still known to the native Highlanders.
The burial place of the Druids in the island

---

[1] See Old Statistical Account of Scotland, vol. xiv., page 100; New Statistical Account of Scotland, vol. vii., part 2. page 313.

had for ages been known and pointed out, and which one of the best Gaelic scholars who ever lived, namely, the Rev. Dr Smith of Campbeltown, in his Life of Columba,[1] mentions, as to the grave or cemetery of the Druids, or as he writes in Gaelic, 'Claodh nan Druithnach.' To test the accuracy of this being, as stated by tradition, a place of interment of the Druids or not, and of which many had expressed an opinion as most improbable, the mound was opened some years ago, and the writer hereof was present with other members of the Iona Club, *and saw* the skulls and other human remains which this examination brought to light. Such a full attestation of the truth of the tradition ought undoubtedly to convince all who are willing to be convinced ; and more cogent proof of the truth of any tradition can scarcely be conceived. These bodies that had been buried there could not have been Christians, as they were not in any of their consecrated burial grounds, but in a mound by themselves, very considerably separated from any of the Christian cemeteries; they could not have been Christians buried there in the time of Columba, or others his successors, as it may be considered *certain* the natives never would have called Christians, *Druids*. The soil was nearly a pure

[1] Life of Columba by Dr J. Smith, page 4.

dry sand, and the number of skulls found were from ten to twenty. This verification satisfactorily establishes the truth of the original name of Iona being 'the island of the Druids.' It is also necessary to say, that, of course, there must have been numbers of Druids buried at their cemetery whose remains had decayed, and were not found. Thus, as we learn in the very ancient Ossianic poem called Carthon, and translated by the learned Dr Smith, one of the characters mentioned is called Dargo, '*Mac dhrui Bheil*,' meaning. Dargo, 'son of *the Druid of Bel*,' and states that he was buried in the Green Isle, that is, Iona, the *place where his fathers rested*.

The heathen worship of the sun—that is, of the god Bel, spelled in Gaelic often Beil, Bheil, and Beal, has already been alluded to; and as it appears in some names of places, it becomes a proof respecting the Pictish language. Thus, in Perthshire there is a considerable property named Tulliebelton, always by the lower orders called Tullie-beltane. Also, most Scotchmen are acquainted with the name of 'Beltane-day';[1] it has become a law term, and is the

[1] Beltane-day is the 1st of May. It is mentioned in several very ancient deeds printed in the Iona Club Transactions, as a term day, for payment of rents, etc., etc.—See the Iona Club Transactions, pages 11, 17, and 20; in the latter

1st of May, the reputed first day of summer. This name is from the ancient Picts language, namely. '*Beal-teine*,' that is, 'the fire of the god Bel or Baal.' This name is a very strong proof of the Pictish language being identical with that of the Highlanders of this day, because the naming of a certain day by the heathen Picts after their god Bel, and the *continuance* of that name among the present Gael, proves that it was derived from the heathen Picts, or their forefathers, the Caledonians. It could not have been derived from the Irish Scots, who were not heathens when they arrived in Alban—they were Christians more than a hundred years before that event; therefore, they had nothing to do with the god Bel. Neither is the name from the Saxons, as it is not their language. The name Beltane, therefore, is clearly from the Pictish language, and the Irish Scots and the Saxon population must have adopted the word from the Picts, the far most numerous race, as also was the custom of keeping the Beltane-day derived from the Picts. These facts are in strict harmony with the historical truth, that there could not possibly have been any kind of con-

---

twice. Tullicbelton means. the 'Knoll of the fire of Bel or Baal,' from the present Gaelic, 'Tulach-beal-teinne,' the name in English being a corruption.

quest of the Pictish nation, and likewise confutes the fable of a new language, and which the author of 'The Early Scottish Church' mainly relies on as having been effected by the Church,[1] that is, by the *Christian* clergymen of the Church; but as they were almost *entirely Irish*, the only Gaelic language they could have brought in would have been *more Irish* than even what the descendants of the Scots in Argyle now speak.

In full confirmation of the foregoing observations, there is a very strong piece of evidence which it is believed will fully satisfy all readers hereof, that Beltane-day is derived from the custom of the Picts, and *from their language.* Among the MSS. of the Highland Society of Scotland, now deposited in the Advocates' Library, Edinburgh, there is one of extraordinary antiquity, in *the Gaelic language,* and of which full proof is given in the Appendix[2] to the Report on Ossian, also fac-similes of the writing engraved therein; and from the able reasons there adduced, we are fully warranted to conclude it must have been written not later than about the middle of the eighth century, that is A.D. 750. Among many other strong

---

[1] See page 31 of that book.
[2] See the Appendix to the Report on Ossian, pages 285 to 293 inclusive.

reasons for this being the latest period to be assigned to it is, that the writer (named Fithil) calls the ecclesiastic with whom he was residing, in a cænobium, or college, in Gaelic thus, 'Mo Pupu Murcuisa,' or 'My Pope Murcus;' but, as after A.D. 730, this title of 'Pope' would not have been accepted or received by the clergy of present Scotland, that term, as the writer in the Appendix shows, was after that date confined to the Pope of Rome, the whole kingdom of ancient Alban having by that year acknowledged the Papal rule, by adopting the new time as to keeping Easter, etc., etc. The writing also establishes it as being of the eighth century, and the orthography corresponds with that period. And lastly, it cannot be claimed as an Irish MS., as it gives *the date* of, and cause of, a most ancient historical tale called the 'Tainbho,' or 'cattle spoil,' which fact proves this MS. was unknown to O'Flaherty, M'Firbis, etc., etc. Having thus endeavoured to make the reader understand the proofs of the immense antiquity of this MS., it is of the highest importance to find that it is written in the *same* language as the Highlanders of Scotland now speak. The writer in the Appendix gives extracts of the Gaelic in which it is written, and which shows there is not a Welsh word among them. How completely this therefore confutes the conjecture that the Pictish Gael spoke Welsh and Gaelic mixed. It is necessary to remember also, for the due estimation of the value of this ancient Gaelic MS., that it was written (as may almost for a certainty be said) probably not less than a hundred years *before* the fabulous Scotch conquest (in A.D. 843), and of the pretended new language, and yet it is proved to be the same Gaelic as now; and lastly, it bears another strong evidence of its *Pictish* origin. The writer dates it as written on ' *Oidche-bealtinne*,' or ' *Beltane-night*.' A piece of evidence so strong as the foregoing, it is hoped, will duly be weighed and considered as a very conclusive proof that the language of the Picts has come down to the present day in that of their real descendants, the Highlanders of Scotland. It is a very remarkable date also, not calling the day the MS. was written, the 1st May, but ' *Beltane-night*,' the word for night being the *same in Gaelic now*. Of course, as Christianity had not been known among the Pictish Gael at this time little more than a century and a half, it is likely Beltane-day would still be regarded as a holiday and important day, though not to the extent of course as in the Druidical times of receiving the Bealteinne, or sacred fire.

Another very ancient Gaelic name, and which must have come down from Pictish times, is the 'Liathfail,' or 'the grey stone of fate,' on which the ancient Caledonian Pictish kings were crowned on; it is now at Westminster Abbey, placed there by Edward I., having been taken from Scotland by him. This stone is fabulously said to have been brought over by the paltry colony of Irish Scots or Dalriads, and that it was the coronation stone *of the monarchs of Ireland*. The latest upholder of the fiction is the author of 'The Early Scotch Church,' to magnify, of course, the Scots rulers that descended from that insignificant Irish colony, and in accordance of placing every thing among the Gael of Alban as coming from the Irish Scots; to believe in the possibility that the sacred coronation stone of the Irish kings should have been allowed by them to have been taken away by the trifling number of emigrants that came over to Argyleshire in A.D. 506, with the three leaders and their fifty men to each would show a wonderful credulity in readers to receive it as in any way possible. And further, when we consider the history of this Irish Scots colony, that for upwards of two hundred years the wretched state of bloodshed that went on between the tribes of Lorn and Kintyre, and the alternation of their petty kings from the one to the other, it may be asked, who held the pretended 'Laithfail' of the Irish kings? Was it given it up as each of these paltry Argyleshire kings got the upper hand? Mr Petrie very properly denies the possibility of 'the stone of destiny' being carried off as pretended, which indeed to believe in, requires more sufficient proof than the most prejudiced extoller of the Irish Scots colony can ever bring forward. It may reasonably and safely be received that this ancient stone was that which belonged to the Pictish kings, and used by them at their coronations, and the attempt to claim it as Irish, is only a portion of the invented fable of a Scots conquest; that having been disproved, we may be satisfied both the stone and the name was handed down by the ancient kings of the Gael of Alban.[1]

There are other words in the present Gaelic derived from the worship of the heathen god Bel, namely, the word for ordeal or jeopardy, '*Gabhadh-bheil*,' literally, 'the jeopardy of the god Bel.' This arose from the Druidical ordeal

[1] Robertson in his Early Kings holds the same views as stated in the text as to how extraordinary it would have been that the Dalriad colonists could have been permitted to carry off 'the sacred stone' of the Irish kings, and that its only removal prior to King Edward's, was from Dunfothir (Forteviot) to Scone.

of passing between two fires, to ascertain the innocence of persons when it was uncertain, and Dr Smith[1] remarked that it was probable St Paul in his travels in the different heathen countries he passed through, might have seen this ordeal by fire,[2] and that he alludes to it in his epistle in 1st Corinthians 3d chap. and 15th verse.

Thus, what was connected in the remote ages of the Pictish language as signifying a particular kind of trial, is now *the same* word at this day (Gabhadh) for jeopardy, or great danger. The present Gaelic word for a year is 'Bliadhna,' in which the god Bel also enters, it being derived, according to Logan,[3] from the words '*Bheil-aine*,' that is, 'the circle of the god Bel,' or the circle of the sun, which is very expressive of what would appear to heathens during the period of a year to have been accomplished by the sun.

In the south-west of Perthshire, and in the parish of Callander, there is situated a very picturesque mountain called Benledi. It has

---

[1] See M'Alpine's Gaelic Dictionary—note on the word 'Gabhadhbheil.'

[2] In another part of this work the author has given the name of a place in the highlands of Perthshire, called 'Dochann le las,' or, 'the agony of the flame of fire,' where, no doubt, this painful trial of heathen times was inflicted.

[3] Logan's Scottish Gael, vol. ii., p. 350.

a very fine appearance, particularly when seen from Stirling Castle; also from the south side of the river Teith, from which position the illustration of it is given. Loch Lubnaig lies due north, and Loch Venacher due south of it. The name of Benledi is a very slight alteration from its Gaelic name, '*Beinn-le-dia*,' or '*the hill of God*,' that is, the hill belonging to the god Bel, or Baal, who thus had this mountain specially dedicated to him,[1] and according to the universal tradition of the country, it was here, on Beltane-day, that the whole people of the adjacent country assembled to worship this deity, and receive from their Druids, that is, their magi or magicians,[2] the 'tiene eigin,' or 'need fire,' or 'fire of exigency,' the heathen custom being, throughout the whole neighbourhood, to put out their fires, and have them relighted from the sacred fire of the god Bel on his day (the Beltane-day) namely, 1st May,

---

[1] There is in Syria, at the foot of Mount Libanus, most magnificent ruins of a temple dedicated to Bel or Baal, and in consequence is called Baalbac or Belbec, and is one of the wonders of the world. Some of the stones of the temple are upwards of twenty feet long.

[2] The word in Gaelic which means a Druid has also the signification of a magician or sorcerer, which the heathen Gael considered all the Druids to be. Thus the Gaelic phrase as to speaking to or asking advice from the Druids, magi, or wise men, was 'dh 'innise siu do *na Druidhean*,' or, '*he told that to the magicians*'

being also considered the first day of summer, when this solemn meeting took place on the top of this mountain.¹ Any one who has ever been at the summit of Benledi must have noticed how very different it is there to almost every other Highland hill. Instead of a mere heap of bare stones or rocks, it is remarkably verdant, having been evidently cleared of stones and smoothed by the hand of man, which is fully accounted for by its Gaelic name, and which, though given undoubtedly *more* than 2000 years ago, it is still the language of the Highlanders of Scotland at this hour. How distinctly, therefore, does this name Beinn-le-dia—or, as in English, Benledi—prove the language of the Picts and present Gael to be identical; and nothing but this identity could have preserved the name through such an immense space of time, and that although the inhabitants have ceased to be heathen for 1300 years. Another corroboration in regard to the

¹ Connected with the sun worship was the heathen practice of the Gael of Alban of what they called the ' *Deiseal*,' that is, ' *the turn sun wise*, a custom much observed by them in heathen times There is a place behind Lude (or properly ' the Druid's • town ') already mentioned, called *Carn-deiseal*, which may have been so named from being connected with the Druidical superstition of ' the turn sun wise.' The mention of this custom occurs no less than four times in Dr Reeves's edition of Adomnan.—See the Index. The ' *Deiseal*' is another undoubted Pictish word.

heathen sanctity of this mountain is that, on its north side there is a hollow, called in Gaelic '*Coire am faidh*,' or '*The Prophets'* [1] *Dell.*'

That the Picts spoke the present Gaelic of the Scotch Highlanders is also proved by the Rev. Dr Thomas M'Lauchlan, who states[2] that the family appellation given to King Brudhi (a Pictish king), was that of 'the greyhound,'[3] which, in the Gaelic of the present day, is 'Mialchu,' and that the father of King Brudhi and his own son bore this name, as also the grandson, though of course the word would be used both in the nominative and genitive cases. In the Irish Annals the appellative name of this king of the Picts often appears both in his own (his reign began A.D. 554), and succeeding times, and chiefly in the genitive.[4] Here then is proved by a Gaelic scholar of high repute, that the Picts gave their king an appellation which *must* have been a word of the Pictish language; therefore those who consider that *only five*

[1] This name also appears heathen. No one in Christian times could possibly pretend to foretell future events. It also is consistent with the heathen name of the mountain.

[2] In 'The Early Scottish Church,' page 33, note.

[3] The appellation of 'the greyhound' was probably to signify swiftness and ability in overtaking his enemies.

[4] The Annals of Tighernach mention, in the year A.D. 752 the death of one of this Royal Pictish race, slain in the battle of Sreith, it is also in the original in the genitive case, being 'Brudhi MacMialchoin.'

words of that language remain ought surely to add this one.

There is a Gaelic word now well known from Ossian, which is indisputably the original of the present word for the region of bliss— the ancient heathen Gael of Alban knew of no greater happiness than to be in the island, far in the west, beyond the setting sun, where all the mighty men of valour went to after death; this they called '*Flath-innis*' or '*the island of heroes;*' likewise the present Gaelic name for heaven, the place of everlasting happiness, is 'Flaith-eanas,' which is but a slight alteration of the heathen name from which it must have been borrowed by the earliest Christian teachers, who would naturally adopt a word[1] which conveyed to the heathen Gael of Alban the greatest possible idea of happiness after death. These words, Flath-innis, or Island of Heroes, *must* have been Pictish, and therefore it is a proof of that language and the Highlanders being identical.

[1] There is a word used in the present Gaelic, which must have been more anciently in use in the language of the Gael of Alban than any that have hitherto been named. It is in English called 'the putting stone,' used in Highland games and sports; but the Gael give it a very different name, they call it the '*Clach-neart,*' or '*the stone of strength.*' This name must have been in use with the Gael *before they came* into the land of Alban, now called Scotland

In this branch, on the subject of the language of the Picts, we have also from the name of the place called Abernethy, in Perthshire, an illustration. In both the New and Old Statistical Accounts of that parish, we find that the name by which it is called by the Highlanders is '*Obair-Nechtan,*' meaning '*Nechtan's work,*' thus clearly identifying it with the Pictish King Nechtan, who sent in A.D. 710 *for architects* to Ceolfrid, Abbot of Jarrow, at the mouth of the Wear, on Tyne, to *build a church, etc.,* and also as to the proper time of keeping Easter, as mentioned by Bede;[1] this Pictish King Nechtan sent the Irish clergy out of his dominions, back to Iona, as they would not hold Easter at what was called Catholic time. The date that this last event happened is mentioned in the Annals of Tigernach as A.D. 717, so we learn the king and Pictish nation bore with them for seven years after having received the very long epistle from Ceolfrid which caused this expulsion. Therefore this King Nechtan, we may be certain, was the founder of the new church, also the curious round tower at Abernethy; and from the above Gaelic word 'Obair' (pronounced Ob-er) meaning 'work,'[2] which

[1] Bede lib. 5, cap. 21, and in A.D. 710.
[2] It was a very great work, indeed, for those remote times. The round tower is still most perfect, and has endured so many ages without any lime, from its good masonry.

being likewise connected with King Nechtan's name, it seems perfectly clear it must have been bestowed on the place at the period of the work *being accomplished*, and the language of course could from the date only be in that of the Picts. The word *obair* is given in one of the Gaelic Dictionaries (M'Alpine's), as signifying 'a confluence,' and he gives several examples of this, it would appear, therefore, that in this case the Gaelic obair, has got corrupted into the Welsh 'Aber.' The pronunciation of both words are certainly very similar, but it must not be understood that there exists any reason for Abernethy being supposed to be at the *confluence* of the Nethy, that place is upwards of a mile off, at the lands of the Gaelic *Innernethy* (properly Inbhirnethy). Many persons unacquainted with the locality would suppose that the Aber, in the name Abernethy, was from the British word signifying a confluence, which it here *cannot*, as there is none, but it is somewhat curious that the Gaelic word '*obair*,' for a confluence (as stated by M'Alpine) should have become the same as the Welsh word '*Aber*.'[1] This corruption

[1] There are many Gaelic words in the topography of Wales, so that some have thought the Gael were there before the Cymri; but in their present language these words may be only obsolete, but have been retained in the language of the present Gael of Alban.

might therefore have taken place in *many other* instances elsewhere, and thereby a Gaelic word came to be considered British, and we may thus understand how many words now obsolete in Gaelic are supposed to be British,[1] the name of the stream 'Nethy,' is derived from the Celtic deity 'Neithe,'[2] the god of the waters. His name enters into several of the rivers in Scotland; thus in the Teith, and in the Nith, there is also another river called the Nethy in Morayshire, all these places testifying it was the same people who originally gave these names. The round tower already mentioned as at Abernethy, is a very great antiquarian curiosity, quite similar to those in Ireland; some years ago, as mentioned in the last Statistical Account its interior was examined, by digging to a considerable depth, when human remains were discovered. These may very probably

[1] We have a very clear example of this in the word 'dur,' which is now obsolete in Gaelic, as mentioned in the dictionaries, and is still retained in the Welsh; therefore in Highland topography streams ending in 'dur' are thus wrongly put down as British. In Perthshire there are two small rivers that give the same name to two small glens, that is, '*Fionn-dur*,' or 'Fingal's water—the Welsh had nothing to do with Fingal. In English these streams are corrupted into 'Fender.' A collection of the obsolete Gaelic words would much clear the ideas held by some as to the Welsh etymologies.

[2] The name Neithe, or the god of the waters of the heathen Gael of Alban, is from a word signifying to purify, as mentioned by Logan in his Scottish Gael, vol. ii., page 332.

have been that of the Saxon Christian clergymen, who had succeeded the Irish ones, whom King Nechtan had banished out of his dominions back to Iona. The round tower was also likely built by him for their security, as appears to have been the intention of the whole round towers, not for a burial place alone, though undoubtedly also used for that purpose by the early Christians, as did the Druidical priests bury within their sacred stone circles. Almost all the round towers have their doors or entrances ten to twelve feet from the ground, proving that security was desired.

But to return to the illustration that the name given by Highlanders of this place (Abernethy), we learn it arises from the Pictish people of the period who called it their king's work; and from the Highlanders of the present day not calling it Abernethy, but 'Obair-Nechtan,' seems a very clear testimony that this designation must have descended from Pictish times.

The strongest proof of all that can be brought forward as to the language of the present Highlanders being the same as the Pictish and Caledonian Gael is the topography of the Highlands. Herein we have a thousand witnesses that the present spoken Gaelic is *the same* as the designations of every object of the features of the country named by the Caledonian Gael, the first settlers of the race, and which names must have been given at latest two thousand years ago, the only exception of the Gaelic names being the topography of the Fingalian heroes of Ossian of the third century. The Gaelic topography of the Highland districts in Scotland, those of Atholl, Lochaber, Lorn, Morvern, Glenelg, and those about Loch Ness, contain the most names relating to the Fingalians, or Feinn heroes, and this topography is mentioned and confirmed by a charter in the Chartulary of Moray of the time of Alexander II., who reigned from 1214 to 1249, and speaks of the 'Tobar na feinn,' or, 'the well of the Feinn.' Near Oban, in Argyleshire, there are several names relating to them mentioned by Skene in his introducduction to the Book of the Dean of Lismore (page lxxxi.), and which were given by the Caledonian Picts *long ere* the Irish Scots came over in A.D. 506. Of those places relating to the children or descendants of Uissneach, there is ' Dun-mhic-Uisneachan ' (which is corrupted by the Guide Books into Dun-mac-Sniachan)—it is a vitrified fort, and means ' the stronghold of the son of Uissneach.' On Loch Etive there is ' Glen Uisneach,' all which proves that the Picts who preceded the Irish

the same as the Highlanders.

Scots in this part of Argyleshire, and gave these names, were a Gaelic race, speaking *the same language* as the present Highlanders of Scotland.

To illustrate this truth would fill a volume to itself; but in this and the former chapter many comparisons of Gaelic names have been given, which prove the identity of the Gaelic-spoken tongue of this day and of the Pictish language, and indeed, of far remoter times than the existence of Picts. As to further examples, a very few more only will be given. Thus, the people who gave the name of a well-known mountain in Ross-shire, called Ben-dearg (the red mountain),[1] were the same Gaelic-speaking people as gave to the two great mountains in Perthshire, called by the same name, and these three are now the same in signification in the Gaelic of this day. The large range of hills in Inverness called the Monadh-*liath*, or grey hills, were the same as is called one of the five highest of the Perthshire hills named the Ben-*liath*. Those who gave the name in Argyleshire of Craig-*Argiod*, also were the same in race and language as

[1] Beinndearg, that is, the red mountain, from the red granite rock and stones appearing on its sides. There is also in Atholl, Perthshire, a mountain situated between Glen Tilt and Glenbruar, called 'Carndeargmor,' or, 'the large red mountain.'

gave Beinn-*Argiod* in Perthshire, and a similar identity of language could be proved and continued through *every county and parish* of what was the dominions of the Picts.

It has already been adverted to that the whole country north of the Moray Firth has *no* British, that is, Welsh names, so that in this large space, which is near a third of Scotland, the Britons had never been, nor apparently in Argyleshire, or the islands. Where, however, it is arrogating far too much for that very circumscribed district, as if the names therein were one particle more genuine Gaelic than the former mentioned great extent of territory, or one atom better than the Inverness or Perthshire Gaelic names, as is stated by the author of ' The Early Scottish Church,'[1] as to ' the whole topography of the county of Argyll,'[2] leaving out the far larger county of Ross, and also all the others just as clear of Welsh names as Argyleshire, which place must also be understood as being intended by this writer to represent that ' the west of Scotland must have been early occupied by a purely

[1] See page 29

[2] In the topography of this county, the obsolete Gaelic word '*dur*,' or, ' water,' appears, and which has been supposed to be British. There is ' the *Durar-water in Argyle*'—see the Rev. Isaac Taylor's second edition of ' Words and Places,' page 199.

Gaelic race.'[1] That is a fact, and cannot be disputed; *but it was before the intrusion* (in A.D. 506) *of the Irish speaking Scots,* so that since that period there never has been any Celtic language spoken in Argyleshire, but *a most impure Gaelic.*

The etymology of Caledonia, given by Logan, Grant, and many other writers on the Gael, is by them all assigned to the native language. This the author of 'The Early Scottish Church'[2] says should be given to the Welsh or British tongue. But there is no reason whatever to receive that writer's conjecture, when we have the root of the word in the Gaelic language of *our fellow-countrymen;* and this preference for Welsh etymology has led this author apparently into many errors as to the Pictish language, equally as it did Chalmers. At page 11 (of 'The Early Scottish Church)' already referred to, the writer himself quotes the root of the word for Caledonia. It is from the Gaelic, as all authors have hitherto stated, namely, ' *Coille,*' a wood, and '*daoine,*' ' men,' or ' people,' hence the word formed is *Coilledaoine,* or ' men of the woods,' and is from the pure Gaelic of ancient Alban, and corresponds far nearer with the Latinised

---

[1] 'The Early Scottish Church,' page 29.
[2] See pages 10, 11.

form of Caledonii, or the Caledonian people, than the Welsh 'Celyddon;'[1] and it is infinitely more reasonable to suppose that Tacitus, who is the earliest writer that names Caledonia,[2] derived it from a native source, as also would all the subsequent Roman writers, as to the Caledonii, or people of the country, than from the foreign Welsh, or British source. With regard to the etymology of Dunkeld, or 'Duncalden,' as it always appears in all the ancient Irish and other Annals, it is past all doubt derived from the language of the ancient Caledonian Gael, namely thus, 'Dun-choille-daoine,'[3] which means, 'the fort or stronghold of the men of the wood,' and this, according to ancient tradition, it was, being the Caledonian capital; likewise, the old Latin Chronicles, and all ancient documents in English, write the name '*Duncalden*,' which comes far nearer the language of our countrymen than going to a Welsh source for it; and further, the attempt to support the Welsh derivation of

[1] This Welsh derivation regarding Caledonia being Celyddon, by the author of 'The Early Scottish Church,' seems clearly borrowed from Chalmers's note, in his Caledonia, vol. i., page 200.

[2] Tacitus Life of Agricola, chapter 26

[3] This word thus written in Gaelic looks very long and formidable in pronunciation; but it is not at all far removed from the name 'Duncalden,' which this well-known place bore to comparatively modern times.

Dunkeld by a reference to the celebrated Perthshire mountain Schichallien,[1] is very surprising, in so good a Gaelic scholar as the author of 'The Early Scottish Church,' and in which he has fallen into great error. Every Highlander in the neighbourhood can testify that they know nothing whatever of this author's Gaelic derivation — that it signifies 'the mountain of the forests.'[2] The name by which this mountain is known and called in the Gaelic language by the native Highlanders is, '*Ti-chaillinn,*' or '*The Maiden's Pap,*' vastly different in words and meaning from '*the mountain of the forests,*' and which gives no countenance whatever to that writer's strange Welsh or British theory, because the above Gaelic words *are the true* native name for this well-known mountain. And the illustration of it in this book will show to everyone how applicable the name is, and most descriptive of its appearance. It has a very peculiar

---

[1] The writer hereof may be allowed a claim to know the true Gaelic name of this noble mountain, having been born and lived within sight of it for years.

[2] See 'The Early Scottish Church,' page 11, by the Rev. Dr Thomas M'Lauchlan; but who, in a note, page 30 of the Book of the Dean of Lismore (in 1862), gives *a very different* etymology for Shichallien, saying it is from 'Sith,' a pointed hill (and challain), which it certainly is, *and for the reason stated in the text.*

sharp peak, and in this it resembles another hill in Glengarry, in the county of Inverness, whose conformation is similar, and has therefore the same name, that of 'Beinn Tï,' which means literally, 'the mountain of the pap.' Thus we have clear proof that Dr Thomas M'Lauchlan is unquestionably in error to make the last part of the name of this mountain 'chaillin' (the maiden's[1]) identical with any part of the name of Dunkeld, or that it is possible in any way to be connected with it. Again, the same writer, in an attempt to make out a British name in the Highlands of Perthshire, 'Trinafour,' is mentioned,[2] and he states that the '*Trin*,'[3] is the Welsh, *Tre*; but such an etymology cannot be received, because no native Highlander ever in Gaelic calls it '*Tre*,' whereby the whole conjecture falls to the ground, and is wrong; besides, there are no well-authenticated British names to be found in the district to which it belongs. An un-

[1] The translation of Schiehallien, '*The Maiden's Pap*,' is the name even in the Lowlands of Perthshire it is known by, where not one word of Gaelic is spoken now, but from whence the singular peak of the noble Schiehallien is visible.

[2] 'The Early Scottish Church,' page 27.

[3] It ought to have been ascertained by the Rev. Dr M'Lauchlan whether the native Highlanders of Atholl ever called this place '*Tre*-na-four,' before he gave such a dogmatical derivation for it, to favour his Welsh theory of the Picts' language.

doubted good Gaelic scholar, who wrote the Statistical Account of the parish,[1] therein states, the *Trin* in Trinafour is derived from a division, or 'the third part,' from the Gaelic '*Trian*,' whereby it would be called 'the cold third part.' This etymology of the first word is certainly nearer by far than the Welsh '*Tre*,' which signifies 'an abode,' or 'dwelling;' and as there is not any Welsh 'Tre' within at least forty or fifty miles, it would therefore prove this place, if we are to believe it was named by the Welsh, to have been in a desert by itself; yet all the large mountains and rivers (the great objects of nature) in sight of it are *in pure Gaelic*, which were of course given by the ancient Gael of Alban, and contradicts the possibility of the name coming from any other people.

A well known Perthshire river is *now* said by the same writer to be from the British or Welsh, namely the Tay. He states,[2] 'The Tay is *the Taw in Wales*.' In refutation of this very dogmatical assertion, the evidence of the Rev. Dr Thomas M'Lauchlan, in his Celtic Gleanings, is, that the name of that noble

[1] See the Old Statistical Account, vol. ii., Parish of Blair-Atholl, by the Rev. Mr M'Laggan, well known from his communications to the Highland Society.

[2] 'The Early Scottish Church,' page 27, by the Rev. Dr Thomas M'Lauchlan.

river the Tay and its Loch, are both from *the Gaelic* and not the Welsh. The word 'Tiber' contains in it the Celtic 'tabh,' 'water,' *a word which we have in our 'Loch Taibh'*[1] *and Uisge Thaibh*—'*Loch Tay*' *and the* '*Water of Tay.*' It was not without reasons of more kinds than one that the Roman soldiers could exclaim as they beheld the Tay, 'Ecce Tiberum.'[2] That the Tay is not the Taw or the Taws of Tacitus, even Chalmers himself disproves. Though no writer was ever more anxious to have made out the ancient Highlanders to be a Welsh race, he clearly proves the Taw of Tacitus to be the Solway Firth.[3] Another very recent and high topographical authority is the Rev. Isaac Taylor. He says, 'some of the names of rivers from the Gaelic Avon (Abhuinn),[4] may be from "*Ta-aon,*" *the "still river;*"' and in another place, speaking of the roots of river names, that the word 'Tam' in them is one meaning *quiet* and *still*, and is related to the Gaelic '*Tav*' (so pronounced, but written 'Tamh'); and he adds, that it appears ' in the Tay (an-

[1] These Gaelic words are pronounced *Tav,* the bh having the sound of v.
[2] See Celtic Gleanings, by the Rev. Dr Thomas M'Lauchlan, pages 37, 38.
[3] See Chalmers's Caledonia, vol. i. page 113.
[4] The writing this Gaelic word for a river ' Amhainn.' is stated in the dictionaries to be erroneous.

ciently the Tavus) in Perth.'¹ Here, then, we have an *unprejudiced* high modern authority who makes the etymology of the river Tay to be from *the Gaelic*, and not the Welsh. The Gaelic word whence the name of the Tay is derived is 'Tamh,' pronounced, as before said, '*Tav*,' and meaning stillness or quietness, which, every one at all acquainted with the noble river Tay can testify, is most applicable to its majestic, calm, flowing current, when in full flood. Besides the latest above modern authority, our own Scotch historians, give the name *Tav* to the Tay, for which see the maps of both Pinkerton and Chalmers, where they only add the Latin termination ' us ' to the Gaelic pronunciation of the word, thereby it is ' *Tavus*.' Ritson likewise calls it Tavus. Our best ancient writer on the geography of Britain is Cambden; he also proves the Tay is Tavus and not Taus. He lived in the reign of Queen Elizabeth, and is thus of higher antiquity than most writers that can be brought forward. He mentions, when speaking of St Andrews in the county of Fife, ' non ita procul a *Tavo* æstuario nunc *Taw* ad quem Perth,' that is, ' not far off *is the Tav* firth, *now* Taw, on which is

---

¹ See ' Words and Places,' by the Rev. Isaac Taylor, pages 209 and 216, 2d edition, 1865.

Perth.'[1] This therefore most distinctly proves that the true, genuine, and native name of the river Tay is from the Gaelic word *Tambh*, pronounced *Tav*, and that calling it *Taw* is but a very *modern* corruption compared to the period when the Caledonian Gael first named the river; and further, that it is only brought forward to try and aid the attempt of making the language of the Caledonian Picts to be a mixture of Welsh and Gaelic, but to which the original name of the river Tay (that wholly flowed through Pictish territory alone) gives no countenance whatever, or to those who we see wish to make the descendants of the noble Caledonians a Welsh-speaking people.

An English chronicle writer in the middle of the twelfth century (1150) is quoted by Robertson in his valuable History of the Early[2] Kings, namely, Henry of Huntingdon, who expressed his wonder as to what had become of the Picts and their language: the extract begins, 'Picti jam videantur deleti,' etc., etc., that is, 'the Picts already appear to be as if blotted out,' etc., etc. This arose from the change of name, the Pictish people, who never were Scots,

---

[1] See this extract from Cambden's Latin edition of his work, quoted by Gordon in his Itinerary, page 34.

[2] Robertson's 'Scotland under her Early Kings,' vol. ii., pages 370, 371, note.

being now so called. This writer heard of nothing but a Scotch king, a Scotch people, and a Scotch language, and from this *change of name* (although the original people remained), has arisen all the fables, and the before-mentioned author (on the Early Scottish Kings), well observes of the ancestors of the Highlanders and the mountainous region they inhabited, that if they '*had spoken* a different language from *Gaelic*, their dialect, whether Cymric or Teutonic, would have lingered amidst the recesses of their wild mountains, long after the days of Henry of Huntingdon.'[1] This is most clear, as it was only in the third century after the pretended date of the fabulous conquest that that writer lived; and when we consider that language is one of the most enduring and unchangeable things known, and whatever alteration of manners or customs among a people may have taken place, so as not to be detected by the closest investigation; yet it is no so with the language of any nation, *that remains* and descends with the people, and neither will it *be lost* even if its use is proscribed, it will still survive; and when we consider that the Gael are, and ever have been in all ages, most dearly attached to their own native tongue the Gaelic of Alban, it is confidently hoped the clear evi-

[1] See Robertson's Early Kings, vol. ii., page 374.

dence herein adduced respecting it, justifies the belief that the present Highlanders speak *the same* Gaelic as their Caledonian ancestors did, who gave those names[1] to every object in their country, from the smallest knoll to the highest of their mountains, from the smallest brook to their largest rivers, and which *same Gaelic* is still their native language.

[1] The topography of the Highlands of Scotland is preserved in Ossian, who lived in the third century, in Adomann who wrote near 1200 years ago, in the Pictish Chronicle of the ninth century, or 1000 years ago; also all the Irish Annals of near 800 years ago, the whole of these authorities proving its identity with that of the present day, and confuting the fable of a *new Gaelic*, as asserted by the Rev. Dr Thomas M'Lauchlan (in his 'Early Scotch Church'), without *any one* *proof or authority being given by him for it.*

BEN LOMOND and LOCH LOMOND from GLENFALLOCH.

CHAPTER X.

The Poetry, National Dress, Arms, and Music of the Gael of Alban.

IF any country possesses a very ancient and historical poetry, and which, with one consent, the inhabitants of that country acknowledge to be composed in their own native language, and which poetry conveys to them infallible proofs of its genuineness and vast antiquity, and at the same time there is an adjoining people and nation who know nothing whatever of the language of the former one, yet deny that their poetry is genuine, a little reflection will show that the truth of the question must be with those to whom the native language belongs. This is precisely the state of the case as to the poems of Ossian, they are received and accepted by the native Gael of Alban, but are not so by some of their neighbours, who may be called foreigners, as they know not a single line, or perhaps a word, of the language in which Ossian's poems were composed; but had the objectors considered that these poems (professing to be of such extraordinary great antiquity) could not have been composed in later ages without betraying to a native clear proofs from the language that they were spurious; and that the closest criticism of the most learned in the Gaelic language have never yet discovered proof that there exists forgery in Ossian's poems, but, on the contrary, that the language is of such a character as carries a conviction of the truth of their extraordinary high antiquity along with them, as also that those who know the Gaelic language best, can discern Ossian's poetry from all imitations by any others; and which poetry never could have received the attention that it does from the native Highlanders, unless it had been undoubtedly genuine. Ossian's poems would never have attained to that high respect and regard they hold in the estimation of the Gael had they been modern, or forged—these considerations give some of the strongest reasons to be assured that this most ancient national poetry is *truly genuine*. Ossian may rightly be called the Homer of the ancient Caledonian Gael; and it should also be remembered that his father Fingal (called also Fionn and Finn), himself, and his son Oscar, were at the same time three of the most illustrious and renowned of the ancient heroes of Alban, and who are still by the Highlanders called 'the Fingalians.' The proofs respecting Ossian's poetry are clearly and most learnedly stated in the Highland Society Report on it, comprising, besides, with it, a most valuable appendix of documents, engravings of ancient Gaelic MSS., the original of the poems, etc., etc., with most numerous letters from parish clergymen of the Highland districts, and others from magistrates, gentlemen of rank and of large property, the whole of them declaring that the poems of Ossian, and partly printed by M'Pherson, they had heard and known from their youth in the *original Gaelic;* and they stated the reciters of these poems to have, in numerous instances, known them *before* M'Pherson was born; and again, many of the reciters could neither read or write, and so could not have learned them in any other way than they were in the remote ages, from which they had been handed down, from one generation to another—here are reasons to believe in Ossian's poetry that surely should make it perfectly satisfactory to do so.

The period of Ossian and when he composed his poems was in the third century, very remote, most undoubtedly; the date that is allowed for the death of his father Fingal is

A.D. 285; his own son Oscar was slain in the battle of Gabhra, the following year, A.D. 286. As there was neither writing or printing known in those times among the Gael, their poetry was preserved from one generation to another by recitation.[1] And there was a profession among the Gaelic people, held in very high esteem, namely, *the bards*, whose duty was to recite and tell of the deeds of their heroes; by them and others the poetry of the Caledonian Gael was kept as it were in one continued stream of remembrance, from one age to another; of course, assuming the poetry was repeated and continued in the *same language* as it was composed in, because, any one advocating *a new Gaelic* language being brought in among the native Highlanders throws the greatest suspicion[2] on the truth of Ossian's poetry. It could not have been transmitted but in the original language it was composed in; and as the

[1] The Gaelic language itself has only been preserved by tradition from one generation to another. They had anciently no books or printing; the language was handed down from father to son exactly in the same manner as were the poems of Ossian.

[2] Those who try to make it believed a *new Gaelic* language came at the time of the fabulous conquest by Kenneth MacAlpin, are doing the worst possible thing to bring Ossian's poetry into discredit. A change of language *is incompatible* with their preservation. They could only remain with any people in the language they *were composed in*.

Gaelic language of the topography of the Highlands *is older* than Ossian's time, and also, when we consider that this topographical language is the spoken tongue of the Highlanders *of this day*, we have thereby an assurance that Ossian's poetry, and now known, is in the same Gaelic as he composed it. As to the supposed difficulty of continuing the repetition of the poems, an example occurs, among many others, in the Highland Society Report, namely, the Rev. Mr M'Diarmid,[1] clergyman of the parish of Weem, Perthshire, who furnished the Highland Society with several of Ossian's poems he had heard recited thirty years before, and the person from whom he so heard them, had received them from another *fifty years before* he recited them to Mr M'Diarmid. Thus, only in *one* generation, we learn the poems had thus existed for eighty years in as great a state of perfection as they did the day they reached the Highland Society. Therefore, we can by reflection understand, that from the endurance of language, and the continual recitation by the bards, etc., it was as easy to carry back the reciting the poems for 1000, as to do so for only 100 years. It is only the multiplying the number of persons; and however strange at first sight this

[1] See the Rev. Mr M'Diarmid's Letter in Highland Society Report on Ossian, page 71.

may appear, it will become evident, when considering the power of the human memory is no more taxed in the one case than the other. With regard to the subject of the powers of the bards to repeat the ancient poetry, there is in the Appendix[1] to the Highland Society Report a clear testimony of it, by one of the M'Murrich's, bard to the family of MacDonald of Clanranald, and of which he declared he was the ninteenth descendant. He repeated the whole of the long poem called Darthula, or the Clan Uisneach, and the parish clergyman certifies he heard him.[2] There was also obtained by the Highland Society of Scotland, from that of London, that most valuable collection of Highland poetry that has been often before mentioned, namely, the Book of the Dean of Lismore, and which contains the poetry of Ossian, and also some subsequent, and the greatest part taken down from reciters more than 350 years ago, namely, in 1512. This collection extends to the vast length of near 12,000 lines; and it contains the greatest portion of the Gaelic poetry known to exist, and is a proof of the highest value to the truth of Ossian, as much of what M'Pherson printed

---

[1] See Appendix, page 20.
[2] See the Appendix to the Highland Society Report on Ossian, page 20.

appears in it, and with only trifling differences; and yet, it ought to be remembered, that what the Dean of Lismore heard and wrote down in 1512, was 250 years before the *same poems* were collected from other native reciters by Macpherson.[1] A fact so strong as this, it is thought, will convince any one as to the truth of Ossian's poems, and likewise prove how faithfully they were handed down by the Highlanders from generation to generation. So great a proof of fidelity, in handing down the poems, it is believed, will be considered conclusive, and that, besides many others, sufficient reasons have now been given to receive Ossian's poetry as genuine, and belonging to the Highlanders,—the real descendants of the Caledonian Gael.

To this poetry, also, it must be remembered that the Highlanders of Scotland are the inheritors from their forefathers, of the third century, and in no way did they derive it from the Irish colony of Scots, who did not come into Argyleshire till the sixth century; the reciting of these Ossianic poems is still conti-

---

[1] The Poems of Ossian, collected by M'Pherson, from reciters in the Highlands, being *identical* with those heard by the Dean of Lismore, and collected by him 250 years before (M'Pherson), should make it very plain how easy it was to transmit the poems for a vast deal longer period of time.

nued in our day.[1] At page 133 of the Gaelic part of the Book of the Dean of Lismore, there is the poem of the battle of Gabhra (in A.D. 286), taken down from the recitation of Christina Sutherland, in the county of Caithness, in 1854, consisting of 200 lines and upwards of closely printed poetry; and in the same work[2] there is a specimen of the poem on this battle, from the oral recitation of the same person in 1856, it begins thus:—

'Is trom an nochd mo chumha fein,
 Guilgeantach mo rian,
 Smuainchadh a chath chruaidh.'

Translation:—

'My mourning is grievous this night,
 Weeping is my condition,
 As I think of the fierce fight.'

The above is translated by the Rev. Dr Thos. M'Lauchlan, and every Highlander should be thankful he undertook the labour, and finished with success, from the Book of the Dean of Lismore, the translation of so valuable a collection of their national poetry, and that whatever

[1] General Stewart of Garth mentions in his work, Sketches of the Highlanders, that there was in Glenlyon, in his immediate neighbourhood, a young woman who could repeat many hundred lines of Ossian's poetry.
[2] Pages 42 and 43, note.

may be the final result of their ancient language, here is a record of it for future generations.

The writer would here venture also to point out the kind meant wishes of the present learned John Stuart Blackie, Esq., Professor of Greek in the University of Edinburgh, in favour of the Gaelic language, on which he gave a lecture some few months ago, showing its distinctive character, etc. A native Highlander (the Rev. D. M'Intyre, Kincardine, has also written an Essay on the antiquity of the Gaelic) it is to be hoped these may be followed by many other similar pamphlets, establishing the identity of the language of the present Highlanders and that of the noble Caledonian, and Fingalian Gael of Alban.

Extracts will now be given of the poems of Ossian, both in Gaelic and English. The oldest of these must unquestionably have been the one mentioned at page 293 of Appendix of the Highland Society Report on Ossian, when he had retired to the forest wilds, then but in his youth, to indulge in his natural propensity to meditation and song, and when his father Fingal found him, Ossian sung a poem of which only the first line is given. The following part of a poem must also have been an early composition of Ossian, in it is the address of Fionn or Fingal (his father) to his grandson Oscar (the son of Ossian) to inculcate in him the principles of valour and honour, by the example of his ancestors. It begins in English, 'Son of my son! said the king.' This poem is given at considerable length in the Appendix to the Report.[1]

Extract from the poem 'Briathran Fhinn re Oscar:'—

'A mhic mo mhich! thu'irt an righ,
Oscair, a righ nan òg fhlath!
Chunnaic mi dearsa do lain, b'i muaill
Bhi ag amharc do bhuaidh sa chath.
Lean gu dluth re clin do shinnsear,
Is na dibir a bhi mar iasdan.
Nuair bu bheo Trenmor na rath
Is Trathal athair nan treunlaoch,
Chuir iad gach cath le buaidh.'

Translation :—
' Son of my son! said the king,
O Oscar, chief of the generous youth!
I saw the gleaming of thy sword,
And I gloried to see thee victorious in the battle.
Tread close on the fame of thy fathers,
And cease not to be as they have been.
When Trenmor of glorious deeds did live,
And Trathal the father of heroes,
They fought every battle with success.'

[1] Appendix to Report, pages 224, 225.

and Music of the Gael of Alban. 207

The following poem by Ossian is in praise of his father, Fionn or Fingal, who by the computation of Irish writers, died, as before said, in A.D. 285. It was composed within a week after that event. It is considered to be of much merit.

The Rev. Dr Thomas M'Lauchlan, who was one of the editors of the Book of the Dean of Lismore (which is a collection of Gaelic poetry, of Ossian, etc., etc., as already mentioned), speaks of this poem in the highest terms, saying,[1] 'In the original' (that is, the Gaelic), 'the poetry is worthy of the name of Ossian, more so, indeed, than any of the pieces in this collection. It is quite impossible to produce in English the effect of the rhythm and alliteration of the Gaelic; but the editor[2] has endeavoured, while giving an exact rendering, to retain, in as far as possible, the peculiar measure of the original. The piece is a fine tribute of filial love and admiration, nor is there room to doubt its genuineness.'

[1] Book Dean of Lismore, page 26. The Gaelic is pages 18, 19.
[2] The Rev. Dr Thomas M'Lauchlan.

Auctor hujus[1] Ossian Mac Fhinn.

Se la gus an dé,
O nach fhaca mi Fionn,
Cha-n fhaca ri 'm ré,
Saoi ba gheire leam ;
Mac nighinn O'Theige,
Rìgh nam buillean tròm.
M'eud 's mo rath,
Mo chiall 's mo chon,
Fa filidh fa flath,
Fa rìgh air gheire,
Fionn flath, rìgh na Feinn,
Fa treabhach air gach tìr,
Fa miall mòr mara,
Fa leobhar air leirg,
Fa sheabhag glan gaoithe,
Fa sith air gach ceairde,
Fa oileanach ceart,
Fa mairg nior mhearbh,
Fa ullamh air ghniomh,
Fa steidh air gach scirm,
Fa fior ceart a bhreth,
Fa tàmhaiche tuaith,

---

[1] Of course it must be apparent to any one that this title was put in by the Dean of Lismore, though a Gaelic title would have been more appropriate.

Fa ionnsaichte 'n a aigh,
Fa brathach air buaidh.
Fa h-e an teachdair ard,
Air chalm 'us air cheol,
Fa diùltadh nan diamh,
O dh' fhàg greagh na clàr,
A chneas mar an caile,
A ghruaidh mar an ròs,
Bu ghlan gorm a rosg,
'Fholt mar an t-òr,
Fa dùil daimh 'us daoine,
Fa aireach nan àgh,
Fa ullamh air ghniomh,
Fa min ri mnathan.

Translation.

The Author of this is Ossian, the son of Finn.

'Twas yesterday week
I last saw Finn;
Ne'er did I see
A braver man;
Teige's daughter's son,[1]
A powerful king;
My fortune, my light,

[1] The mother of Finn or Fingal was Muirne, daughter of Teige, a celebrated Druid. Others think her of a royal family called Bregia —See note, page 26, Book Dean of Lismore.

My mind's whole might,
Both poet and chief.
Braver than kings,
Firm chief of the Feinn,
Lord of all lands,
Leviathan at sea,
As great on land,
Hawk of the air,
Foremost always.
Generous, just,
Despised a lie.
Of vigorous deeds,
First in song.
A righteous judge,
Firm his rule.
Polished his mien,
Who knew but victory.
Who is like him
In fight or song?
Resists the foe,
In house or field.
Marble his skin,
The rose his cheek.
Blue was his eye,
His hair like gold.
All men's trust,
Of noble mind.
Of ready deeds,
To women mild.

Is e ughdair so Ossian.[1]

Is fad an nochd na neula faim,
Is fada leam an oidhche an raoir,
An la an diugh ge fada dhomh,
Do bu leor fada 'n la an dé,

Fada leam gach la a thig,
Ni mar sin bu chleachdadh leam
Gun deabhtha gun deanamh catha,
Gun bhi foghlum cleas dlù.

Gun nigheanaibh, gun cheòl, gun chruit,
Gun phronnadh cnaimh, gun ghniomh gré,
Gun tuilleadh fhoghlium gheire,
Bhi gun fheill, gun òl fleidh,

Gun chion air suiridh, no air sealg,
An da cheard ri an robh mi,
Gun dol an gleò no an cath,
Ochan! ach is deurach domh,

Gun bhreith air eilid no air fiadh,
Ni h' amhuil sin bu mhiann leam,
Gun luaidh air chonbheart no air chon,
Is fad an nochd na neula faim.[1]

[1] This is the Gaelic title for Ossian's poems.
[2] See Gaelic part of the Book of the Dean of Lismore, page 3.

It will be seen that this poem is a lament by Ossian in his declining years, it is very pathetic and descriptive of the effects of age.

The author of this is Ossian.

Long do the clouds this night surround me—
Long to me was the night that is past—
For the day that has come I have longed—
While slowly rolled the day before.
Tedious to me is each day that comes,
For it is not as it was wont!
Gone are the heroes, my friends in war,
And feats of strength are no longer performed:
Generosity, the will and the deed have failed.
Sad is my heart without an object for its love,
Nor power to avenge the feeble.
Hospitality and the drink of the feast are no
  more;
No more the love of the fair or of the chase,
In which I was wont to take delight.
On the sword, or the dart I no longer rely.
I do not come up with the hind or the hart,
Nor do I traverse the hills of the elk.
I hear not of hounds nor their deeds.
The night of clouds to me is long![1]

The following lines taken from Ossian's

[1] Translation in Highland Society Report on Ossian's poems, page 94.

and Music of the Gael of Alban.   213

poem of Ca-Lodin, commencement of Duan 3d, is considered the grandest and most sublime of all his compositions :—

' Whence have sprung the things that are ?
And whither roll the passing years ?
Where does time conceal its two heads,
In dense impenetrable gloom,
Its surface marked with heroes deeds alone ?
I view the generations gone ;
The past appears but dim—
As objects by the moon's faint beams
Reflected from a distant lake.
I see indeed the thunderbolts of war ;
But there the unmighty joyless dwell,
All those who send *not down their deeds
To far succeeding times.*

The following very ancient poem is printed in the Appendix[1] of the Report of Highland Society on Ossian, the MS. from which it is taken is also of very high antiquity, namely, written in 1238, and is now deposited with the other even more ancient Gaelic MSS. in the Advocates' Library, Edinburgh.

This highly beautiful poem is called Deardir or Darthula, and is exceedingly tender and pathetic, and shows it was composed on her

[1] Appendix, pages 297, 298, 299.

leaving her native[1] land Alban,—the only thing which appears to have reconciled her to it being that she departed with her lover Naos, who also, it would appear, had resided in Glenurchy. The Gaelic topographical names are but slightly changed from the time of the writing of the poem, more than *six hundred years* ago, a strong proof how they pass *correctly* from one generation to another.[2]

The following is from the Gaelic MS., dated 1238:—

Do dech Deardir ar a heise ar crichibh
Alban .... agus ro chan an laoidh.

Inmain tir an tir ud thoir
Alba cona lingantaibh
Nocha ticfuin eisdi ille
Mana tisain le Naise.

Inmain Dun Fidhgha is Dun Finn
Inmain in Dun os a cinn
Inmain Inis Draignde[3]
Is inmain Dun Suibnei.

[1] Probably to settle in Erin, as in another part of the poem she says herself and her lover are going west, and to leave Alban for ever.

[2] There is also a very fine translation of this poem in the introduction to the Book of the Dean of Lismore, see page lxxxvii.

[3] Inisdrailhn, now called Inistrynich, and near Loch Awe.

Caill cuan gar tigeadh Ainnle mo nuar
Fagair lim ab bitan
Is Naise an oircar Alban.

Glend Laidh do chollain fan mboirmin caoimh
Iasg is sieng is saill bruich
Fa hi mo chuid an Glen laigh

Glend masain ard a crimh geal a gasain
Do nimais colladh corrach
Os inbhar mungach Masain

Glend Eitchi ann do togbhus mo ched tigh
Alaind a fidh iar neirghe
Buaile grene Glend eitchi

Mo chen Glend Urchaidh
Ba hedh in Glend direach dromchain
Uallcha feara aoisi ma Naise
An Glen Urchaid

Glend da ruadh
Mo chen gach fear da na dual
Is binn guth cuach
Ar craeib chruim
Ar in mbinn os Glendaruadh
Inmain Draighen is tren traigh
Inmain Auichd in ghaimimh glain
Nocha ticfuin eisde anoir
Mana tisuinn lem Inmain.

Translation.

Darthula looked behind her towards
The land of Alban, and raised the strain.

Lovely land is that eastern land,
Alban with all its lakes,
O that I might not depart from it!
But I depart with Naos.

Lovely is the tower of Fidga, and the tower of
    Fingal.
Lovely is the tower above them,
Lovely the Isle of Dragno
And lovely the tower of Suvno.[1]

But alas! the wood, the bay which Ainle would
    approach,
Are left by me and Naos for ever
Upon the coast of Alban.
O vale of Laith![2] would I were sleeping by its
    soothing murmur!

Fish and venison, and the choice of the chase
    prepared,
Would be my repast in Glenlaith,[2]

---

[1] Now in English called Castle Sween.
[2] Glenlaith, now in English Glenlochy, but there is Benaoidhe there still.

Glenmasain![1] high grow its herbs, fair wave its
    branches,
Steep would be the place of our repose
Over the grassy banks of Masan.

O vale of Etha! where a first house has been
    built for me,
·Delightful were its groves when the sun risen
    to his height
Would strike his beams on Gleneiti.

How I long for the vale of Urchay!
Straight vale of the fairest hills
Joyful were his companions around Naos
In Glenurchay.
Vale of Daruadh!
Pleasant to me would be each of its people.

Sweet is the note of the cuckoo
From the bending tree of the mountain
Above Glendaruadh [2]
Lovely is Dragno of the sounding shore!

---

[1] This name remains even in English the same. It is a valley in Cowal, in Argyleshire, which, with Glenurchay and Gleneitive, two other valleys in Argyleshire, is celebrated in this poem, and was the scene in which the sons of Uisneach, or Usnoth, followed the chase.—See Appendix, Report on Ossian, page 207.

[2] Called in English Glendaruel.

Lovely is Avich of the brightest sand!
O! that I might not depart from it west,
But I depart with my love!

The first person who ever thought of printing and translating Gaelic poetry was a young man of twenty or twenty-one, named Jerome Stone.[1] This was exactly one hundred and ten years ago. He went to reside at Dunkeld, and got so fond of the Gaelic language, that he acquired it, and was not only able to translate, but to render it into poetry. This took place in 1755; and, after he had been at the pains to collect several of the ancient poems of the Highlands, he sent a copy of one of them to the only periodical that then existed in Scotland, namely the 'Scots Magazine,' along with a very modest, becoming letter, to the editor of the magazine; and it so attracted his attention, that he published the letter, Gaelic poem, and translation in verse by Stone, in the 'Scots Magazine' for the month of January 1756. An extract of the original Gaelic, as written down by Stone,[2] will be given, and three translations of it will also,—one by the Highland

---

[1] See the Highland Society Report on Ossian, page 23.

[2] There were no dictionaries or grammars of the Gaelic as yet, when this young man wrote, and, though not a native, shows how near the writing of Gaelic then is to the present.

and Music of the Gael of Alban.   219

Society Committee, one by Stone in verse, and
another from the Book of the Dean of Lismore. The name of the poem, which is very
pathetic, is called 'Bàs Fhraoich,' or 'The
Death of Fraoch.' The scene of it by many is
thought to be Loch Fraoch, called in English
Loch Fruchie, in Glenquaich, Perthshire. The
name of the loch corresponds, and there is an
island in it. Tradition also places it here.

Bas Fhraoich.[1]

Osan caraid ann cluain Fhraoich,
Osan laoich ann caiseal chro,
An osan sin ou tuirseach fear,
Son tromghulanach bean og.

Sud e shiar an Carn am bheil,
Fraoch MacFedhich an fhiult mhaoidh,
Am fear a rinn buidhheachas do Mhei,
Sann air a shloinnte Carn Fhraoich.

Gul nam ban on Chruachan shoir,
Is cruaidh an Fath mam guil a bhen
Ise fhag a hosan go trom, trom,
Fraoch MacFedhich na colg sean.

[1] This is the original Gaelic, as collected by Jerome Stone, and printed in the Appendix of the Report on Ossian, page, 99.

Gur i an ainir a nith an gul,
Tighin ga fhios do chluain Fhraioch.
Doun abhradh an fhuilt chais aill,
Aon inghean Maidhe ga m bidh na laoich.

Aon inghean Choruil is grinne falt,
Taobh re taobh anochd is Fraoch,
Ga h-iomad fear aghradhuigh i,
Nior ghaoluigh i fear ach Fraoch.

Literal Translation of the Poem on the Death of Fraoch, in Report of Highland Society.[1]

The sigh of a friend in the grove of Fraoch!
A sigh for the hero in its rounded pale,
A sigh which causes each man to mourn,
And which makes each maiden weep!

There, to the westward, is the Carn,[2]
Which covers Fraoch, son of Fiach, of the soft hair,
He who obeyed the call of Mey,
And from whom the Carn of Fraoch has its name.

---

[1] See Appendix, page 112.
[2] A monumental heap of stones, to mark a grave.

The maids from Cruchan weep,
Sad is the cause of their woe,
For their mournful sighs are occasioned,
By Fraoch, son of Fiach, of the ancient weapons.

Him most bewails the maid
Who comes to weep in the grove of Fraoch,
The brown-eyed fair of curling locks,
Only daughter of Mey, whom the heroes obey.

Only daughter of Corul, of finest hair,
Whose side to-night is stretched by the side of
    Fraoch;
Though many were the men who sought her love,
She loved none but Fraoch.

The Death of Fraoch.[1]

Whence come these dismal sounds that fill our
    ears!
Why do the groves such lamentations send!
Why sit the virgins on the hill of tears,
While heavy sighs their tender bosoms rend!

They weep for Albin with the flowing hair,
Who perished by the cruelty of Mey;
A blameless hero, blooming, young, and fair;
Because he scorned her passions to obey.

[1] This is the translation in verse by Jerome Stone.

See on yon western hill the heap of stones,
Which mourning friends have raised o'er his bones!

O woman! bloody, bloody was thy deed;
The blackness of thy crime exceeds belief;
The story makes each heart but thine to bleed,
And fills both men and maids with keenest grief!
Behold thy daughter, beauteous as the sky,
When early morn ascends yon eastern hills,
She loved the youth who by thy guile did die,
And now our ears with lamentations fills:
'Tis she, who sad, and grovelling on the ground,
Weeps o'er his grave, and makes the woods resound.

The Death of Fraoch.

'Tis the sigh of a friend from Fraoch's green mound,
'Tis the warrior's from his lonely bier,
'Tis a sigh might grieve the manly heart,
And might make a maid to weep.

Here to the east the cairn, where lies
Fraoch Fitheach's son of softest locks,
Who nobly strove to favour Mai,
And from whom Cairn Fraoch is named.

In Cruachan east a woman weeps,
A mournful tale 'tis she laments;
Heavy, heavy sighs she gives
For Fraoch MacFithich of ancient fame.

She 'tis in truth who sorely weeps
As Fraoch's green mound she visits oft;
Maid of the locks that wave so fair,
Mai's daughter so beloved of men.

This night Orla's soft-haired daughter
Lies side by side with Fraoch MacFithic.
Many were the men who loved her,
She of them all *loved Fraoch alone*.[1]

The following Gaelic poem is called 'Oran nam Beann,' or, 'the Song of the Mountains.' It is given because it mentions so much of Highland topography in Atholl, Perthshire, and refers to several of the mountains that appear in the illustrations. It is understood

[1] See the Book of the Dean of Lismore, English part, page 55.

to have originally been composed in very remote ages by an ancient warrior, on the prospect of his return to his native hills, after an expedition in which he had been engaged, and he names mountains in Atholl that are chiefly close together, and he rejoices at the prospect of again beholding them. The hills all bear the same names now. Its antiquity is evidenced by one of the mountains being called that of the Roaring of the Wolves, which animals have been nearly extinct in Atholl the last three hundred years. The song now passes in the district for the composition of a celebrated deer-stalker, who, early in the seventeenth century, helped himself and friends to venison from the adjoining deer-forests,[1] and, with alterations, he suited the song to his own circumstances, when having the prospect of again receiving his liberty,[2] so as to return to his accustomed haunts among his native hills. The song is well known in that part of the Highlands. The literal translation of the fifth verse is as follows:—

---

[1] He must have frequented the royal forest of Benachromleg (Beinncrombeag, or, the little crooked mountain), as he speaks of Carurigh, or, the King's Hill, which is near the centre of the forest.

[2] He is said to be in prison when he composed this song.

'I shall see the dim hazy mountain of the
  pointed¹ tops,
The little mountain, and the silver mountain,²
The mountain of the roaring of the great wolf,
And the little brook with the bird's at its side.'

Oran nam beann.

Chorus.

En min o iri horo
En mino horo iri
En min o iri horo
'Saoibhinn leam an diugh na chith.

Chith mi 'n Dūn, Chith, mi 'm meadar,
Chith mi eadar dha Ghaig.
Chith mi thall an coire creagach.
Gu tric san robh an eilid ga sarach.
    En min o, etc.

Chith mi 'n dubh lochan uaine.
Chith mi Chruach 's a Bheinn bhreac.

---

¹ 'Beinn na Ghlonaneag,' or the dim hazy mountain of the pointed, or indented tops.

² The names of all these mountains, though given no doubt at least two thousand years ago, are still the Gaelic of the present day in the Highlander's language, a positive proof of the people and language *being the same.*

Chith mi gleann Oisin nam Fionn,
'Seirigh greine air meal nan Leachd.
  En min o, etc.

A 'bheinn uaine ma tha thu torrach
Gur eutrom chuireas tu dhiot t'eallach,
Is ioma damh ruadh rangach.
Thig stigh an gleann gun cheannach.
  En min o, etc.

'S ann sinn bhan comunn bris-deach,
Eadar mise 'us chreig shulich,
Mise gu brath cha diriadh,
'Us ise gu dilinn cha tearnadh.
  En min o, etc.

Chith mi Beinn Ghlo nan eag,
Beinn bheag, 's Argiod bheann,
Beinn bhuirich nam madadh, mōr,
'S allt a nid an eun ri taobh.
  En min o, etc.

A choilich sinn, 'us a choilich dhubh,
Chunnaig mi thu 'n diugh 's an de,
Nám biodh mo ghun a Carnanrigh,
Bhrisinn an it 'thu shios fo'd sge.
  En min o, etc.

The following is from the fragment of a Gaelic song of the island of Lewis, and is only given as showing that the same language prevails in the islands—it likewise refers to names of places in the island.

'A Mhor! a Mhor! till ri d' machan.
'S gheibh thu goidean bric o' n' lochan,
O' Loch Nidir 's o' Loch Naidir,
'S o' chean Loch Eit nam bradan.'

Translation.

' O Sarah, Sarah, return to thy son,
And thou shalt get a string (or withe) of
trouts (from the lakes);
From Loch Nidir, and from Loch Naider,
And from Loch Eit of the salmon.'[1]

The National Dress & Arms of the Highlanders.

There is nothing which so much distinguished the Gael of Alban as their highly picturesque costume, and which has been for so many ages peculiar to them. Proofs and

[1] See Proceedings of the Society of Antiquaries, Scotland, vol. iii., part 1, page 132, collected by Captain Thomas, R.N., and is supposed by him to refer to the walrus, called by the Highlanders the 'Each Uisge,' or 'Water-horse,' which is rarely, or even ever seen in the course of a whole generation.

authorities respecting it will be given to the reader from the most remote times, and which it is considered must, from such a connected series of evidence, demonstrate the unquestionable great antiquity of the Highland garb. It has already been mentioned that there was a wall built by the Romans between the rivers Forth and Clyde, going across present Scotland. It was called the wall of Antonine[1] (and for which see the Map), being named after that Roman Emperor. The date of the construction of it was A.D. 140. From a part of its ruins there was dug up, some years ago, a piece of sculpture (and which is now preserved at Croy), that represents three figures exactly dressed in the national garb of the Highlanders, and an account of this piece of sculpture is given in the Archæologia.[2] This is the earliest piece of evidence the writer has met with of a representation of the Highland dress. The classical author Herodian, when speaking of the dress of the Caledonians in or about the year A.D. 204, says they were only partially clothed, which statement exactly accords with the appearance of the native dress at this day, and is precisely similar to what almost all sub-

---

[1] This wall can be seen in the map, where it is inserted.
[2] See Archæologia xxi., page 456, as quoted by Logan in the Scottish Gael, vol. i., page 243.

sequent writers on the subject[1] have said of it. Grant, in his work on the Gael, translates a passage from Diodorus Siculus, stating that the natives of Gaul (from whence, no doubt, the Gael of Alban emigrated) wore a sort of tartan, or clothing of different colours. The translation given is, 'they wear coats stained *with various colours.*'[2] Thus we see the Caledonian Gael, when they first arrived in Britain, wore clothing exactly answering to the Highland tartan of this day, but of course *not of the modern* distinctions as to clans. We are entitled to believe the calling the Highland dress 'the garb of Old Gaul' is not an unfounded boast, when we remember that Cæsar and Tacitus both declare that the Britons (the latter writer had full information and accounts of the natives of the North, or Caledonians) were precisely the same people as *the Gauls* in manners, religion, *appearance*, and customs, and, of course, if there had not been a similarity of clothing between the Gauls and the Britons, both Tacitus and Cæsar would have had much cause to observe a very remarkable difference between the inhabitants of Gaul

---

[1] The classical writer Dio says the Caledonians are hardly clothed (he wrote A.D. 230), and dwell in tents, and without shoes.—Dio, lib. 76, cap. 12, as quoted by Ritson in his Caledonian Annals, vol. i. page 12.

[2] Diodorus Siculus, lib. v., cap. 30, quoted by Grant on the Gael

and Britain. Cæsar arrived in the latter country fifty-five years before the Christian era, and Tacitus wrote of the country of Caledonia from the first campaign of Agricola, in A.D. 78. Camden, a very learned antiquarian, is also quoted in Grant's Gael as saying that the Gauls wore a garment they called 'Brachæ,' and which word appears almost identical with the Gaelic word 'Breacan,' meaning 'the Highland plaid' or coloured dress used and worn by the Gael of Alban from the earliest times. The learned Gaelic scholar Dr Armstrong, in his Gaelic Dictionary, speaks of the 'breacan Gaidhealach,' or 'Highland plaid,' and mentions some particulars,—thus the Ardrigh, or supreme king had seven different colours in his dress, the Druidical tunic had six, and that of the nobles or maormors had four, and although this information is derived but from tradition,[1] it would be a point so well and generally known. there seems good reason to believe it is correctly founded, as although the Druidical times are now very remote, still the topography of

[1] Almost the whole topography of the Highlands chiefly rests on tradition, which alone has handed down the names of hills and rivers, etc., from the remotest times. Many hundred places were never named in charters or books, and as to maps there *were none* almost, it may be said, giving the names of the mountains till last century, yet the present topography of the Highlands is in general more than 2000 years old.

the Highlands and Ossian's poems are quite as ancient, and came down to modern times by tradition alone. The next writer that alludes to the dress of the inhabitants of Caledonia is the orator Eumenius, who, in the year A.D. 296, in his oration in praise of the Emperor Constantius, says that the Britons were only accustomed to encounter the Picts 'hostibus seminudis,' or 'half naked enemies,' exactly corresponding with the description always applied to the Highlanders' dress. Logan, in his work on the Gael, also quotes from the very ancient classical author (namely, Herodian) to the same effect that from the apparently scanty clothing of the Caledonian Gael, the expression naked was not inapplicable.[1] We have next the testimony of the earliest of British writers. Gildas, who wrote about A.D. 550, and he says that the Picts were only dressed with cloth round the loins.[2]

In the sculptured stones of Scotland we have most clear and decided evidence of the antiquity of the national dress of the Gael— they bear clear testimony to the dress of the

[1] Herodian, lib. iii., cap. 47, quoted by Logan, Scottish Gael, vol. i., page 222.

[2] Gildas, cap. 15. The Antiquarian Library published by Bohn, London, is a most valuable collection for all who wish to make references to, or quotations from, the earliest writers we possess, and all of them taken from the very best editions that exist.

Gael, and these monuments are all within the ancient territories of the Caledonian Picts, *none* of the same antiquity exist within the boundaries of the country of the Irish Scots of Argyleshire. The date assigned to these ancient stone monuments is, to some of them, undoubtedly from their symbols, prior to Christianity. Their period may therefore be said to extend from the sixth to the ninth century. Of those in which certain symbols appear, and which represent the national dress, there is one at Dupplin,[1] in Perthshire, and another at Forres, in Morayshire, both probably not later than the eighth century. There was discovered within the last four or five years at Dull, in Perthshire, a sculptured stone slab, and on which is a representation of many figures in the Highland dress, and there are two figures mounted on horseback, those on foot have their round shields on their left arms, evidently prepared to make an attack, and the leaders, probably intended to represent the maormor of Atholl, and another chieftain close to the footmen, who could not be sup-

---

[1] In the cross at Dupplin, besides the figures being in the Highland dress, they are represented also as armed with the round target of the Gael, and spears. There is also a fine sculptured stone that is thought to be not later than the seventh century, at Nigg—the figure is in the Highland dress, with the 'purse,' or 'sporan.'

posed to be represented as if on the line of march, as then the shield or target was always carried slung on the back, this, therefore, would show that it was intended to represent their being prepared for combat, and in close contact with an enemy. The bonnet is very distinctly portrayed in one of the figures. The date of this sculpture[1] may be as ancient as the eighth century, considering it has already appeared in a previous part of this work, that there were personages called kings of Atholl so far back as A.D. 736. The appearance of the tunic in some of these ancient monuments arises from the intended representation of what is called the belted plaid;[2] this applies to the Forres obelisk, and some others, in most of the sculptured stones, both the legs and feet are represented bare, which indicates

[1] This very curious ancient sculpture found at Dull, has, within these few months, been deposited in the museum of the Society of Antiquaries at Edinburgh, as it is a representation of the dress from a place in the country that ever formed part of the territory of the Picts, it becomes a very strong proof indeed of their dress.

[2] The Gaelic name for the Highlanders' dress has already been mentioned—this one was called the 'breacan feile,' or, 'the belted, or chequered plaid,' and consisted of twelve yards of tartan, worn round the waist, and obliquely across the breast, and over the left shoulder, and partly depending backwards. This was the Highlanders' full dress; the 'feilebeag' was the undress, and is now the kilt.—See Dr Armstrong's Dictionary.

that it was chiefly in winter weather the 'osan,' or hose, would be worn. There is a natural representation of the dress of the Gael in the Isle of Skye, that must be a vast deal more ancient in name than even the antiquity of the sculptured stones of Scotland, namely, in the parish of Kilmuir,[1] in that island, there is a rock named '*Creag na fcile*,' or, 'the rock of the kilt,' which it bears from its exact resemblance to a Highlander in his native dress. This name must be coeval with the arrival of the Caledonian Gael in Skye, which was probably not less than four centuries before the Christian era, and the name itself would be one of the very first names likely to be imposed on so striking an object to the primitive settlers—it is therefore a very strong proof that the earliest inhabitants wore the Highlanders' dress, and must have brought it with them, and it likewise proves they must have spoken the *same Gaelic* as the present Gael. The upper part of the native dress was secured on the left shoulder with a large pin or broach; and with regard to these it is right to remark, that during the whole of this century, and towards the end of last, the remains of very numerous

---

[1] See the New Statistical Account, volume for Inverness-shire, page 246.

Pictish houses[1] have been opened and examined, and in every one of them, almost without exception, there has been found large pins made of bone, and sometimes of bronze,[2] generally three inches and more in length, within all these ancient dwellings of the Pictish Gael, these, it can scarcely be doubted, were used by them in wearing their national dress. There are numerous examples of these pins, and also broaches, found in Pictish houses, to be seen in the Antiquarian Museum[3] in Edinburgh; and these discoveries in such ancient places, and undoubtedly connected with the dress, is a very great evidence of its high antiquity; from the preceding proofs and remarks, which go back to the remotest ages, we see that the Highlanders' garb was as ancient as anything we know of the race of the Gael of Alban, and that with this very *distinguishing feature,* the dress of the people and nation, the Irish Scots cannot intermeddle, and

[1] The writer is aware that in general they are called '*a Pict's house,*' as if only a single Pict lived in them, yet as habitations in England are called '*an English house,*' so those in the land of the Picts may also be called '*a Pictish house*'—thus, it is common to say '*an English house* is more comfortable than a French one.'

[2] Though they would likewise wear wooden ones, these have decayed, but the bone and bronze have resisted the waste of ages.

[3] See the Catalogue of that Museum also, at pages 33-35

the most extreme prejudiced advocate, who ever wrote respecting the Scots in Argyleshire, can never with truth make out that the Highlanders of present Scotland ever derived their native dress *from that source;* but that on the contrary, as the Scots or Gael in Ireland never wore the chequered plaid, therefore the Irish Scots or Dalraids must have received it from the Caledonian Picts.

With regard to the arms of the ancient Caledonian Gael, we have the authority of Tacitus that in the first century[1] they were precisely the same as their descendants, the Highlanders of Scotland wore, and used up to the year 1745, namely, long broad swords, and small round shields, and also 'pugiones,'[2] or the dagger or Highland dirk, called in Gaelic the 'biodag'— there will be given hereafter further details as to the arms of the Highlanders. There is mention made also of the dress and arms at a very ancient period of Scotch history, and which is given in Ritson's Caledonian Annals,[3] who mentions that

---

[1] The writer Herodian, in the year A.D. 207, also describes in his third book, the arms of the Caledonians (exactly as does Tacitus) when he speaks of the expedition of the Emperor Severus in that year.

[2] As called by Tacitus and all Latin writers.

[3] This evidence as to the antiquity of the Highland dress at this date, as here mentioned by Ritson in his Caledonian Annals, is taken from Æthelred's Chronicle, but the editor of

Walter Espec, a great Norman baron (who came over with William the Conqueror in 1066), in a speech by him to the Anglo-Norman army, previous to the battle of Cowton-moor, after after mentioning the former successful exploits by them against the Scots, added, that they should rather laugh than fear against such as *the vile Scot*,[1] who half naked comes forward to fight, and that to the Norman swords and spears they oppose their naked hide, using a calf skin for a shield.[2]

Next in date there is another ancient piece of evidence contained in the history or Saga of Magnus King of Norway, which was translated and printed in the Iona Club Transactions, and from which valuable collection of highly curious documents many very interesting ones will be given hereafter. The following is the passage from the Norse Saga (and it is useful to remember that this Norwegian king was contemporary with our King Malcolm Canmore),—'A.D. 1093—It is said when King

the Iona Club Transactions does not seem to have been aware of it, yet it forms a link in the history of the Picts, *now called Scots*, as wearing the identical dress of their ancestors, the Caledonian Gael, who always by the 'gall' or foreigners were called 'half naked,' and from the same cause, their dress.

[1] It was the object of this leader to cast ridicule, if possible, on the national dress, and which to him would appear very strange.

[2] See Ritson's Caledonian Annals, vol. ii., pages 18, 19.

Magnus returned from his expedition to the west,[1] that he *adopted the costume in use in* the western lands, and likewise many of his followers.'[2] Our own race of Celtic kings likewise wore the national garb. The most ancient evidence we have of this is in the case of King Alexander I., whose reign began in 1107. This monarch's seal represents him in the Highland dress, and not only with the 'feilebeag,' but also with the round Highland target or shield, and from the proof afforded by this seal, its high antiquity and official authority, it is engraved by Dr Meyrick in his splendid work, as mentioned by Logan[3] in his book. Pinkerton, in his 'Iconographia Scotica,' states[4] King David I., who came to the throne in 1124, and King Malcolm IV., who succeeded in 1153, that both these monarchs used a seal *identical* with that of Alexander I., and their adopting it proves conclusively they must have

---

[1] That is, when he conquered the Western Isles of Scotland and the Dalriad country, and made them a dependency on Norway.

[2] The editor of the Iona Club Transactions, at page 26 of the notices on the Highland dress, says, that after this notice as to Magnus, three centuries intervene as to the Highland dress, but the evidence respecting King Alexander I. and the other subsequent monarchs as to the Highland dress, by the writers, Pinkerton and Meyrick, prove this to be an error.

[3] See Logan's Scottish Gael, vol. i., p. 247.

[4] In the letterpress descriptions, page 78, note.

used the dress their seals represented. That
this was the fact, is further proved by an en-
graving of Pinkerton in his work before mentioned (Iconographia Scotica), wherein King
David I. is represented in the national dress,
so also is King Malcolm[1] IV. In the case of
King David, the kilt appears to reach a little
below the knee, and the 'bhrògan,' or brogues,
reaching to the ankle. Above the native dress
he has on a robe or cloak, called the 'Sagum.'
King Malcolm is attired in a similar manner,
and his cloak or robe of state is fastened in the
usual manner of the Highlanders, with a broach
on the left shoulder. King Alexander II., whose
reign began in 1214, also given in this work, appears evidently to be also in what is intended
to represent the national costume, from the belt
round the body fastening the plaid into plaits
round the waist, but the robe in this case is
over the limbs down to the ankles, both apparently bare. Of the date of the middle of
the following century, there is a very fine
sculptured specimen of a chieftain in what is
called 'Macmillan's cross.' This monument
represents him as at the chase; and the way he
is attired is in the Highland dress, very dis-

[1] The delineations Pinkerton very properly states are not to
taken as portraits of these monarchs, but *as representing the
costume*.

tinct. The date is not given, yet the inscription of 'Crux Alexandri Macmillan,' etc., etc., that is on it, prove from the character it could not be later than 1350. The complete and clear evidence from this fine sculpture is situated at Kilmory, Argyleshire ; there are also very perfect specimens carved in stone of other chieftains in the Highland dress to be seen at Iona, but their dates are uncertain.

The next authorities are chiefly from the Iona Club Transactions. *Andrew Wyntown*, Prior of Lochleven, who wrote about 1400, speaks on more than one occasion in his metrical Chronicle of 'the wyld wykkyd Helandmen ;' and under the year 1396, in reference to the celebrated combat of thirty Highlanders against thirty, fought on the North Inch of Perth in that year, in presence of King Robert III. and his court, in order to settle the disputes of two contending clans, he uses these words :—[1]

> At Sanct Johnestone beside the Freris [2]
> All thai entrit in Barreris [3]
> Wyth Bow and Ax, Knyf and Swerd,
> To deil amang thaim *thar last werd*.

Abbot Bower or *Bowermaker* (the continua-

[1] Vol. ii , page 374.
[2] The Friars.
[3] The barriers.

and Music of the Gael of Alban. 241

tor of Fordun's Scotichronicon) wrote in the reign of James II. of Scotland; and, in describing the arrangements for the above-mentioned noted combat in 1396, says[1] that it was to be fought —

triginta personis adversus triginta de parte contraria, gladiis tantum, arcubus et sagittis, absque deploidibus vel armaturis aliis, praeter bipennis: et sic congredientes finem liti ponerent et terra pace poteretur.

Translation.

by thirty men against thirty of the opposite party, armed only with swords, bows and arrows, without mantles or other armour except axes; and thus encountering that they should end their disputes, and that peace should be established in the country.

The Historian *John Major*, who wrote in 1512, notices the Highland dress in two different parts of his[18]work. At p. 84,[2] talking of the Highlanders generally, he thus describes their dress and armour :—

A medio crure ad pedem caligas non habent, chlamyde pro veste superiore et camisia croco tincta, amiciuntur. Arcum et sagittas, latissimum ensem cum parvo halberto, pugionem grossum ex solo uno latere scindentem sed acutissimum, sub zona semper ferunt. Tempore belli loricam ex loris ferreis per totum corpus induunt et in illa pugnant. In panno lineo multipliciter intersuto et coerato aut picato cum cervinae pellis coopertura vulgus sylvestrium Scotorum corpus tectum habens in praelium prosilit.

[1] Vol. ii., page 420.
[2] Edit. Edinburgh, 1740, 4to.

Translation.

From the middle of the thigh to the foot they have no covering for the leg, clothing themselves with a mantle instead of an upper garment, and a shirt died with saffron. They always carry a bow and arrows, a very broad sword with a small halbert, a large dagger, sharpened on one side only, but very sharp, under the belt. In time of war they cover their whole body with a shirt of mail of iron rings, and fight in that. The common people of the Highland Scots rush into battle, having their body clothed with a linen garment manifoldly sewed and painted or daubed with pitch, with a covering of deerskin.

At page 302, after mentioning the defection of the Clanchattan and Clanchameron from Alexander Lord of the Isles, who in 1429 had raised the standard of rebellion against James I., *Major* thus describes *the customs of these Clans,* and thereby it may be presumed of the Highlanders at large :—

Laetos dies in ocio ducunt, de pauperum bonis victitantes. Arcu, pharetra et halbarda optime scindente, quia bonas mineras ferri habent, utuntur ; grossos pugiones sub zona positos ferunt ; frequentur nudis tibiis sub cruribus ; in hyeme chlamydem pro veste superiori portant.

Translation.

They pass their days merrily in idleness living upon the goods of the poor. They use a bow and quiver, and a halbert well sharpened, as they possess good veins of native iron. They carry large daggers placed under the belt ; their legs are frequently naked under the thigh ; in winter they carry a mantle for an upper garment.

In 1471, John, Bishop of Glasgow, treasurer to King James III., gives in his account for tartan for the use of the King. For a yard and a-half the price was £1. 10s. Scots, and the colour blue. Also half a yard of what is called 'double tartane' for the Queen is eight shillings. This is from Logan's Gael.[1]

In the *Accounts of the Lord High Treasurer of Scotland* in August 1538, we find the following entries regarding a Highland dress made for King James V., on the occasion of that Monarch making a hunting excursion to the Highlands :—

Item in the first for ij elnis ane quarter elne of variant cullorit velvet to be the Kingis Grace ane schort *Heland* coit price of the elne vj^{lib} summa . . xiij^{lib} x^s.

Item for iij elnis quarter elne of grene taffatyis to lyne the said coit with, price of the elne x^s summa, ... xxxij^s vj^d.

Item for iij elnis of *Heland tertane* to be hoiss to the Kingis grace, price of the elne iiij^s iiij^d summa . xiij^s.

Item for xv elnis of holland claith to be syde[2] Heland sarkis to the Kingis Grace, price of the elne viij^s summa . . . . vj^{lib}.

Item for sewing and making of the said sarkis. ix^s.

Item for twa unce of silk to sew thame, . . x^s.

Item for iiij elnis of rubanis to the handis of thame, ... ij^s.

The following passage, showing how the Highlanders came to be denominated *Redshanks*, is extracted from the curious letter of

---

[1] See Logan's Gael, vol. i., page 230.
[2] *Syde i e.* long, or hanging low.

John Elder, a Highland priest, to King Henry VIII., anno 1543. The letter itself has been printed at full length in the Collectanea de Rebus Albanicis.[1]

Moreover, wherefor they call us in Scotland Reddshankes, and in your Graces dominion of England, roghe footide Scottis, Pleas it your Maiestie to understande, that we of all people can tollerat, suffir, and away best with colde, for boithe somer and wyntir (exceptc when the froest is most vehemonte), goynge alwaies bair leggide and bair footide, our delite and pleasure is not onely in huntynge of redd deir, wolfes, foxes, and graies, whereof we abounde, and have greate plentie, but also in rynninge, leapinge, swymmynge, shootynge, and thrawinge of dartis: therfor, in so moche as we use and delite so to go alwaies, *the tendir delicatt gentillmen* of Scotland call us *Reddshankes.* And agayne in wynter, whene the froest is mooste vehement (as I have saide) which we can not suffir bair footide, so weill as snow, *whiche can never hurt us whene it cummes to our girdills,* we go a huntynge, and after that we have slayne redd deir, we flaye of the skyne, bey and bey, and settinge of our bair foote on the insyde therof, for neide of cunnyge shoemakers, by your Graces pardon, we play the sutters; compasinge and mesuringe so moche thereof, as shall retche up *to our anclers,* pryckynge the upper part therof also with holis, that the water may repas when it entres, and stretchide up with a stronge thwange of the same, meitand above our said ancklers, so, and please your noble Grace, we make our shoois: Therfor, we usinge such maner of shoois, the roghe hairie syde outwart, in your Graces dominion of England, we be callit roghe footide Scottis; which maner of schoois (and pleas your Highnes) in Latyne be called perones, whereof the poet Virgill makis mencioun, sayinge, That the *olde auncient Latyns in tyme of warrs* uside suche maner of

[1] Vol. i., pages 23 to 32.

schoos. And althoughe a great sorte of us *Reddshankes* go after this maner in our countrethe, yeit never the les, and pleas your Grace, whene we come to the courte (the Kinges grace our great master being alyve) waitinge on our Lordes and maisters, who also, for velvettis and silkis be right well araide, we have as good garmentis as some of our fellowis whiche gyve attendaunce in the court every daye.

In the year 1552, an *Act of Privy Council* was passed for the levy of two regiments of Highlanders, and it is inserted at full length in the appendix, to form part of a body of Scotch auxiliaries about to proceed to the assistance of the King of France; and the Earl of Huntly being Lieutenant of the North Highlands where these men were to be raised, was directed to see that the Highland soldiers were

Substantiouslie accompturit with jack and plait, steill-bonett, sword, bucklair, new hois and new doublett of canvouse at the lest, and slevis of plait or splenttis, and ane speir of sax elne lang or thairby.

An *Act of Parliament*, anno 1574, under the regency of the Earl of Morton, directing a general *weaponshawing* throughout Scotland, makes a distinction between the arms of the lesser gentlemen and yoemen in the Lowlands and those in the Highlands, as under:—

Lowland Arms.

Brigantinis, Jakkis, steilbonettis, slevis of plate or mailye, swerdis, pikkis or speris of *sex elnis lang*, culveringis, halbertis or tua handit swerdis.

Highland Arms.

Habirschonis, steilbonettis, hektonis, swerdis, bowis and dorlochis,[1] or culveringis.

In a *MS. History of the Gordons*, by W. R., preserved in the Advocates' Library,[2] the following anecdote is given, as occurring about the year 1591 or 1592:—

Angus, the son of Lauchlan Macintosh, Chiefe of the Clanchattan, with a great party attempts to surprise the Castle of Ruthven in Badenoch, belonging to Huntly, in which there was but a small garrison; but finding this attempt could neither by force nor fraude have successe, he retires a little to consult how to compass his intent. In the meanetime, one creeps out under the shelter of some old ruins, and levels with his piece at one of the Clanchattan *cloathed in a yellow warr coat*[3] (which, amongst them, is the badge of the Cheiftanes or heads of Clans), and, peircing his body with the bullet, stricks him to the ground, and retires with gladness into the castle. The man killed was Angus himself, whom his people carry away, and conceills his death for many yeirs, pretending he was gone beyond seas.

John Taylor, 'the King's Majesties Water Poet,' made an excursion to Scotland in the year 1618, of which *he published an amusing narrative* under the title of '*The Pennylesse Pilgrimage.*' He describes the dress of the Highlanders in the following account he gives of his visit to Braemar for the purpose of pay-

[1] *Dorloch*, a Gaelic word, properly *Dornlach*, a quiver.
[2] Jac 5th, 7, 11.
[3] In another and later copy of the MS., the Editor finds *waist coat* instead of *warr coat*.

ing his respects to the Earl of Mar and Sir William Moray of Abercairney.[1]

Thus, with extreme travell, ascending and descending, mounting and alighting, I came at night to the place where I would be, in the Brae of Marr, which is a large county all composed of such mountaines, that Shooters hill, Gads hill, Highgate hill, Hampstead hill, Birdlip hill, or Malvernes hills, are but mole-hills in comparison, or like a liver, *or a gizzard* under a capon's wing, in respect to *the altitude of their tops, or perpendicularite of their bottomes.* There I saw mount[2] Benawne with a furrd'd mist upon his snowy head instead of a night-cap; for you must understand, that the oldest man alive never saw but the snow was on the top of divers of those hills, (both in summer as well as in winter). There did I find the truely noble and Right Honourable Lords John Erskine, EARLE OF MARR, James Stuart, EARLE OF MURRAY, George Gordon, EARLE OF ENGYE, sonne and heire to the Marquise of Huntley, James Erskin, EARLE OF BUGHAN, and John, LORD ERSKIN, sonne and heire to the Earle of Marr, and their Countesses, with my much honoured, and my best assured and approved friend, Sir William Murray, Knight, of ABERCARNY, and *hundred of others*, knights, esquires, and their followers; *all* and every man in generall, *in one habit*, as if Licurgus had been there, and made lawes of equality. For once in the yeere, which is the whole moneth of August, and sometimes part of September, many of the nobility and gentry of the kingdome (for their pleasure) doe come into these Highland countries to hunt, where they doe conforme themselves to the habite of the Highland men, who, for the moste part, speake nothing but Irish; and in former time were those people which were called the *Red-shanks*. Their habite is shooes with

[1] Taylor's Works, London, 1633, folio.
[2] He no doubt means the mountain called in English Benavon (in Braemar); in Gaelic, 'Beinn-abhuinn,' or 'the mountain of the river'.—J. A. R.

but one sole apiece; stockings (which they call short hose) made of a warme *stuffe of divers colours*, which they call tartane. As for breeches, many of them, nor their forefathers, never wore any, but a jerkin of the same stuffe that their hose is of, their garters being bands or wreathes of hay or straw, with a plaed about their shoulders, which is a mantle of divers colours, much finer and lighter stuffe than their hose, with blue flat caps on their heads, a handkerchiefe knit with two knots about their necke; and thus are they attyred. Now, their weapons are long bowes and forked arrowes, swords and targets, harquebusses, muskets, durks, and Loquhabor-axes. With these armes I found many of them armed for the hunting. As for their attire, any man of what degree soever that comes amongst them, must not disdaine to weare it; for if they doe, then they will disdaine to hunt, or willingly to bring in their dogges; *but if men be kind unto them, and be in their habit, then are they conquered with kindnesse, and the sport will be plentifull.* This was the reason that I found so many noblemen and gentlemen in those shapes. But to proceed to the hunting.

My good Lord of Marr having put me into that shape.[1] I rode with him from his house, where I saw the ruines of an old castle, called the castle of Kindroghit.[2] It was built by king Malcolm Canmore (for a hunting house), who raigned in Scotland when Edward the Confessor, Harold, and Norman William raigned in England; I speak of it, because it was the last house that I saw in those parts; for I was the space of twelve dayes after, before I saw either house, corne-field, or habitation for any creature, but deere, wild horses, wolves, and such like creatures, which made me doubt that I should never have seene a house againe.

[1] It must have been very amusing to the Highland noblemen, gentlemen, etc., when they saw this cockney '*put into that shape,*' as he calls it.

[2] These ruins of King Malcolm's Castle still exist.—J. A. R.

and Music of the Gael of Alban.

In the beginning of 1678, a body of Highlanders, 'the Highland Host,' as it was called, amounting to about 10,000 men, were brought from their native mountains and quartered upon the western counties, for the purpose of suppressing the field meetings and conventicles of the Presbyterians. But their irregular and disorderly conduct, soon made it necessary for government to disband them; and therefore we need the less wonder that they should on this occasion *be represented in satirical colours.* The following is an extract from a letter,[1] dated February 1, 1678, and evidently written by an eye-witness. The entire letter will be found in Blackwood's Edinburgh Magazine, April 1817, page 68.

We are now all quartered in and about this town, [Ayr?] the Highlanders only in free quarters. It would be truly a pleasant sight, were it at an ordinary weapon-shaw, to see this Highland crew. You know the fashion of their wild apparel, not one of them hath breeches, yet hose and shoes are there greatest need and most clever prey, and the spare not to take them everywhere: In so much that the committee here, and the Counsel with you (as it is said) have ordered some thousands of pairs of shoes to be made to stand this great spoil. As for their armes, and other militarie accoutrements, it is not possible for me to describe them in writing; here you may see head-pieces and steel-bonnets raised like pyramids, and such as a man would affirme they had only found in chamber-boxes; targets and shields of the most

---

[1] Wodrow MSS. Advocates' Library, 4to, vol. xcix., No. 29.

olde *and antique forme*, and powder horns hung in strings, garnished with beaten nails and burnished brass. And truely I doubt not but a man, curious in our antiquities, might *in this host finde explications* of the strange pieces of armour mentioned in our old lawes, such as a bosnet, iron hat, gorget, pesane, wambrassers, and reerbrassers, panns, leg-splents, and the like, above what any occasion in the Lowlands would have afforded for *several hundreds* of yeers. Among the ensigns also, besides other singularities, *the Glencow men* were very remarkable, who had for *their ensigne a faire bush of heath*, welspred and displayed on the head of a staff, *such as might have affrighted a Roman eagle*.

William Cleland, Lieutenant-Colonel to the Earl of Angus' regiment, who was killed whilst gallantly defending his post at Dunkeld against a party of Highlanders, soon after the Revolution, *wrote a satirical poem* upon the expedition of the Highland Host in 1678,[1] from which the following extracts are taken:—

> But to discrive them right surpasses
> The art of nine Parnassus Lasses.
>
> * * * * *
>
> Their head, their neck, their legs and thighs
> Are influenced by the skies,
> Without a clout to interrupt them
> They need not strip them when they whip them;
> Nor loose their doublet, when they're hang'd
> If they be miss'd, its sure they're wrang'd.
>
> * * * * * *
>
> But those who were their chief Commanders,
> As such who bore the pirnic standarts,
> Who led the van, and drove the rear,
> Were right well mounted of their gear;

[1] Collection of poems, etc., 12mo, 1697, page 12.

With brogues, trues, and pirnie plaides,
With good blew bonnets on their heads,
Which on the one side had a flipe
Adorn'd with a tobacco pipe,
With durk, and snap work, and snuff mill,
A bagg which they with onions fill,
And, *as their strick observers say,*
A tupe[1] *horn fill'd with usquebay;*
A slasht out coat beneath her plaides,
A targe of timber, nails and hides;
With a long two-handed sword,
As good's the country can affoord;
Had they not need of bulk and bones,
Who fight with all these arms at once?
It's marvellous how in such weather,
Ov'r hill and hop they came together;
How in such stormes they came so farr;
The reason is, they're smear'd with tar,
Which doth defend them heel and neck,
Just as it doth their sheep protect;
But least ye doubt that this is true,
They're just the colour of tar'd wool.

William Sacheverell, Esq., Governor of the Isle of Man, who was employed in 1688 in the attempt to recover the stores of the 'Florida,' one of the great vessels of the Spanish Armada (which was blown up and sunk in the harbour of Tobermory in Mull exactly a hundred years before), made in that year an excursion through the Isle of Mule, and thence to Icolmkill. In 1702, he published at London an account of

[1] A ram's horn filled with whisky, here named 'usquebay,' and called by the Gael, Uisge-beatha, or water of life, Latin acquavitæ, French eau-de-vie, etc., etc.

this excursion, along with an account of the Isle of Man. At page 129 of this volume, he thus describes the dress, armour, and general appearance of the Highlanders as he saw them in the Isle of Mull in 1688:—

During my stay, I generally observed the men to be large-bodied, stout, subtle, active, patient of cold and hunger. There appeared in all their actions *a certain generous air of freedom,* and contempt of those trifles, luxury and ambition, which we so servilely creep after. They bound their appetites by their necessities, and their happiness consists, not in having much, *but in coveting little.* The women seem to have the same sentiments with the men; though their habits[1] were mean and they had not our sort of breeding, yet in many of them there was a natural beauty *and a graceful modesty,* which never fails of attracting. The usual outward habit of both sexes is the pladd; the women's much finer, the colours more lively, and the squares larger than the men's, and put me in mind *of the ancient Picts.* This serves them for a veil, and covers both head and body. The men wear theirs after another manner, especially when designed for ornament: it is loose and flowing, like the mantles *our painters give their heroes.* Their thighs are bare, with brawny muscles. Nature has drawn all her strokes bold and masterly; a thin brogue on the foot, a short buskin of various colours on the legg, tied above the calf with a striped pair of garters. What should be concealed is hid with a large shot-pouch, on each side of which hangs a pistol and a dagger, as if they found it necessary to keep those parts well guarded. A round target on their backs, a blew bonnet on their heads, in one hand a broadsword and a musquet in the other. Perhaps *no nation goes better armed;* and I assure you *they will handle them with bravery and dexterity,* especially the sword and

[1] That means their dress.

target, as our veterane regiments *found to their cost at Gillecrankee.*¹

In Martin's description of the Western Isles of Scotland² we find the following among his accounts of the dress :—

When they travel on foot, the plad is tied on the breast with *a bodkin of bone* or *wood* (just as the *spina* wore by the Germans, according to *the description of C. Tacitus*). The plad is tied round the middle with a leather belt; it is pleated from the belt *to the knee very nicely.* This dress for footmen is found much easier and lighter than breeches or trowis.

* * * * *

The ancient way of fighting was by set battles; and for arms some had broad two-handed swords and head-pieces, and others bows and arrows. When all their arrows were spent, they attacked one another with sword-in-hand. Since the invention of guns, they are very early accustomed to use them, and carry their pieces with them wherever they go: they likewise learn to handle the broadsword and target. The chief of each tribe advances with his followers within shot of the enemy, having first laid aside their upper garments; and after one general discharge, they attack them with sword-in-hand, having their target on their left hand (*as they did at Kelicranky*), which soon brings the matter to an issue, and verifies the observation made of them by your historians :—

'*Aut Mors cito, aut Victoria læta.*'

There is another authority which speaks of the Highland dress, and appears to have been

¹ That is Killiecrankie, where Dundee, with the Atholl Highlanders, etc., gained his victory over General Mackay and his Southern forces, in 1689.
² 2d Edition, London, 1716, page 206.

unknown to the editor of the Iona Transactions, namely, Chamberlayne, who, in his account of Britain, printed in 1710, under the head of Perthshire, says, 'The people *call themselves Albanach.*' And of their dress, he states, they wear 'stripped mantles of divers colours called plaids.'[1]

There has thus been laid before the reader a complete series of evidence that proves the antiquity of the Highlander's dress, and arms, beyond dispute. In the unfortunate civil wars of 1716 and 1745, it is notorious that the dress was worn by the whole Highland army who followed 'Bonnie Prince Charlie.' The English Parliament adopted the cruel measure of proscribing it, as, if possible, they also would the language of the Gael; but we may be glad to think these feelings are long since gone, and the national dress is now admired and encouraged.

National Pipe Music.

The great Highland bagpipe is peculiarly a national instrument of the Gael of Alban. It is evidently of the most remote antiquity, and though the Irish have pipes, they are but *a very feeble* imitation of that of

[1] See page 329.

the Highlanders, and not, like it, suited for the battle-field, or suited to inspirit a clan on the line of march. It has well been said, that 'in halls of joy and scenes of mourning it has prevailed; it has animated her warriors in battle, and welcomed them back, after their toils, to the homes of their love and *the hills of their nativity*. Its strains were the first sounded on the ears of infancy, and they are the last to be forgotten in the wanderings of age. Even Highlanders will allow it is not the gentlest of instruments, but when far from their mountain homes, what sounds, however melodious, could thrill round their heart like one burst of their own wild native pipe? The feelings which other instruments awaken are general and undefined, because they talk alike to Frenchmen, Spaniards, Germans, and Highlanders, for they are common to all, but the bagpipe is sacred to Scotland, *and speaks a language which Scotchmen only feel.*[1] The most sweet and plaintive airs of the bagpipe are the laments. Thus the 'Cumh mhic 'an Tosach, or Macintosh's Lament,' and 'Lord Rae's Daughter's Lament,' are both very fine examples. The Gathering, or Cruineachadh, of each tribe was composed usually from the event of some battle gained by the clan. The 'failte,' or salute, was an-

[1] Preface to Macdonald's Ancient Martial Music of Caledonia.

other class of the native melody. A very
ancient piece of pipe music is still preserved
called 'The Battle of Harlaw,' and dates back
to the year 1411, composed by the chief piper
of the Lord of the Isles on that occasion, when
he endeavoured by arms to enforce his right to
the Earldom of Ross. Another, and still more
ancient, piece of pipe music was some time ago
printed by Macdonald, called 'Cumha Somhairle'—that is, 'Somerled's Lament.' He
was the great founder of the family of all the
Macdonalds, and was assassinated in the year
1164 near Renfrew, immediately after he had
arrived and invaded Scotland with a large army.
The chiefs of the clans who descend from any
of the petty Dalriad princes were *all* followers
of Macdonalds, the Lord of the Isles. As said
before, the instrument and martial music of the
great Highland bagpipe has been ever peculiar
to the Gael of Alban, unknown among the
Gael of Erin, therefore the Dalriads or Irish
Scots must have learned it and adopted it
from the Caledonian Picts. There was great
encouragement given in ancient times to the
performers on this national instrument, and
they were of high value in all the expeditions
of the Gael; and they, along with the bards,
greatly added to incite the combatants before
and during the tumult of battle.

In the Isle of Skye was situated the college for the instruction of the 'Piob-mor,' or 'great Highland bagpipe.' There was a family named M'Crimmen, who, for many generations, were the chief professors and teachers of the pupils at this college, who went when young, and were not considered to have attained to a proper proficiency under seven years' attendance and instruction. M'Leod of M'Leod gave a farm, in the Isle of Skye, named Boreraig, for the support of this college.¹ There are many more celebrated 'piobaireach,' or 'pipe tunes' than those already spoken of: among them may be mentioned the '*a ghlas mheur*,' or, '*the finger lock*,' which is considered a master-piece, and is of high antiquity. There is, however, a far more ancient one, called '*cogadh na sith*,' meaning 'alike to me is peace or war.' It is very gratifying to all Highlanders the encouragement given to their ancient national instrument and its martial music. The Highland regiments and various societies greatly keep up these laudable feelings in the Highlanders' breast.

¹ See New Statistical Account, vol. Inverness-shire, and Parish of Duirinish, Isle of Skye, pages 339, 340.

CHAPTER XI.

Short Notices of the Highland Clans.

IT is not generally understood that there were *no clans* among the Gael until after the great Celtic Earls became extinct, and which began in the thirteenth century. Before the Earls appear, the tribes that inhabited the various districts of the Highlands were under leaders or nobles, who were called Maormors, these, we have good reason to believe, existed among the Caledonian Gael from the most remote period, though the native name for the dignity was not known; but Tacitus is a clear authority that in *the first century* the inhabitants of Caledonia had nobles or leaders among them who ruled the tribes and elected the Ardrigh, or supreme king, as he states that the choice of Galgacus as sovereign was from among 'many leaders' ('inter plures duces'); and in the year A.D. 563, the year Columba arrived in Alban, Adomnan also tells us of 'quendam

CAIRN GORM from the north side of Loch an-eilean.

de nobili Pictorum genere,[1] proving there were nobles among the Picts. The Irish Gael appear not to have had this title (Maormor) among them; but of course it had been so often heard of by those who wrote the Irish Annals, that in those of Ulster, so far back as A.D. 917, the Maormors are mentioned. In the fourteenth century the clans then appear to have commenced pretty generally over the Highlands; and to place before the reader a clear view of what they became two centuries afterwards, the writer considers that this will be properly and best effected by giving an Act of Parliament, which recites *the whole* of them, and to which is appended the roll of their chieftains, etc., etc., thereby the short notices proposed to be given respecting them will be placed upon an *authentic* and undeniable *foundation*. The date of this very interesting Act of Parliament is almost 300 years ago, being in 1587, and is contained in the 3d volume of the Scots Acts. It was also printed by the Iona Club, with notes, which is here given with additions to both. Another roll of the clans, dated 1594, will also be given, with explanatory additions.

The following and the ROLL OF CLANS are (as before alluded to) appended to a long and

[1] Adomnan, lib. ii., cap. 24.

important Act of Parliament regarding the police of the country, entitled, ' For the quieting and keeping in obedience of the disordourit subjectis inhabitantis of the Bordouris, Hielandis, and Ilis,' but commonly called, from one of its most important provisions, 'THE GENERAL BAND,' or Bond. As this Act of Parliament is very frequently referred to in documents connected with the Highlands, the curious reader is referred to the latest edition of the Acts of the Scottish Parliament, vol. iii., pages 461 to 467, where it is printed entire.

For the sake of convenience, the illustrative notes to these Rolls, and to that contained in the Act of 1594, will be given at the end of the last-mentioned Roll, and will be *easily found by attending to the numerical references* placed before each name. *The words within a circumflex are added* to the old Acts to give further information.

The Roll of the names of the Landlislordis and Baillies of Landis in the Hielandis and Iles, quhair brokin men hes duelt and presentlie duellis, 1587.

Londislordis and Baillies.

1 The Duke of Lennox.
2 The Laird of Buchananc.

3 The Laird of M'Farlane of the Arroquhar.
4 The Laird of Luss.
5 The Laird M'Cawla of Ardincaple.
6 The Laird of Marchinstoun.
7 The Laird of Glennegyis.
8 The Earle of Glencarne.
9 The Laird of Drumquhassill.
10 The Laird of Kilcreuch.
11 The Tutour of Menteith.
12 The Laird of Knockhill.
   Harry Schaw of Cambusmoir.
13 The Laird of Kippanross.
14 The Laird of Burley.
15 The Laird of Keir.
16 The Master of Levingstoun.
17 The Lord of Down.
18 The Lord Drummond.
19 The Laird of Tullibardin.
20 The Laird of Glenorquhy.
21 The Laird of Lawaris.
22 The Laird of Weyme.
23 The Abbot of Inchaffray.
24 Coline Campbell of Ardbeich.
25 The Laird of Glenlyoun.
26 The Erle of Athoill.
27 The Laird of Grantullie.
28 The Laird of Strowane-Robertsoue.
29 The Laird of Strowane-Murray.
30 The Laird of Wester Wemyss.

31 The Laird of Abbotishall.
32 The Laird of Teling.
33 The Laird of Inchmartine.
34 The Laird of Purie-Fothringhame.
35 The Laird of Moncreiff.
36 The Laird of Balleachne.
37 The Barroun of Fandowie.
38 The Erle of Erroll.
39 The Erle of Gowry.
40 The Laird of Cultybragane.
41 The Lord Ogilvy
42 The Laird of Clovay.
43 The Laird of Fintray.
44 The Laird of Edyell.
45 The Erle of Mar.
46 The Master of Elphingstoun.
47 The Erle Huntlie.
48 The Master of Forbes.
49 The Laird of Grant.
50 Makintosche.
51 The Lord and Tutour of Lovate.
52 Cheisholme of Cummer.
53 The Larde of Glengarry.
54 Mackanyie.
55 The Laird of Fowlis.
56 The Laird of Balnagown.
57 The Tutour of Cromartie.
58 The Erle of Suthirland.
59 The Laird of Duffus.
60 James Innes of Touchis.

61 The Erle of Caitlines.
62 The Erle of Merschall.
63 The Lord Oliphant.
64. The Laird of Boquhowy.
65 The Laird of Dunnibeyth.
66 Macky of Far.
67 Torquill M‘Cloyd of Cogoych.
68 The Laird of Garloch.
69 Makgillichallum of Raarsay.
70 M‘Cloid of the Harrich.
71 M‘Kynnoun of Strathodell.
72 M‘Cleud of the Lewes.
73 M‘Neill of Barray.
74 M‘Kane of Ardnamurchin.
75 Allane M‘Kane of Ilanterum.
75 The Laird of Knoydert.
76 M‘Clane of Dowart.
77 The Lard of Ardgowir.
    Johnne Stewart of the Appin.
78 M‘Coull of Lorne.
79 M‘Coull of Roray.
80 The Laird of Lochynnell.
81 The Laird of Caddell.
82 The Laird of Skermourlie, for Rauchry.
83 M‘Condoquhy of Innerraw.
    Angus M‘Coneill of Dunyveg and Glen-
    nis.
84 The Laird of Lowip.
85 The Schiref of Bute.
86 The Laird of Camys.

87 Erle of Ergile.
88 Laird of Auchinbrek.
89 The Laird of Ardkinglass.
90 M'Nauchtane.
91 M'Lauchlane.
92 The Laird of Lawmont.
92 The Laird of Perbrak.
94 The Laird of Duntrune.
95 Constable of Dundy, Laird of Glastry.
96 The Laird of Elanegreg.
97 The Laird of Otter.
98 The Laird of Coll.
99 Makclayne of Lochbuy.
100 M'Fee of Collowsay.
101 The Lord Hamiltoun.

The Roll of the Clannis [*in the Hielandis and Iles*] *that hes Capitanes, Cheffis, and Chiftanes quhome on thay depend, oft tymes aganis the willis of thair Landislordis: and of sum speciale personis of branchis of the saidis Clannis*, 1587.

 Buchananis (in Monteith and the Lennox).
 M'Ferlanis Arroquhar (in the Lennox).
 M'Knabbis (in Glendochart, Perthshire).
 Grahmes of Menteth.
 Stewartis of Buchquhidder.
 Clangregour (M'Gregors in Monteith and Rannoch, Perthshire).

the Highland Clans.

Clanlawren (M'Larens, Balquhidder, Perthshire).
Campbellis of Lochnell.
Campbellis of Innerraw.
Clandowill of Lorne (M'Dougals).
Stewartis of Lorne, or of Appin.
102 Clane M'Kane of Avricht.
Stewartis of Athoill, and pairtis adiacent.
Clandonoquhy, in Athoill, and pairtis adiacent.
Menyessis, in Athoill and Apnadull.
Clan M'Thomas in Glenesche.
Fergussonis (in Glenshee, Perthshire).
Spaldingis (in Glenshee, Perthshire).
Makintoscheis, in Athoill (in Glentilt).
Clancamroun (Lochiel, Argyleshire).
103 Clanrannald, in Lochquhaber.
Clanrannald of Knoydert, Modert, and Glengaray.
Clanlewid of the Lewis.
Clanlewyd of Harray (that is, Harris).
Clanneill (Isle of Barra).
Clankynnoun (Strathordill, Isle of Skye).
104 Clan Icane.
Clanquhattan (M'Intoshes, Inverness-shire.
Grantis (Strathspey, Inverness-shire).
Frasseris (Lovat, Inverness-shire).
Clankayne (M'Kenzies, Ross-shire).

105 Clanandreis.
Monrois (Fowlis, Cromarty).
Murrayis, in Suthirland.

Roll of the Broken Clans in the Highlands and Isles,[1] 1594.

OURE SOVERANE LORD and his estaitis in this present Parliament, considering that, nochtwithstanding the sindrie actis maid be his Hienes, and his maist nobill progenitouris, for punischement of the authoris of thift, reiff, oppressioun, and sorning, and masteris and sustenaris of thevis;. yit sic hes bene, and presentlie is, the barbarous cruelties and daylie heirschippis of the wickit thevis and lymmaris of the clannis and surenames following, inhabiting the Hielandis and Iles; Thay ar to say :—
106 Clangregour (M'Gregor's).
Clanfarlane (M'Farlane's).
Clanlawren (M'Laren's).
Clandowill (M'Dougal's).
Clandonochie (Robertson's).
107 Clanchattane (M'Intoshes).
108 Clanchewill (or Clanquhale).
Clanchamron.
Clanronald, in Lochaber.

[1] From an Act of Parliament, 'For punishment of thift, reiff, oppressioun, and sorning.'—Vol. iv., p. 71.

the Highland Clans.

Clanranald, in Knoydert, Modert, and Glengarie.
Clanleyid of the Lewis.
Clanlewid of Harriche.
109 Clandonald, south and north.
Clangillane (M'Lean's).
110 Clanayioun.
Clankynnoun (M'Kinnon or M'Fingon).
Clanneill.
Clankenyie (M'Kenzie's).
Clanandries (Rosses).
111 Clanmorgan (Mackays).
Clangun.
112 Cheilphale (Mackays).
And als many brokin men of the surnames of—
Stewartis, in Athoill, Lorne, and Balquhedder.
Grahames, in Menteith.
Buchannanis.
M'Cawlis.
Galbraithis.
M'Nabbis.
113 M'Nabrichis.
Menzeis.
Fergussonis } (both in Glenshee, Perth-
Spadingis }   shire).
M'Intoscheis, in Athoill.
M·Thomas, in Glensche (Perthshire).
Ferquharsonis, in Bra of Mar.

114 M'Inphersonis (Badenoch).
   Grantis.
   Rossis.
   Frasseris.
   Monrois.
115 Neilsonis.
And utheris inhabiting the Schirefdomes of Ergyle, Bute, Dunbartane, Striviling, Perth, Forfar, Aberdene, Bamf, Elgin, Forres, Narne, Inuernes, and Cromertie, Stewartries of Stratherne and Menteith,[1] etc.

Notes to the two preceding numbers of the Miscellaneous Documents.

1 Ludovick, second Duke of Lennox; whose father, Esme, Lord of Aubigny in France (son of John, Lord of Aubigny, third son of John, third Earl of Lennox, of the Stewarts), was created by King James VI. *Earl* of Lennox, 5th March 1579-80, and *Duke* of Lennox, 5th August 1581.
2 Sir George Buchanan of that ilk, second of that name, and, according to Auchmar, nineteenth Laird of Buchanan. The

---

[1] The details of this Act, which is very long, and refers, like the Act 1587, to the broken or disorderly Clans in the Borders, as well as the Highlands, will be found as above in the printed Acts, vol. iv., pages 71 to 73.

lands of this ancient family lay chiefly in the Highland districts of Menteith and Lennox, in the vicinity of Loch Lomond and Loch Katrine, and are now possessed by the Duke of Montrose.

3 Andrew Macfarlane of that ilk, chief of his ancient clan, descended, in the male line, from *Gilchrist*, a younger son of Alwyn, second Earl of Lennox, of the old family.

4 Humphrey Colquhoun of Luss.

5 Awlay, afterwards Sir Awlay Macawlay of Ardincapill, one of the principal vassals of the Duke of Lennox.

6 Sir Archibald Napier of Merchistoun and Edinbellie, father of John Napier of Merchistoun, the celebrated inventor of the Logarithms. He possessed considerable lands in the earldoms of Menteith and Lennox, and likewise at Ardownane (or Ardeonaig), in Glendochart, in virtue of his descent from Elizabeth, daughter of Murdac de Menteth, and sister and one of the co-heiresses of Patrick de Menteth of Rusky.

7 John Haldane of Glenageis (*now called Gleneagles*), descended from Agnes, the other co-heiress of the above-mentioned Patrick Menteth of Rusky, through whom he possessed considerable lands in the districts

of the Highlands mentioned in the preceding note.

8 James, seventh Earl of Glencairn. Not yet discovered what possessions this nobleman had in the Highlands. Perhaps he is only brought here as answerable for his relation, Drumquhassill—(*See next note.*) Glencairn was, moreover, connected with the Highlands by marriage, his first wife being eldest daughter (by the second marriage) of Sir Colin Campbell, sixth laird of Glenurchy.

9 John Cunningham of Drumquhassill was served heir to his father, John C. of D., in the £5 lands, old extent, of Portnellan, Galbraith, and Tullochan, with the Islands of Loch Lomond, adjacent to the same, in the Dukedom of Lennox, 1613.—(*Special Retours, Co. Dunbarton, No. 15.*)— This ancient family descended from *Andrew* Cunninghame, said to have been a younger son of Sir Robert Cunningham of Kilmaurs, and to have lived in the reign of David II.

10 James Galbraith of Kilcreuch, in the Lennox, is mentioned 1584-5, and Robert Galbraith was laird of Kilcreuch *anno* 1593.—*Registrum Secreti Concilii.*—The Galbraiths are, by tradition, said to

descend from the Britons of Strathclyde.
11 George Graham, Tutor or Guardian to John, sixth earl of Menteith, of the Grahams.— *Registrum Secreti Consilii,* 1584-5.
12 James Shaw of Knockhill, in Menteith, is mentioned in 1584-5, *Reg. Sec. Con.;* and William Shaw of Knockhill in 1599. —*Compota Thesaurarii Scotiæ.*
13 —— —— Stirling of Kippanross.
14 Sir Michael Balfour of Burleigh, who was superior, if not proprietor, at this time of the lands of Mochaster, etc., in Menteith.
15 Sir James Stirling of Keir.
16 Alexander, afterwards seventh Lord Livingston. This family possessed the lands of Callander and Corriechrombie in Menteith, with other lands in the Highlands of Perthshire.
17 James Stewart, first Lord Doune, father of the 'bonny Earl of Moray.'
18 Patrick, third Lord Drummond.
19 Sir John Murray of Tullibardin, in Strathearn. This baron also possessed lands in Balquhidder, and was the ancestor of the Duke of Atholl.
20 Duncan, afterwards Sir Duncan Campbell of Glenurchy, seventh laird—one of the

most potent of the Highland barons, ancestor of the Earls and Marquis's of Breadalbane.
21 John, afterwards Sir John, Campbell of Lawers (whose ancestor was a cadet of the family of Glenurchy). He possessed considerable lands both in Breadalbane and Strathern.
22 James Menzies of that Ilk, or of Weem, proprietor of extensive lands in Breadalbane, Strathtay, and Rannoch.
23 James Drummond, Commendator of Inchaffray, and laird of Innerpeffry, possessor also of lands in Balquhidder. He was brother of Patrick Lord Drummond, and was created, in 1609, Lord Maderty. His grandson, William, fourth Lord Maderty, was created Viscount Strathallan in 1686, he is now represented by William, present Viscount Strathallan.
24 Brother to Sir Duncan Campbell of Glenurchy. His lands lay in the vicinity of Lochearnhead.
25 Colin Campbell of Glenlyon, descended from the house of Glenurchy.
26 John, fifth Earl of Atholl, of the Innermeath line.
27 Sir Thomas Stewart of Grandtully, descended

likewise from the house of Innermeath, proprietor of lands in Strathtay.

28 Donald Robertson of Strowan, one of the most extensive baronies in Perthshire.

29 John Murray of Strowan, in Strathearn. His daughter was married after this period to *Eoin dubh* Macgregor (afterwards killed at Glenfrune, in 1603), brother to Allaster Macgregor of Glenstray, chief of the Clan Gregor.

30 31 The editor was unable to say who these individuals were, or what was their interest in the Highlands.

There were two families in Fife, *Wemyss of Wester Wemyss,* and *Scott of Abbotshall,* the heads of which are probably meant here. The family of Wemyss acquired right to an estate in Atholl, called Kinnaird, by marriage of the heiress of De Inchmartin, Perthshire, which family had married a daughter of John Earl of Atholl, who was beheaded in 1306. The family of Wemyss sold the property of Kinnaird to Stewart of Rosyth, but retained the superiority, and a younger son of Rosyth was the ancestor of the Stewarts of Kinnaird.

32 Sir David Maxwell of Teling, in Forfarshire. He may have possessed lands in the Brae

of Angus, and this family had large property in Strathardle, Perth.
33 Patrick Ogilvie of Inchmartine, proprietor of lands in the south-eastern Highlands of Perthshire; he had also rights in the lands and Barony of Lude, Perthshire.
34 Thomas Fothringham of Powrie, also a proprietor in the Brae of Angus.
35 William Moncrieff of that ilk, proprietor of the lands of Culdares and Tenaiffis in Atholl, which he afterwards sold to Sir Duncan Campbell of Glenurchy. These lands had been possessed by the family of Moncrieff for several centuries, by a grant from Menzies of that ilk.
36 Sir James Stewart of Ballechin, in Atholl, descended from a natural son of King James II. This family was also formerly styled of *Stuiks*, also in Atholl.
37 John Macduff, alias Ferguson, Baron of Fandowie, in Atholl, was executed for his accession to Gowrie's Conspiracy, 1600.
38 Francis, eighth Earl of Errol. This nobleman possessed Logyalmond, part of Inchmartine, and other lands on or near the Highland line.
39 James Ruthven, second Earl of Gowrie, and fifth Lord Ruthven. He possessed

lands in Strathardill and all Strathbran, in the south-eastern highlands of Perthshire. He died in 1588, in his fourteenth year.

40 Alexander Reidheuch of Cultebragan. His lands lay in and near Glenleidnoch, in the Earldom of Strathern. Edward Reidheuch, fiar of Cultebragan, is frequently mentioned in the records at this period.

41 James, sixth Lord Ogilvy of Airly. This nobleman had large possessions in Glen-Isla and other parts of the Brae of Angus.

42 Alexander Ogilvy of Clova was alive in 1557. James Ogilvy was served heir to James Ogilvy of Clova, his father, in the lands of Clova, etc., 1623. The lands of this family lay principally in the Brae of Angus.

43 Sir David Graham of Fintry, Knight, a considerable proprietor in Forfarshire, was alive in 1577. This family descended, it is said, from a younger son of the Grahams of Kincardine, afterwards Earls of Montrose.

44 Sir David Lindsay of Edyell, proprietor of Glenesk, and other lands in the Highlands of Forfarshire.

45 John Erskine, seventh Earl of Mar, proprietor of Braemar, Aberdeenshire, etc., etc.
46 Alexander, afterwards fourth Lord Elphinstone. This noble family seem to have possessed Corgarff, in Banffshire, Kildrummy, etc., etc.
47 George, sixth Earl, and afterwards first Marquis of Huntly, Lord of Badenoch and Lochaber, a most potent noble.
48 John, afterwards eighth Lord Forbes. This family possessed large Highland estates near the sources of the river Don, in Aberdeenshire.
49 John Grant of Freuchy.
50 Lauchlan Macintosh of Dunauchton, Captain of the Clanchattan.
51 Simon, eighth Lord Lovat, and Thomas Fraser of Knockie and Strichen, his uncle and guardian.
52 Alexander Chisholm of Strathglass was alive *anno* 1578. John Chisholm of Comer is mentioned *anno* 1613.
53 Donald Macangus [Macranald] of Glengarry, proprietor also in right of his grandmother (Margaret, sister and co-heiress of Sir Donald de Insulis of Lochalsh) of the half of the lands of Lochalsh, Lochcarron, and Lochbroom, in Ross-shire.

54 Colin Mackenzie of Kintail, whose grandfather had acquired from Dingwall of Kildun, half of the lands of Lochalsh, Lochcarron, and Lochbroom, which Dingwall inherited from his mother Janet, the other co-heiress of Sir Donald of Lochalsh.
55 Robert Munro of Fowlis, said to have been the 15th Baron of that ancient house.
56 Alexander Ross of Balnagown, descended in a direct line from Hugh Ross of Rariches, second son of Hugh, the sixth Earl of Ross, of the old family.
57 John Urquhart of Craigfintry and Culbo, guardian to his grandnephew Thomas, afterwards Sir Thomas Urquhart of Cromarty.
58 Alexander, eleventh Earl of Sutherland.
59 Alexander Sutherland of Duffus was alive in 1555. William Sutherland of Duffus, probably his son, is mentioned in 1605.
60 Not yet ascertained what lands in the Highlands this individual possessed.
61 George Sinclair, fifth Earl of Caithness.
62 George, fifth Earl Marischall.
63 Lawrence, fourth Lord Oliphant. He possessed, among other lands, Berrydale in Caithness, on account of which he appears to be included in this Roll.

64 Patrick Mowat of Boquhally, a considerable proprietor in Caithness, is mentioned in 1564. Magnus Mowat of Boquhally is mentioned in 1598.
65 William Sinclair of Dunbeath, in Caithness.
66 Hugh Mackay of Far, father of Donald, first Lord Reay.
67 Torquil Macleod was the eldest son of Roderick Macleod of the Lewis, by that Baron's second marriage with a daughter of Mackenzie of Kintaill. During his father's lifetime he held the estate of Cogeache, and was known by that title; but on his father's death, he claimed the estates and style of Macleod of Lewis, his title to which was disputed.
68 John Mackenzie of Garloch.
69 Malcolm Macleod, or Macgillechallum of Rasay, nearest heir male at this time of the Macleods of Lewis, after the descendants of the body of Roderick Macleod of Lewis.
70 William Macleod of Harris, Dunvegan, and Glenelg, chief of the *Siol Tormaid.*
71 Lauchlan Mackinnon of Strathwardill in Skye, and of Mishnish in Mull, chief of his ancient tribe.
72 Roderick Macleod of the Lewis, Cogeache and Assint, chief of the *Siol Torcuil.*

73 Roderick Macneill of Barray.
74 John Maccoin, or Macian, of Ardnamurchan, chief of an ancient tribe sprung from the family of the Isles.
75 Alexander Macranald of Knoydert, chieftain of his tribe, an ancient branch of the Clanranald.
76 Lauchlan, afterwards Sir Lauchlan Maclean of Dowart, a brave and gallant soldier, as he proved himself by his conduct at Glenlivat in 1594.
77 Ewin Maclean of Ardgour, representative of an ancient branch of the family of Dowart.
78 Dougal Macdougal of Dunolly.
79 Allan Macdougal of Raray.
80 Archibald Campbell, second Laird of Lochnell, killed at the battle of Glenlivat, 1594.
81 John Campbell of Calder or Cadder, frequently written Caddell.
82 Sir Robert Montgomery of Skelmorlie, who seems, at this time, to have possessed the small island of Rachry, or Rachrin, lying near the coast of Antrim.
83 Dougal Macconachy (Campbell) of Inveraw, head of an ancient sept of the Campbells.
84 Alexander Macallaster of Loupe, in Kintyre.
85 John Stewart, sheriff of Bute.

86 Hector Bannatyne of Kames, in Bute.
87 Archibald, seventh Earl of Argyll, then a minor. His principal guardian was John Campbell of Calder.
88 Duncan Campbell of Auchinbreck.
89 Sir James Campbell of Ardkinlass.
90 Malcolm Macnauchtane of Dundaraw.
91 Archibald Maclauchlan of Stralauchlan, or of that ilk.
92 James Lamont of Inveryne, or of that ilk.
93 Colin Campbell of Barbrek.
94 John Campbell of Duntrune.
95 James, afterwards Sir James, Scrymgeour of Dudhope, constable of Dundee, and proprietor of the barony of Glasry in Argyleshire, which had been in the possession of this family for many generations.
96 —— Campbell of Elangreg.
97 Archibald Campbell younger of Otter is mentioned in 1580.
98 Hector Maclean of Coll.
99 John Maclean of Lochbuy.
100 Murdoch Macfee of Colonsay.
101 Lord John Hamilton, afterwards Marquis of Hamilton. He is brought in here as proprietor of the Isle of Arran.
102 The Clan Eoin, or Macdonalds of Glenco, whose chief is patronymically styled '*Mac Eoin Abrach.*'

103 The Macdonalds in the Braes of Lochaber, commonly called the Macdonalds of Keppoch.
104 The Clan Eoin of Ardnamurchan.
105 The Rosses, of whom Balnagowan was the chief.
106 An undesirable precedence seems to be assigned to the Clan Gregor in this Roll.
107 It will be observed that the Clanchattan and Macphersons are distinguished from each other in this Roll.
108 It is doubtful, at present, what tribe is indicated by '*Clan Chewill.*' The Clanquhale are named in the year 1392 as followers of the De Atholia family, the ancestors of the Robertson's of Atholl. See 1st vol. Scots Acts Parliament, page 217, when the whole chieftains of the Clandonachy were forfeited for the two battles in which they had defeated the Lindsays, etc., etc., in 1391. The locality of this tribe seems to have been somewhere in Badenoch or Lochaber.
109 The Clandonald South were the Clan Eoinmhor of Isla and Kintyre. The Clandonald North were the Clan Huistein of Sky and North Uist.
110 Clan Eoin of Ardnamurchan, probably.
111 The Mackays of Strathnaver.

112 A sept of the Mackays, descended from one Paul Macneill Mackay.
113 '*M'Nabrichis*,' a contraction probably for '*Mac Eoinabrichis*,' the Glenco Macdonalds.
114 See note 107.
115 '*Neilsonis*,' probably intended to mean another sept of the Mackays, called by Sir Robert Gordon *Seill Neill*.

Some interesting particulars will now be given of the force and strength of the various Highland Clans, and showing the power of the various chiefs throughout the country of the Highlanders; also the badges of the clans, and their different war-cries, or rallying words, handed down from the remotest times by their forefathers, who formed the original tribes of the different districts of the Caledonian Picts.

The oldest notice yet discovered in the public records of raising a force by the Government from the Highlanders is dated more than three hundred years ago, namely, in 1552, when two regiments of Highlanders were ordered to be raised, within the boundaries of which, the then Lord Huntly was Lord Lieutenant. The manner in which the Highlanders were to be armed has already been noticed:

the Highland Clans.

and as it is very curious, the Act itself of the Privy Council, ordering the levy, is printed in the Appendix.[1] The next notice, as showing the relative power of the chiefs, is contained in a public document dated in January 1602, being an Act of Privy Council for a levy of Highlanders to assist the Queen of England in her wars in Ireland, it is also given in the Appendix; and as an abstract of it has not yet appeared, it is here inserted. The information is highly curious; and as the Act itself expresses it, His Majesty the King (that is, King James VI.) had placed the burden of levying this force of Highlanders upon such of his subjects 'within the Hielandis *as ar of maist power to furncis thame*,' namely, by

	MEN
The Duke of Lennox,[2]	200
The Earl of Argyll and Laird of Glenorchy,	300
The Earl of Atholl,	100
The Laird of M'Gregor,	50
The Abbot of Inchaffray, Lairds of Lundy	

[1] From the Iona Club Transactions—which are almost as unknown as if never printed—the writer is glad to make known such curious, indeed, historical, old documents as are printed in the Appendix.

[2] Almost all here mentioned have been spoken of in the Notes of the Roll of the Clans, where they will be found on reference to it.

and Tullibardine, for Menteith and Strathearn,	50
The Marquis of Huntly,	100
M'Intosh,	100
The Laird of Grant,	100
The Laird of Balnagown,	100
Lord Lovat and the Laird of Fowlis,	100
The Earl of Caithness,	100
The Earl of Sutherland and Mackay,	100
Glengarry,	100
The Captain of Clanrannald,[1]	200
M'Conal Dhu—Allan Cameron of Lochiel, and M'Ranald—Allaster M'Donald of Keppoch,	100
M'Kenzie—Colin M'Kenzie of Kintail,	100

Strength of the Clans to be raised for King James II. in the year 1704.

M'Donalds,	1800
M'Phersons,	700
M'Kenzies of Seaforth,	1200
M'Leods,	700
Frasers,	1000
Roses of Kilravock,	500
Rosses of Balnagowan,	300
Duke of Gordon,	1000
Grant of Balindalish,	300

[1] The proportion assigned to the Captain Clanranald seems very large compared with others in this levy.

Stewart of Appin,	200
Farquharsons,	700
Chisholms,	200
M'Dulothes,	500
Earl of Perth Highlanders,	600
The Horsemen of Inverness and Morayshires,	1000
	10,700

General Wade gives the following statement of the Highland forces in 1715 who fought for King James.

The Islands and Clans of the late Lord Seaforth,	3000
M'Donalds of Slate,	1000
M'Donalds of Glengarry,	800
M'Donalds of Moidart,	800
M'Donald of Keppoch,	220
Camerons of Lochiell,	800
The M'Leods, in all,	1000
The Duke of Gordon's followers,	1000
Stewarts of Appin,	400
Robertsons of Strowan,	800
M'Intoshes and Farquharsons,	800
M'Ewen, in the Isle of Skye,	150
The Chisholms of Strathglass,	150

The M'Phersons, ... 220

The following Clans, he adds, joined *without*
 their superiors with them:
The Atholl men, one-half of whom nearly
 were Robertsons, . . . 2000
The Bredalbane men, . . . 1000

                                              14,140

The following Clans were believed to be well
 affected to the Government:
The Duke of Argyll, . . . 4000
Lords Sutherland and Strathnaver, . 1000
Lord Lovat's Frasers, . . . 800
The Grants, ... 800
The Ross's and Munroes, . . 700
Forbes of Culloden, . . . 200
Rose of Kilravock, ... 300
Sir Archibald Campbell of Clunes, . 100

                                               8000

The number of Highlanders properly armed and fit for the field in 1745, on the side of Prince Charles, was estimated at the lowest to be 12,000 men, and those on the opposite side were nearly equal.[1]

---

[1] See the Stuart Papers, vol. ii., page 117.

Suaicheantas[1] nan Gael,

Or the Badges of the Highland Clans, in Gaelic and English.[2]

Buchanans,	Dearc; braoileag,	The Bilberry.
	Also Darach	The Oak.
Camerons,	Dearc, Fitheach,	The Crowberry.
Campbells,	Garbhag ant sleibh,	Fir Club Moss.
Do.,	Roid,	Wild Myrtle.
Chisholms,	Raineach,	The Fern.
Colquhouns,	Braoileag nan con,	The Dogberry.
Cummings,	Lus mhic Cuiminn,	Cummin Plant.
Drummonds,	Lus na Macraidh,	Wild Thyme.
M'Farquhar or Ferguson, and Farquharsons,	Ros-grian,	Little Sunflower.
	Lus-nam-ban-sith,	Fox Glove.
Forbes & Mackays,	Bealaidh,	Broom.
Frasers,	Iubhar,	Yew.
Grants, M'Gregors, M'Kinnons, and M'Quarries,	Guithas,	The Scotch Fir.
Gordons,	Iadh shlat Eithann,	Ivy.
Grahams,	Buaidh craobh, na laibhreis,	Laurel, the Tree of Victory.
Hays,	Uile-ic,	Misletoe.
MacAulays and Macfarlanes,	Muileag	Cranberry.
MacDonalds, MacAlastairs, & MacNabs,	Fraoch,	Common Heath.
MacDougals,	Fraoch-dearg,	Bell Heath.

[1] Aodach suaich cantas, means the national costume or dress complete, with the badge, etc.

[2] Both Logan, Skene, etc., have been consulted to form this list.

Clan	Gaelic	English
Mackenzies and MacLeans,	Cuilioun,	Holly.
MacLauchlans,	Faochag,[1]	Lesser Periwinkle.
Do., Do.,	Uinnse,	The Mountain Ash.
Macleods, Gunns and Ross,	Aiteann,	Juniper.
MacNauchtans,	Lus Albanach,	The Trailing Azalia
M'Neills and Lamonts,	Luigh na tri beann,	Trefoil.
Mackays,	Luachair-bhog,	Bull Rushes.
MacPherson, M'Intosh, MacDuffs, MacBeans, Shaws, Farquharsons, M'Queens, & many others, as belonging to the Clanchattan,	Craobh aighban,	Boxwood. This is said to be the oldest badge.
Do., do.,	Lus na'n Craimsheag na Braoilaig,	Red Whortleberry.
Menzies's,	Fraoch na Meinearach,	The Menzies Heath
Munro's,	Garbhag au gleann	Common Club Moss.
Murrays and Sutherlands,	Bealaidh.	Broom.
Ogilvies,	Lus Boglus,	Evergreen Alkanet.
Oliphants,	Luachair,	The Bull Rush.
Robertsons,	Dluith Fraoch,	Fine Leaved Heath. This is said to be the oldest badge.
Do.,	Raineach,	The Fern.

[1] According to Logan.

Rose's,	Ròs-mairi fiad-haich,	Wild Rosemary.
Stewarts,	Darag,	The Oak; also Cluaran, the thistle, the present national badge. That of the Pictish kings was Rudh, rue, and which is joined with the thistle in the collar of the order.
Urquharts,	Lus-lethn't-samh-raidh,	Wallflower.

War Cries,

Or Rallying Words of some of the Clans.

Buchanan's, 'Clāre Innis,' an island in Loch Lomond.

Campbell's, 'Cruachan,' a well-known mountain in Argyleshire.

Farquharson's, 'Carn na Cuimhne,' 'the Cairn of Remembrance' in Strathdee.

Fraser's, anciently 'Mor-faigh,' or 'Get more;' later, Castle Downie.

Forbes's, 'Lonach,' a mountain in Strathdon.

Grant's, 'Craig Elachaidh,' or 'Craig Eagalach,' 'the Rock of Alarm,' Strathspey. A portion of the Grants called Clan Chirin have 'Craig Rabhach,' 'the Rock of Warning;' and add, Standsure.

Macdonald's, 'Fraoch eilean,' 'the Heathy Island.'

Macdonnel's, 'Craig an Fitheah,' 'the Raven's Rock.'

Macfarlane's, 'Loch Sloidh,' or 'Loch Shuagh,' the Loch of the People or Host.

MacGregor's, 'Ard-coille,' 'the High Wood.'

MacIntosh, 'Loch Moy' or 'Loch na Maoidh,' 'the Loch of Threatening.'—a lake near the seat of the Chieftain,

M'Kenzie's, 'Tulach Ard,' a mountain near Castle Donnan, the stronghold of the clan anciently.

M'Pherson's, 'Creag dubh Clann Chattan,' 'the Black Craig of the Clan Chattan.'

It is related of a 'creagh' or 'spoil,' made by three of the Macdonalds of Glenco into Strathspey, the Grant's country, that on their way back to Glenco, and while asleep, they were overtaken by the Grants, and two of the Macdonalds were bound, but the third one escaped. The Grants, after proceeding homeward a very short distance, sat down to partake of some refreshment. In the meanwhile the Macdonald who escaped had observed at a distance what had passed, and returned and released the other two; and the three then suddenly came upon and attacked the Grants, killed seven, and wounded sixteen of them, and rescued the cattle. The Grants were not only surprised, but of course had been taken at an immense disadvantage, by thinking themselves perfectly secure, and doubtless had likewise taken off their arms and accoutrements. The writer mentions this occurrence, because during the fight the Macdonalds used this war cry, which was of course a well known one among the Highlanders :—

'A mhic, a mhic, luathich do lamh,
Cruadhich do buille.'

Which means—

'My son, my son, quicken thy hand,
And harden thy blows.'

This Gaelic war cry must have been very ancient, and there is no reason to doubt but that it had been in use in most remote times among the Caledonian Picts, which is the reason it is here mentioned. The word 'son' is not to be taken literally; it is only a term of endearment, quite common in many languages.

The MacDonalds.

Of all the clans, that of the MacDonalds is by every rule of antiquity, power, and numbers, fully entitled to be spoken of before any other. Their founder was named in Gaelic Somhairle, and also by the Norsemen Somerled (very possibly a corruption of his Gaelic name), both words having the same meaning, namely, Samuel.[1] This hero, for such he undoubtedly was, did more to free his countrymen from the rule of the Danes and Norwegians than any other and, in consequence attained to a power greater than has fallen to the lot of any subject of present Scotland. Of course, his family

---

[1] See 'Gregory's Highlands and Isles, page 10.

being claimed by the grasping Irish writers as descended from their race, was to be expected; and according to others, he was a Norwegian by descent, and for which they have nothing to offer in proof of it but his name, Somerled, Samuel; but that name was as well known, and perhaps better, to the Gael of Alban than to the Norwegians; and Somerled's whole exertions were *against* the Norwegians, and to raise a Gaelic race in the isles, etc. As to the Irish claims, though they brought Somerled and his forefathers from a race of Irish kings,[1] yet this Irish descent has ever been rejected by the chieftains and heads of the name, as also by the whole clan themselves. His origin, as stated by Gregory, seems to be clearly Pictish. His father was named Gillebrede, a very common Pictish name, meaning the servant or follower of St Bride or Bridget, and his grandfather was called Gilladomnan, with quite a similar signification, as to the name of Adomnan. There is a most remarkable document, printed in the Iona Club Transactions,[2] of a Highland writer who flourished in the reign of Henry VIII., and

---

[1] This was the usual plan whenever any family rose to power, for the Irish Senachies, or the Irish Scots clergy, to hold out as an inducement that they came of Irish kings.

[2] Iona Club Transactions, page 23, and many following pages.

who gives a very long account of the Highlanders of Scotland, in which he declares the MacDonalds to be of '*the ancient stoke,*' that is the Pictish. Another authority is that of the chieftain of the Kintyre MacDonalds, who declared his race had been settled in Scotland in Pictish times, as he says they dated back from the time he wrote[1] (which was in 1615), a thousand years, or, as he expresses it, 'tenne hundred years.' The period assigned at which Somerled became first powerful, and called Thane or Lord of Argyle, is 1135, and that he married a daughter of the King of Man and the Isles, named Ragnhildis,[2] in 1140. By this marriage he gained great extent of territory, in addition to his own paternal and acquired possessions. Somerled died in 1164, and he left by this marriage four sons. 1st, Dugall, from whom descended the Lords of Lorn, a powerful family, but ended in heiresses, who married the ancestors of the family of the Earls of Argyll and Breadalbane; the male line is continued in the family of 'the M'Dugall,' designed of Dunolly; 2d, Angus, who had three sons, but they died without issue in 1210, and an only daughter, who married the Steward of Scotland; 3d, Olave, who left no issue; 4th,

---

[1] Skene's Highlanders, vol ii., page 37.
[2] Gregory's Highlands and Isles, page 12.

Reginald, and who had two sons,—Roderick, the eldest, whose race ended in an heiress, and Donald, the youngest, from whom come all the families of the name of Macdonald. Reginald's great inheritance consisted of the Island of Islay, Jura, and others, also Kintyre, and most part of Lorn.[1] After his elder brother's death, he was called 'Rex insularum,' or 'King of the Isles.' His second son Donald, above named, had a son called Angus Mor, who had two sons—1st, Alexander, whose race ended in an heiress called Amy de Insulis, who married John de Insulis, who was the male descendant and representative of the second son of Angus Mor, and was called Angus Og, that is, the younger Angus, his father being Angus mor. The marriage mentioned of John de Insulis with Amy (the heiress) was *his first*. By her he had three sons, the youngest alone, named Ranald, left issue. From him descend the Clan Ranald, and called of Glengarry, and Clan Ranald. For the latter there is a bar to the chieftainship, the ancestor of the family having been illegitimate. This has been very lately denied by the writer of the 'Scottish Nation,' and in *very*

---

[1] Thus he was proprietor of what had formed nearly *the whole* of Dalriada, called the country of the King of Scots (before he succeeded to the Pictish dominions), as the Map clearly shows.

positive terms; but had he searched the public records, he would have written differently. He says of the ancestor of the family of Clan Ranald being a natural son, the statement 'appears to be *founded on an assumption* that has been followed by almost every succeeding writer on the Highland clans, *without being once satisfactorily proved.*'[1]

That the writer of this book may not be included, there is the following in the Public Records as here given:—' Preceptum legitimationis Johannis MacAlestar de Casteltirrim, *bastardi filii naturalis* quondam Alexandri MacAllan de Casteltirrim in Communa forma. Apud Striviling xv. Januarii Anno predicto,'[2] (that is 1531, the last date named). For the above, see 'The Record of the Privy Seal,' vol. ix., and the back of folio 72.

It is very remarkable that the writer in 'The Scottish Nation,' in continuation, after the extract before given from his book, makes mention of some entries from the Privy Seal, but leaves out the above far more important one.

Lord Macdonald[3] unquestionably represents

---

[1] The Scottish Nation, Supplement, page 722.

[2] This legitimation the writer copied from, and compared with the entry in the Public Record, and vouches for its accuracy; and the reference to it is given herewith.

[3] Lord Macdonald is called by the Highlanders, '*Mac-Dhonuill na'n Eilean*,' or 'Macdonald of the Isles,' thus recognising his representation of the Lords of the Isles.

the Lords of the Isles, but they descended from the *second* marriage of John de Insulis, with Margaret, daughter of King Robert II.; therefore, as long as any male descendant of the first marriage exists, they are the representatives of Reginald, Rex insularum. And the Clanranald family being excluded for the reason proved above, the representation is therefore with the family of Glengarry. The representation of the senior branch, and thereby of Somerled, the founder, and of course, the chieftainship of the Clan Dugall or Dougal, is with 'the Macdugall,' styled of Dunolly, provided that they do not descend from Dugall de Insulis, a younger son of Roderick, eldest son of King Reginald. The son of the Dugall above named was Duncan, and it has been stated he died without issue; if so, the descent of the Clan Dugall or Dougal must be from the Duncan, son of Dugall, the *eldest* son of Somerled, and from whom descended the Lords of Lorn. Gregory, in his work, gives the representation as heir-male to Macdugall of Dunolly.[1]

[1] See 'Gregory's Highlands and Isles of Scotland,' page 420. Dunolly is an exceeding ancient place. It is mentioned in the Annals of Ireland as 'Dunollaig' in very remote times, and has appeared in a former part of this work under the year A.D. 734.

The MacLeans.

This numerous clan has been seated in the Island of Mull from the earliest date, that they appear as an independent clan, which was not till after the forfeiture of the Lord of the Isles in 1476,—of course they existed as a tribe long ere that, and under their own chiefs, who were the vassals of the Lords of the Isles; they are mentioned in the ancient MS. (called that of 1450),[1] printed in the Iona Club Transactions, page 359—this genealogy brings them from Gilleain (or Gille-eon), son of Icrath, etc., etc.. they are always called in Gaelic and also in the ancient public records, the Clan Gilleain and Macgilleain, the chieftainship of the whole clan is undoubtedly with the MacLean's of Dowart. Lachlan, the founder of that house, so far back as 1366, obtained a dispensation for marriage with Margaret, the daughter of John, first Lord of the Isles,[2] this proves a former relationship with the family of the Lord of the Isles, the

---

[1] The writer of the Scottish Nation says, the M'Lean's are *not* mentioned in the genealogy of the 1450 MS.—he could have seen that they were if he had read the Transactions of the Iona Club.

[2] A. Stewart's History of the Stewart's, page 447, and the late Professor Munch also in a Communication to the Society of Antiquaries of Scotland speaks of this dispensation which he had seen at the Vatican.

pretended Irish descent for this family is wholly fabulous, and was unknown prior to the seventeenth century;[1] but the entry already given from the ancient genealogy is the true descent. The family of Lochbuy were of contemporary antiquity with that of Dowart, and also very powerful, and descend from Hector, a brother of Lachlan, the founder of Dowart.[2] There was a third branch of the MacLean's, that of Coll, and descended of a common ancestor with the house of Dowart; and it has been disputed which brother was the eldest; Gregory is of opinion, from evidence he had seen, that the ancestor of the family of Coll was by a prior marriage, and was disinherited to make way for a half brother who was ancestor of Dowart.[3]

The M'Kenzies.

The descent of the chieftains of this clan is unquestionably pure Gaelic, and not Irish, as has been pretended—their descent in 1450 is thus given, 'the genealogy of the Clan Ken-

[1] Skene's Highlanders, vol. ii., page 205.
[2] We are told that the chiefs of this ancient Gaelic clan are (see the Scottish Nation, vol. iii., page 38) probably of Norman or of *Italian* origin ! ! and that the Gaelic MacGilleain 'may mean the great stranger, from *Magnus* great, and *alienus* a foreigner,'—a truly strange piece of information for Highlanders to believe in.
[3] See Gregory's Highlands and Isles, page 71, note.

neth—Murdoch son of Kenneth, son of John, son of Kenneth, son of Angus, son of Christian, son of Adam, son of Gilleoin-og, son of Gilleoin of the Aaird.'[1] The last named means Colin of the Aird; and the same ancient MS. makes him to be head of the ancient Ross tribe, and thus the M'Kenzies are identified with them. A clumsy invention of a charter for the lands of Kintail, in Ross-shire, was made out for this name, purporting to be dated in 1262; but in Robertson's Index of the Missing Charters, there is a Crown Charter of Confirmation by King David II., for the lands of Kintail, nearly a hundred years after that date, namely 1344, where a grant of Kintail and many other lands by William, Earl of Ross, to Reginald, son of Roderick de Insulis, dated in 1342,[2] is confirmed. The earliest date which has been assigned to the M'Kenzies acquiring Kintail (and that derived only from a private history of the name),[3] is 1463 from John, Earl of Ross; the M'Kenzies, after the forfeiture of the Lords of the Isles, became like all the other Western Clans, independent, and rose to great power, and became ennobled in the peerage as Earls of Sea-

[1] Iona Club Transactions, pages 54, 55.
[2] See Robertson's Index of the Missing Charters, page 100.
[3] Dr George M'Kenzie; MS. History of the M'Kenzies, quoted by Gregory, page 83.

forth. The M'Kenzies of Gerloch are the next oldest family. An ancient feud between this family and the M'Leods of Rasay was ended in 1611 by the death of the latter in a skirmish for the lands of Gerloch, after which the MacKenzies held Gerloch without further interruption.[1] The heir-male of the Earls of Seaforth is stated to be M'Kenzie of Allan Grange, and the M'Kenzies of Tarbat of the Earls of Cromarty.[2]

The Clanchattan.

This numerous clan includes the *M'Phersons*, *M'Intoshs*, *Shaws*, *Farquharsons*, *MacBeans*, and others. The seat of these tribes is the extensive districts of Badenoch and Lochaber[3]—the two great branches are the M'Intosh's and the M'Pherson's—their descent is given in the ancient genealogy of 1450, and deduced in the male line from Gillichatan, 'from whom came the Clan Chattan;' a far more intelligible account than that they descend from a thane of Fife, and named *M'Duff*. There has long existed a rivalry between the chiefs of the M'Intosh's and the M'Pherson's, without pronouncing positively, it does look from the proofs brought forward for the chief

---

[1] Gregory's Highlands and Isles, page 341.
[2] Gregory's Highlands and Isles, page 425.
[3] These are marked in the Map.

of the latter name, by Skene,[1] as affording a strong presumption in his favour, from the fact of M'Intosh calling himself *Captain* of the Clan, and also claiming a foreign origin—however, they are both extremely ancient, and the old genealogy (of 1450) makes them come of two brothers. This account may be therefore so far received, though it, in the usual style of the Senachies, traces these chieftains to one of the petty Irish Scots or Dalriad kings, but it would be a fiction to suppose the clan itself had any descent from *that quarter*. The chiefs of the M'Intosh's have certainly held their chiefship over that name, and many followers, for upwards of four hundred years; and Skene considers it was after the battle on the North Inch of Perth, in 1396, and fought between the M'Pherson's and M'Intosh's, that the latter assumed the title of Captain.[2] The M'Pherson's are called in Gaelic the 'Clan Mhurich,' (pronounced vuirich), and have for long been independent, and their chief is called Cluny M'Pherson, in English.

M'Leods.

They were divided into two tribes—the M'Leods of Lewis, called the tribe of Torquil,

---

[1] Skene's Highlanders, vol. ii., page 171 to 175.
[2] Skene, vol. ii., page 177.

and the M'Leods of Harris, the tribe of Tormod, both were very powerful and independent of each other, they are mentioned in an ancient Gaelic genealogy of 1550, and descend from the son of Leod, 'from whom the clan is named,'¹ and his pedigree goes very far back to an ancestor named 'Laigh the Strong.' In Robertson's Index of the Missing Charters, page 100, are two charters to Torquil, M'Leod's ancestor of the Harris branch, by King David II. probably dated in 1344, as that is the date to other charters in the same roll, for the lands of Glenelg, and for which he was to render to the king a ship with 26 oars—the other charter grants Tormod the lands of Assint. This branch (that of Harris) is considered from these and other facts to have been the senior tribe, and M'Leod of Lewis the oldest cadet,—of course both families held under the Lords of the Isles; and at the early part of King David the Second's reign, both the Islands of Lewis and Skye belonged to the Earl of Ross. After the forfeiture of the Lord of the Isles the MacLeod's assumed independence. The M'Leods of Harris had also large possessions in Skye. The rival family of Lewis became extinct, but the heir-male is M'Leod of Rasay.

¹ See the translation of this ancient MS. Iona Club Transactions, page 361.

The Camerons.

The earliest notice that has been discovered as to the original seat of the Camerons (also sometimes spelled Chameron) was Lochaber. They are, by the best authorities considered as of the same origin as the Clanchattan; and John Major, an old Scottish writer, quoted by Gregory,[1] declares they were of the same blood; they separated, however, in the end of the fourteenth century, probably directly after the battle on the North Inch of Perth. The Camerons were at first in three septs, the M'Martins of Letterfinlay, the Camerons of Strone, and the Camerons of Glenevis. The Lochiel family are considered to belong to the second named branch, and it is likely they declared themselves independent of the Clanchattan, and this they have ever since maintained. Donald Dubh led the clan at the battle of Harlaw in 1411. It would therefore appear that though the Letterfinlay branch were the eldest, and adhered to the Clanchattan, yet the Lochiel family obtained the following of the clan with them, from their declaration of independence. Thus they have been designed only *as captain* of the clan; and

---

[1] Gregory's Highlands and Isles, page 75; and John Major's History of Scotland, page 302.

from the above named Donald Dubh, the
Lochiel branch are called 'MacDhonuill Dubh,'
or, the son of dark or black Donald. In the
civil wars the Camerons were ever on the
side of the Stewarts; and in the 1745, their
chief was called 'the gentle Lochiel,' and was
the same who said to Prince Charles Stewart,
'Come weal, come woe, I'll follow thee.'

The M'Neills.

The clan Neill were divided into two
branches, the M'Neills of Giha or Taynish,
and M'Neill of Barra, being two islands off the
coast of Argyle. The oldest crown charter to
the name is for the Isle of Barra, and was a
confirmation of a charter from Alexander, Lord
of the Isles, dated 1427, and is granted to
Gilleonan, son of Roderick, son of Murchard,
the son of Neill. The Giha branch were, so
far back as 1472, keepers of Castle Swen, in
Knapdale, under the Lord of the Isles. The
M'Neills of Barra have, in recent times, been
always held as the chiefs.

The Macquarries.

This clan claims to be descended from one
of the Dalriad princes; and the ancient Gaelic
genealogy, assigns it to them also, thus,—
Cellach, son of Paul, son of Cellach of the

islands, son of Torquil, son of Cellach, son of Guaire,[1] son of Cormac, son of Oirlertaigh son of Murdoch, son of Ferchar, son of Bethach, son of Finlay, son of Fercharfada,[2] son of Feredoch, son of Fergus.[3] The first of the name yet known is John M'Quarrie of Ulva, and who died in 1473. The clan, of course, followed the Lord of the Isles. Afterwards they had possessions in Mull. Though a small clan, they are of very great antiquity.

The Clan Duffie, or Macfie's.

Their possessions were the Island of Colonsay. They are mentioned in the old MS. of 1450, Donald being the first name given in it, and he is witness to a charter of John, Earl of Ross, and Lord of the Isles, dated at the Earl's Castle of Dingwall, 12th April 1463;[4] this clan also is traced up to the Dalriad prince Fercharfada, or Ferchar the tall or long. The M'Duffies or Macfies are stated to have buried in Iona, and on the principal tomb-stone there is this inscription:—'Hic jacet Malcolumbus M'Duffie de Colonsay.' In 1623 Malcolm M'Fie was proprietor of Colonsay, and was

---

[1] It would appear it is from this ancestor the name was derived.

[2] This is the Dalriad prince.

[3] Iona, Club Transactions, page 57.

[4] See the Register of the Great Seal, Book vi. No. 17.

killed that year by the well-known Coll Macdonald, called Colkitto.

The M'Kinnons.

This is also a very ancient clan, and are named in the old genealogy of 1450, and traced to Ferchar Og, and includes Finlay, the son of Fingon, 'from whom sprung the clan Fingon,' and which they are always called in Gaelic. They appear as early as 1354 in an indenture between the Lord of the Isles and the Lord of Lorn.[1] They had property in Mull at that period, and likewise about the same time the lands of Strathordill in Skye, and which they retained till comparatively recent times.

The Macnabs.

They are named in the ancient Gaelic genealogy of 1450, and brought from Ferchar, son of Feredach. They certainly belong to the old Gaelic race, notwithstanding the author of 'The Scottish Nation' asserting[2] 'the Macnabs *are erroneously* held to belong to the old Celtic race.' For this contradiction he gives no authority whatever. They are called in Gaelic the Clan-an-Aba, or the descendants of the Abbot. This arises from their chief ances-

---

[1] See Gregory's Highlands and Isles, page 80.
[2] Vol. iii., page 50.

tor having been Abbot of Glendochart. He
flourished between 1150 and 1180. His lands
would of course be within Glendochart, and
these his descendants, the Macnabs, inherited.
It does not follow that being an Abbot he was
prevented from marriage, or holding property;
the contrary was common in these remote
times. The author of 'The Scottish Nation'
also, under the head of the name of Macnab,
tries to make his readers believe there never
was an Abbot of Glendochart. Had this writer
read the Public Records he would not have
made this very erroneous statement. In
Douglas's Baronage he will see the descent of
the Macnabs; and in the first volume of the
Scots Acts of Parliament, he will find there
was an Abbot of Glendochart, who was of such
consequence as to be joined with the Earl of
Atholl in the reign of King William the Lion,
in having the management and rule over
Argyleshire at that time, as the Royal authority was not then entrusted to any one belonging to that county. Another most imaginary
statement is made by the writer of 'The Scottish Nation,' at the same name (that of Macnab), when he would have the Highlanders of
Scotland believe that the name of Macnab is
'the great *Nab* or *Nob*,' may not improperly
be held to mean the district around or near

the mountain *now called* Benmore (or *great head*), which is conspicuous all along the glen of the Dochart, and very near its source.' It is hardly possible to conceive a greater stretch of imagination. This writer asserts here, that the mountain *is now called* Benmore, that is, the great or large mountain, from the Gaelic Beinn-mōr. Where did he discover it was ever called anything else? This great mountain is among the most majestic and highest in Britain, being very near 4000 feet in height. To carry out his extraordinary theory, as to the country being a Nab or Nob, he translates Benmore to signify 'great[1] head!!' The Macnabs having joined the Macdougals, Lords of Lorn, against King Robert Bruce, suffered

[1] This specimen of this writer's Gaelic and etymology of the Highland mountain Benmore cannot be surpassed, except by his still more extraordinary Gaelic teaching, which requires the Highlanders of Scotland to believe they are altogether unacquainted with the true meaning of their own language in the word 'Mac,' which this writer says is a contraction of the Latin word Magnus, and means 'great,' and not 'son,' to be noticed hereafter. Many who have only *a very limited knowledge* of the origin of Latin, fancy the Gaelic is partly derived from it. The direct contrary is *the fact*. The Celtic tribes who established themselves in Italy 500 years before Christ, gave a great foundation of Gaelic words in the Latin language. And in only 260 years before Christ, in the Latin inscription on the Columna, rostrata, at Rome, and in the ablative case, the Latin bears the exact Gaelic form of *Pucnandod*, and *Prædad*, instead of *Pugnando* and *Prædo*. See more particulars Highland Society Report on Ossian, Appendix, page 263.

the loss of the greater part of their Glendochart property. They retained a small portion called Bowaine or Bovan; but the Campbells coming in shortly upon them, they could not long resist the grasping policy of that clan. The descendant of their ancient chiefs is now said to be settled in Canada.

The MacLauchlans.

The genealogy of this clan is given with greater fulness in the ancient MS. history[1] of the clans, than any other, whereby it is most reasonably supposed *a MacLauchlan* wrote it. Whoever it was, he was an unscrupulous advocate for extolling the insignificant Irish Scots, or Dalriads, of Argyleshire, of which his *false* pedigree for King David I., is a clear testimony of one of his fabrications. He makes that monarch not to descend from Crinan,[2] Abbot

---

[1] The writer gives always the date 1450 to this MS. history, as part of it may have been written *prior* to that date, and also part subsequently, for the later date 1467 is affixed at one part, therefore 1450 appears a medium date.

[2] Dr Reeves, in his edition of the Life of Columba, by Adomnan, and in his table of the Petty Irish Scots or Dalriad kings, follows this, which was not to be expected from any one who was desirious of the *accuracy and impartiality* necessary in such an historical document respecting the descent of the Celtic kings of Scotland; but the far greater blame rests with the *fabricator* of this spurious descent, and who is a mere prejudiced inventor of tales to magnify the insignificant kings of the Scots in Argyleshire, and of which there are followers up *to the present day.*

of Dunkeld, but from certain other quite imaginary personages.

The genealogy of this clan is in the Gaelic MS., headed as that of 'Lachlan oig,' who is named in the account at a remote time, and states that his mother was 'Elizabeth, daughter of the Lord of Cowal;' and this corresponds with the tradition of this clan deriving their possessions in Cowal through an heiress of the Lamonts, and who have always been considered the ancient Lords of Cowall. After being followers of the Lords of the Isles, the MacLauchlans became dependent on the Campbells. Besides MacLaughlan of that ilk, there was a very ancient branch in Lochaber (which has been considered the original[1] seat of the clan). They were called of Cornanan.

The Lamonts.

This clan is unquestionably of great antiquity. Their genealogy is given in the ancient history of 1450, and begins with Murdoch, son of Ferchar, who appears to have died without issue, and been succeeded by another son of Ferchar, called Duncan, who was father of Malcolm, the father of Lauman, or Laumanus, as he is called in the Latin of the Book of Paisly, and from this Lauman, or Lamont,

[1] Skene, vol. ii., page 119.

the surname of the family came. The period of Lauman was 1295. In the same way as other smaller clans, the Lamonts suffered from the encroachments of the Campbells; but still a portion of their ancient territory remains with the name.[1] A very ancient family of the name were the Lamonts of Inverin.

The Robertsons.

They are called by the Highlanders the Clandonachy of Atholl (properly Clanndonnachadh), being descended of the family of de Atholia, which was the designation of the ancestors of the chieftains of the clan for four generations; and it distinctly points out that they must derive from the ancient Celtic Comes de Atholia, and, like other clans, they appear in independence upon the extinction of the Celtic Earls,[2] and were in possession of very large landed properties in the north and west

---

[1] In a charter by Stewart Ardgowan, dated at Dunoon in 1402, Celestine Lamont, son and heir of Robert Lamont, and also Christian Lamont, appear as witnesses.

[2] They first appear in history as a clan when they attacked the Lindsays in 1391 for depriving them of property in Glenesk, Aberdeenshire. They were opposed by Ogilvie, the sheriff of Angus, and many others. Ogilvie was slain, and numerous other Lowland barons, at the battle of Glascluny, in the Stormount; and again, when the clan were followed to their own country, at a second battle in Glenbrerachen, in Atholl, again the Clandonachy were victorious.

of Perthshire. For full proofs of the early extent of the possessions of this clan it will be found in a work on the Ancient Earldom of Atholl, written by the author of the present book. As to the descent of the chiefs of the clan, and which has been *always* allowed by themselves, it is from the Macdonalds,[1] and

[1] A MS. history, printed in the Iona Club Transactions, from pages 282 to 324, contains a great deal about the origin of the Robertsons of Atholl. It was written in the reign of King Charles, and derives the chiefs from Reginald, King of the Isles. Again, *so far back as* 1549, Dean Monro, in his History of the Macdonalds, makes the Robertsons to descend from them. It would therefore appear that Andrew de Atholia, the father of Duncan, had married the Atholl heiress, she being daughter of Ewan, son of Conan, son of Henry, the last Celtic Earl of Atholl; that Andrew was the same person called son of Gilmur, in the Register of the Priory of St Andrews, in 1269, and also 'Clerauch,' or clerk of Dull, and his father Gilmur, was in and before 1200 seneschal of the earldom of Atholl. And according to Buchanan of Auchmar, there was a Gilmur, son of Maoldonach, administrator of Dull, who may have been a son of Reginald. The lands of Apnadull were the most ancient of the possessions of the clan, the ancestors of whom had held their lands by crown charters at a remote period. The writer found in the Public Records, four years ago, a crown charter by James IV., dated in 1501, wherein it appears that Donald of Lude (the fifth laird), had been fined 100 merks, and till he paid it, the Crown took possession of the lands of Balnegrew, part of his barony, and conveyed them to Lord Ruthven, sheriff of Perthshire, who, the charter says, is to hold them as freely ('sicut dicti Donaldi libere tenuit') as said Donald of Lude and his predecessors had held them of us, '*and our predecessors*,'—clear proof the ancestors of the Robertsons held the lands of the crown for many past generations. — See the Great Seal Book 13, Number 408.

when it is considered, that, instead of being derived from another clan, but to have been descended from an original and independent stock, is always much preferred, it lends truth to the constant and invariable tradition of a Macdonald descent to the founder called Duncan de Atholia, whose father Andrew was also so designed. Duncan died in or about 1355. His sons were Robert de Atholia, ancestor of the Robertsons of Strowan; and Patrick de Atholia, ancestor of the Robertsons of Lude, who got a crown charter in 1448 for that barony. The next oldest families of the name were the Robertsons of Strathloch, Robertson of Fascally, etc., etc.

The Campbells.

This powerful clan rose upon the ruins of the Macdonalds, and their whole policy for ages was to supplant and ruin that race. The earliest spelling of the name is in the Ragman Rolls of 1292 to 1296—it is Cambel,[1] and

[1] The Norman, or Campo-Bello origin, is thereby a fiction, and the Gaelic cam-beul, or the crooked mouth, is so also, as that could not go to a son. The name is to be looked for as territorial; and the Gaelic for it being *Caimbal*, is very near *Caimgill*, or Caimgilla, a word for Cowal.—(See the Gaelic in the Iona Club Transactions, page 52.)—The M'Ivor Campbells were most undoubtedly in Cowal anciently. It does seem a very probable origin for the name always anciently spelled Cambel, therefore, possibly, some of the early ancestors belonged to Cowal.

Kambel, and *the first* crown charter of the Argyll or MacCailean Mor branch of the name for lands in Argyleshire was one by King Robert Bruce to his nephew Sir Colin, and whose name is also written '*Cambel*' therein—it is for the lands of Ardsonnachan,[1] and dated at Arbroath, 10th February 1316. In the ancient MS. history of 1550, the Campbells are traced to Colin Mor, etc., etc., and the ancestors of the M'Arthur Campbells likewise appear in it; this last family were undoubtedly independent, and must have been chieftains of the clan at the time that King David II. granted them a charter,[2]—'quod nulli subjiciter, pro terri nisi Regi,' that is, 'they were to be subject to no one for their lands except the king.' The whole of the Clan Campbell have also another designation in Gaelic, namely, the 'Clan Diarmad Na'n Tore,' or, 'Diarmad of the Wild Boar,' an ancient and celebrated Pictish hero, and on which account the Campbells all carry the boar's head for their crest. The Cailean Mor family rose to great power and influence,[3] and obliged many

---

[1] This is a well known ferry on Loch Awe, and is called Port Sonnachan.

[2] See Robertson's Index of the Missing Charters, page 68.

[3] In 1420 to 1423 the ancestor of this branch was designed *of Lochawe*, and became first Lord Campbell. He was

small clans to take the name of Campbell. Of this the family of the Clan Dougall Craignish were probably of the greatest antiquity and of property, but do not appear to have been of the same race. The extraordinary assertion put forward by the writer of 'The Scottish Nation,' at page 544, on the name of Campbell, where he attempts to teach the Highlanders of Scotland Gaelic, by informing them that 'Mac' does *not mean* a son, but is from the Latin Magnus, and that it means great,[1] is perfectly ludicrous. The word 'Mac' did, and always must, signify a son in Gaelic, and will continue to do so as *long as the language lasts*. This same writer at the same page says, the designation of the Duke of Argyll, 'Mac Cailean Mor,' is not the true Gaelic, 'Son of the great Colin,' but '*the great stranger chief.*' In charity, the Highlanders must suppose this writer mistook 'Mor' for 'Mac.' The Breadalbane family appear the next oldest to the family of Argyll.

reputed one of the most wealthy of the barons of Scotland—his income is stated to have been the very large sum for those times of 1500 merks.—See Rymer's Fœdera x., 302.

[1] Another most ridiculous etymology this writer gives at the same page on the Campbells, is that of 'Mucross,' in Fifeshire, which, he says, is '*the great cross*,' whereas it is from the Gaelic, 'muc,' a sow, and 'ros,' a promontory, and Mucross was anciently the name for St Andrews.

The Macnaughtans.

This clan appears in the old MS. history of 1450, and begins with Moris son of Malcolm, and traces them up to Fercher fada, a petty prince of the Irish Scots in Argyleshire, and goes still farther back to Lorn, a reputed son of Erc, and one of the leaders of the colony from Ireland in A.D. 506. The lands and possessions of the clan were within Lorn on Lochawe side. On the forfeiture of John, grandson of Alexander de Insulis, Alexander, then chief of the name, got a charter of his lands, dated in or about 1344, from King David II. See Robertson's Index of the Missing Charters, page 100. Again, in the reign of Robert III., Sir Colin Campbell of Lochow, that is, Lochawe, granted to Moris, or Maurice M'Naughtan, one of the succeeding chiefs, sundry lands in Over Lochow.—See the above-mentioned Index at page 149 for the charter, and in it, it is stated as to the lands 'which are evill to be copied.' In Douglas's Baronage a still more ancient grant by charter from King Alexander III. (reigned from 1249 to 1285) to Gilchrist MacNaughtan of the custody of the Castle and Island of Fraoch, in Lochawe. The name is derived from Nechtan or Nacthan, of which there were many Pictish kings so called. The best known was the King Nechtan who founded Abernethy. The name is also sometimes spelled M'Naughton.

The Clan Anrias or Ross's.

The Highlanders design the Ross's, Clan Anrias, altogether different from their name, as, in a precisely similar manner the Robertsons are called the Clandonachy. In the ancient genealogical history of 1450, they are also called 'Clann Anrias,' and it begins with ' Paul MacTire,' etc., to him William Earl of Ross granted a charter[1] for the lands of Gerloch in 1366. The name of Ross is exceedingly ancient, and the Celtic Earls can be traced back to the year 1160. In the time of the first Earl of Haddington, and whose MS. collections and notes on the Missing Charters are so valuable and copious,[2] among them the writer met with an entry in the reign of King Alexander II., dated in or about 1220, of a ' charter to Ferquhard Ross of the Earldom of Ross.' This Ferquhard or Ferchar was called *Mac an t-Sagart,*'

---

[1] See Iona Club Transactions, page 62.

[2] There is a most valuable MS. in the Advocates' Library, Edinburgh, in two large folio volumes in this Earl's hand writing of the Missing Charters. The writer has to acknowledge the kindness and courtesy of S. Halkett, Esq., the librarian, to have been enabled often to peruse this and the other MSS. containing so much valuable historical information.

or the priest's son, and has with reason been supposed to be the son of Gille-Anrias, from whom the clan took the name. From Lord Haddington's entry it is certain that crown charters of King Alexander II. were then in existence— now all unfortunately lost. The Ross's of Balnagowan were very ancient, springing from a William de Ross, son of Hugh de Ross, in King David II.'s reign. The Ross's had great feuds with the Mackays; and the Earls of Sutherland appear to have assisted in the strife. The ancient Ross's of Balnagowan failed, and by an unusual circumstance, the estate came by purchase to a family of the Ross's of Hawkhead of the same name only, last century. Ross of Pitcalnie is stated to represent the ancient Ross's of Balnagowan.

The Macfarlanes.

This name and clan are descended in a similar manner as the Robertsons, from the ancient Celtic Earls of the district to which they belonged, namely, from the old Earls of Lennox. The chiefs of the Macfarlanes were designed of that ilk, and also of Arrochar, where was their seat, at the head of Loch Long. The eminent and most zealous antiquarian, Walter Macfarlane of that ilk, has left numerous MSS. relating to his family and the Earls from whom they descend, namely, Gilchrist, a younger brother of Malduin, Earl of Lennox, and who is a witness to his charters. Duncan was his son, and got a confirmation of the family lands of Arrochar. This Duncan appears in the Ragman Roll of 1296. His grandson was Bartholomew, which, in Gaelic is Parlan, from whom the clan are designed; the letters P and F are easily convertible. Malcolm was the sixth laird, and who got from Duncan, Earl of Lennox, a charter for the lands of Arrochar, dated at the Earl's Castle of Inchmurrin in 1395. The direct male line of the ancient chiefs failed, and their estates forfeited. A member of a junior branch, named Andrew M'Farlane, by a marriage with the daughter of the Stewarts, Earls of Lennox, regained the old family property, but his son was only allowed the title of Captain of the Clan: this was in 1493—the Macfarlane's appear in both the Acts of Parliament given in this book, namely, in 1587 and 1594. The last descendant of the chiefs is said to have gone to America at the end of last century.

The Munros and M'Millans.

These are supposed to descend from the old Moray tribes. The ancient genealogy makes them come first from Ewen, son of Donald

dubh, and traces them to *Millan*, son of Neil.
The Munros are called in Gaelic the Clan roich,
their possessions were on the north side of the
Cromarty Firth—the chiefs title was Munro of
Fowlis. George Munro of Fowlis is stated to
have got a charter from the Earl of Sutherland
in the reign of Alexander II. 'Robert de
Monro' gets a charter from King Robert Bruce
in 1309 for lands in Strathspey, Robertson's
Index, page 2. The Munro's held their lands
of, and were followers of, the Earl of Ross. This
clan seem to have preserved their estates in the
civil wars by opposing the cause of the Stewart
family, the only Gaelic clan almost, except the
Campbells, who did so. The Munros of Fowlis were created Baronets in 1634. Munro of
Milton is considered the next oldest house.

The Macmillans have always held a tradition that they were proprietors of lands on
Loch Tay, namely, Lawers, but were driven
out by Chalmers of Lawers in the reign of King
David II. They seem then to have gone to
Knapdale, and held considerable property
therein: the Latin inscription on the tombstone of one of the chieftains of the Macmillans
has already been mentioned; one of them is
also stated to have had the lands named in his
charter for his estate cut on a rock in Gaelic,
at the extremity of his property.

The Macgregors.

The descent claimed by this clan is from Alpin, father of King Kenneth, who was the first Scot that succeeded to the throne of the Pictish dominions, but this tradition was unknown in 1450. The genealogy of that period, and printed in the Iona Transactions (pages 52, 53) does not mention Alpin as one of their ancestors. The title in Gaelic claimed by the M'Gregors is, 'S'rioghail mo dream'—'Royal is my race.' Sir Walter Scott says of them that they were 'famous for their misfortunes and the indomitable courage with which they maintained themselves as a clan.' It is certain the M'Gregors were the most persecuted and oppressed clan in all Scotland, when the cruel laws passed against them are considered, and the harsh severity with which they were enforced, the very name being even proscribed. They appear to have been in possession of the lands of Glenurchy towards the end of the thirteenth century, and that according to the Ragman Roll of 1296, John de Glenurchy appears. In the genealogy of the name, John is called son of Griogair, or Gregor. In the reign of King David II., the direct and oldest line of chiefs would appear to have ended in an heiress, who married, it is said, a

Campbell, a younger son of the house of Argyll; but the next heirs-male of the chiefs appear still to have remained in Glenurchy, though only as tenants to the Campbells, whose whole efforts were to grasp all the lands in their neighbourhood from this oppressed clan. John dubh M'Gregor of Glenstrae, and Gregor M'Gregor of Roro, in Glenlyon, were both younger brothers of the chief named Patrick, who had succeeded in 1390. His family became extinct, and the chieftainship came to the M'Gregors of Glenstrae, but they only had the title of captain of the clan. In 1502 the M'Gregors of Roro lost their lands by the Campbells of Glenurchy, though remaining as tenants, their descendants still survive. The battle of Glenfruin in 1603 was brought about by the Colquhoun's cruel severity in executing those barbarous laws against the M'Gregors, who retaliated, and under Alexander M'Gregor of Glenstrae, invaded their lands. Colquhoun of Luss assembled a force double the number of the M'Gregors, even getting the citizens of Dumbarton to join them, and marched so as to try and surprise the M'Gregors, but the result was a complete defeat of the vastly larger numbers by the M'Gregors. The vanquished Colquhouns then resorted to a device of appearing before the king at Stirling, with the pretended shirts of the slain, smeared with blood; this succeeded, and the M'Gregors were still further proscribed. In the end of last, and beginning of the present century, these laws were repealed, and Sir John Murray M'Gregor[1] of Lanrick, Bart., descended of the ancient stock, was acknowledged as chief by no less than 826 M'Gregors capable of bearing arms. Sir Malcolm M'Gregor, Bart., is his direct descendant and representative.

The Grants.

The origin of this clan, whose territory has always chiefly been in Strathspey, is purely Gaelic. As to the chiefs being of French descent it may be dismissed, as the clan themselves have always, from the most remote times, acknowledged they are of the same stock and race as the M'Gregors. The mention of the name of the chiefs is very ancient; it is never till the fifteenth century '*de* Grant,' but '*le* Grant,' and the earliest notice is '*dictus* Grant,' all which goes to disprove the French origin of the chiefs, for no one has yet pretended the clan or Grants themselves are Frenchmen. The name, it is not impossible, may be originally territorial, from possessing the lands of

---

[1] His grandfather was A.D.C. to Prince Charles Stewart at the battle of Prestonpans, in 1745.

Grantach, or Griantach, being from the Gaelic,
and meaning the field of the sun, as mentioned
by Dr John Macpherson and quoted by Logan,[1]
and certainly is not improbable, as the Grants
possessed these lands, and the people of the district
were of course the descendants of heathen
Gael, worshippers of the sun. Lawrence and
Robert 'dicti Graunt' appear in 1258. Lawrence
was Sheriff of Inverness in the reign of
Alexander III. (from 1249-1285), and by
marriage of the heiress of Glencharny, they
acquired many lands; indeed, the greater part
of Strathspey came to belong to the Grants.
In the year 1338 '*Patrick le Graunt*' is a witness
to a charter of Duncan, Earl of Fife, and
which is contained in No. 57 of the collection
of original charters belonging to the Advocates'
Library, Edinburgh (No. of the MS. 15-1-18.)
The first of the Grants of Freuchy was Duncan
le Grant. The writer met with a notice in the
Privy Seal regarding the Grants, which shows
how crown lands, etc., granted to chiefs increased
their clans by the inhabitants on them,
it is a letter or gift by the king to John Grant
of Freuchy, son of the above Duncan, for the

[1] The writer of the 'Scottish Nation' of course sneers at
this, as he does at every thing else connected with the Highlanders;
his own etymologies for the clans are more deserving
of the terms he employs about this derivation of the Grants
from Grantach by Dr M'Pherson and Logan.

lands of Ballyquharn, Erricht, and others in the county of Inverness, extending to a 12 merk lands; and it adds, that the king's whole lieges, inhabitants, and tenants on the whole said lands are for the future to obey the said John Grant of Freuchy, it is dated[1] at Stirling 4th August 1499, thus the whole inhabitants became part of the clan Grant. The chiefs not very long afterwards came to be called Grant of Grant, and rose to very considerable power, and by a marriage with a daughter of the Earls of Findlater and Seafield, the family succeeded to that last title and estates in 1811. The Grants of Tullochgorum are said to be the next oldest family.

The Mackays.

They are called in Gaelic the Siol Mhorgon, or clan Morgan. They are no doubt the descendants of the pure Gaelic race, who had retired to the interior of the country from the Norwegian invaders. Several of the ancient ancestors were called Y or I Mackay. They held extensive estates, and were designated of Strathnaver. In 1427 Angus dubh Mackay was leader of no less than 4000 men. In after times they had constant feuds with the Earls of Sutherland and Caithness. In the reign of

[1] See the Privy Seal, vol. iv., folio 17.

Charles I. the chief was raised to the peerage as Lord Reay in 1628. Their property now belongs to a different race and name. The Mackays of Scourie and Auchness are considered the next oldest.

Sutherlands.

This clan are descended apparently of the remnants of the Gaelic population that fled from the Norwegian invaders, and afterwards Hugh Freskin getting a grant of the territory of Sutherland from King William (said to be in 1197), was founder of the great and powerful Earls of Sutherland, which name the inhabitants of that earldom seem to have adopted.

The Menzies, Stewarts, Frasers, and Chisholms.

All the chieftains of these clans are not of original Gaelic descent, but the whole clan themselves are the descendants of a pure Gaelic race. The Menzies had very large possessions in the Highlands of Perthshire; so also the Stewarts of Atholl and Lorn, the former almost all descended of Duncan Stewart, a natural son of Alexander Earl of Buchan. The Lorn Stewarts also from a natural son of John Lord Lorn, the chief of the descendants of the above-named Duncan, were the Stewarts of Garth,

the Highland Clans.

Perthshire, and even the Rev. Dr Thomas MacLauchlan admits that in the Highlands of that county 'we have the purest Celtic blood in Scotland,'[1] therefore, whatever the chiefs of all the above clans were by original descent, it could not affect the Gaelic race of people that formed all these clans, they were as much the true and genuine descendants of the ancient Caledonian Gael as any other of the clans in Scotland.

[1] Book Dean of Lismore, page 34, note.

CHAPTER XII.

Historical and Antiquarian Descriptions of the Illustrations.

I. THE PASS OF KILLIECRANKIE, AND THE FIVE BENAGLOE'S.

THE Pass of Killiecrankie is one of the most picturesque in the Highlands of Scotland. The grandeur of its scenery has obtained for it the name of the Caledonian Thermopylæ. To appreciate it properly it should be traversed on foot by the old road. The one which appears in the illustration was made by Marshal Wade[1] about 1732. The steep sides of the Pass are beautifully covered with fine natural woods, and the river Garry passes at the bottom between two walls of rock, as partly can be seen to the right hand

[1] The old rhyme is—
' If you had seen this road *before* it was made,
You would take off your hat and bless General Wade.'

BENA...UE from the ...

of the illustration.[1] The historical importance of this Pass renders it highly interesting. So late as the civil war of last century, such was the striking and imposing grandeur of this defile, that a detachment of Hessian cavalry, which had been ordered to reinforce Sir Andrew Agnew, who held Blair Castle as a government garrison, that on reaching the entrance of the Pass, refused to proceed any further. The name given by the ancient Caledonian Gael also marks their idea of it, as the present English for it (Killiecrankie) is a corruption from the Gaelic 'Coille-Criothnachadh,'[2] or 'the wood of trembling,' the last word being expressive of their terror; and indeed the *first time* the human foot trod this Pass, feelings of awe would naturally arise. It is also possible a storm of thunder might have passed over at the period, which, to superstitious heathens, would further increase their sense of dread. This Pass likewise gives name to a battle gained in 1689 by the Highlanders under Viscount Dundee (whose spirited exertions kept up the cause of King James II.), and who, having obtained possession of Blair Castle, the English troops under General Mackay marched to dispossess him. Dundee also marched to meet

[1] A railroad now goes through the Pass.
[2] Pronounced somewhat like Creeonachie.

him, and a desperate conflict ensued, in which
the Highlanders gained a signal victory, but
their noble commander received a mortal
wound, and died the following day, and was
buried in his armour at the church of Blair
Atholl. To all who would wish to read details
of this event, will find it and much interesting
particulars in the well written book on Lord
Dundee by Mark Napier, Esq. In the illustration there is represented the five towering
summits of the five Benagloe's, to which, as to
one mountain, the name is applied. The word
is derived from the Gaelic, and is 'Beinn na-
ghlo,[1] nan-eag,' or 'the dim hazy mountain of
the pointed or indented tops,'—a most descriptive name of these mountains, as the illustration
fully exhibits.[2] The whole five have different
names: the one nearest, and near the centre,
is called the ' Beinn-liath,' or ' the Grey Mountain ;' the next to the right is ' Beinn Mhuil,'
which, probably from the drifting snow in
winter, got its name of 'the Mountain of the

[1] The Gaelic word 'gleo' is in some parts of the Highlands
used as to dimness of sight, but this Atholl name shows it was
applied anciently to objects where a haziness appeared frequently, as it does on these mountains in summer, and mist in
autumn and winter.

[2] The Gaelic 'Oran nam Beann,' or 'the 'Song of the
Mountains,' which is given in another part of this book. It
will at once be seen from this illustration that they well deserve
to be called ' of the pointed tops.'

Chaff;' the centre one the 'Beinn-beag,' or 'the Little Mountain,' which certainly it appears (though upwards of 2000 feet above the sea) among its lofty neighbours; the fourth is the next one, and is named 'Airgiod Beinn,' or the 'Silver Mountain,' from the greater part of its steep sides being covered with whitish stones, which, when the sun is shining on it, gives it a bright glittering appearance; the furthest off, and which is the highest of them all (being upwards of 3700 feet above the level of the sea), though from its distance does not look so, is called 'Carn-na-goibhre,' or 'the Mountain of the Goat.' These distinct members combine, forming a majestic group of mountains,[1] the base of which is not less than from thirty-five to forty miles in circumference, which will give the reader a better idea of the magnitude of this, 'the Mountain of the Pointed Tops.'

[1] To the east of the Benagloe mountain called Carngower in English, is the Royal Forest of Benchrombeg, where, in 1529, King James V. went to hunt with 'his Queen, and the Pope's Ambassador, and remained there three days, entertained by John Stewart, Earl of Atholl; and there was killed 'thirty score of hart and hynd, with other small beasts, as roe and roebuck.'—See Lindsay of Pitscottie, History of Scotland, page 225, Edition 1778. Again, in Queen Mary's time, she was in Atholl when there was a far greater hunting held, and an enormous number of deer, etc., were killed. This took place in 1562. Pennant gives an accurate description of it with authorities.—See Pennant, vol. ii., page 64.

They are all situated within the district of Atholl, Perthshire.

II. DUNKELD.

Dunkeld is unquestionably of most remote origin, and, from tradition, is held to have been the capital of the ancient Caledonian Gael; and the name certainly favours that opinion, it being, until very modern times, always written and called 'Duncalden.' The learned Rev. Isaac Taylor, a high authority on the etymologies of places, says, in his second edition in 1865, on 'Words and Places,'—it is his opinion that the word Caledonia appears to contain the root of the word 'Gael,'[1] although he also states the usual etymology is 'the Men of the Woods,' as has appeared in another part of this work. The idea of this writer seems perfectly feasible, and Duncalden would thereby be the corruption of the Gaelic, signifying the fort or stronghold of the Gael people; the letters g and c are interchangeable, therefore, instead of Gael we have Cael, the word becomes 'Dun-cael-daoine,'[2] or, 'the

[1] See the Rev. Isaac Taylor's work on 'Words and Places,' edition 1865, and page 65.

[2] The pronunciation of this would, in course of time, easily become in English 'Duncalden.'

stronghold of the Gael people,'—the etymology, therefore, seems quite possible upon the view of the author above named, besides its supposed antiquity in the remote ages of the Caledonians.

St Columba in or about A.D. 570, is stated to have resided, with his reputed nephew, Drost or Drostan, for some time at Dunkeld, and founded a Christian establishment there. Constantine, the king of the Picts, as has been already mentioned, founded, and, no doubt, largely endowed, a royal monastery at Dunkeld; in consequence of the ravages of the Danes on Iona, this was likely to have been in or soon after A.D. 806, as the whole clergy had been murdered by these Northmen, as the Annals of Ulster tell us. In them we are also told of the death of the Primate ('Primus Episcopus') of the Pictish kingdom and Abbot of Dunkeld, called Tuathal (and which name is now considered to be represented by Dugald), in the year A.D. 865, and in A.D. 873 the same Annals mention the death of the Bishop of Dunkeld (called in the original 'Princeps Duincaillden'). These notices seem clearly to establish that the Abbots of Dunkeld preceded St Andrews, as holding the Primacy. Crinan was the Abbot of Dunkeld between the years 1005 and 1034; and from his marriage with

Beatrice, eldest daughter of King Malcolm II., descended the last of Scotland's race of Celtic kings. The town of Dunkeld, according to the Pictish chronicle, was burnt in A.D. 905 by the Danes. In A.D. 965 the Mormaor of Atholl, and Duncan, the Abbot of Dunkeld, were killed at the battle of Duncrub.[1]

In the early part of the reign of David I., namely, in 1127, the monastery of Dunkeld was made the seat of a very large diocese, embracing not only all the greater part of Perthshire, but also the county of Argyle. The present cathedral[2] of Dunkeld was begun in 1318, but was not wholly completed till 1464. The bishops had palaces at the castle of Cluny, near Dunkeld, also at Perth and Edinburgh, and the See was endowed with most ample revenues. Dunkeld gave a higher tax to the Pope in 1270 to 1280 than almost any other diocese in Scotland; this appears

---

[1] See Robertson's Early Kings of Scotland, vol. i., page 77. The Rev. Dr Thomas M'Lauchlan in 'The Early Scottish Church,' page 311, most improperly calls the battle of Duncrub as it were the battle of Crieff, which are places twelve miles apart.

[2] The cathedral is very prominent in the illustration. The oldest tombstone remaining within it is that of Prince Alexander Stewart, Earl of Buchan, died in 1394, as stated in the inscription. The small church at the end of the bridge, on the left of the illustration, is that of the parish of Little Dunkeld.

from the MSS. in the Vatican[1] codex at Rome. In the Appendix will be found a very curious and ancient charter by a Bishop of Dunkeld, copied by the writer hereof from the original; it is of great antiquity, having been granted in or before 1165. The scenery about Dunkeld is very picturesque. The name of the hill immediately behind it is in Gaelic, 'Creig-bearn,' or, 'the notched or indented craig,' which is very descriptive, though this appearance is now obscured by the woods—in English, the name is corrupted into 'Craig-barns.' The handsome bridge, so prominent in the illustration, over the Tay,[2] was built by the assistance of a Government grant of £5000 in the year 1809. In the Dunkeld grounds of the Duke of Atholl are two of the first seven larch trees brought from the Tyrol in a portmanteau, by Menzies of Culdares, in 1738— they are the largest in Scotland. The five

---

[1] They were inspected by Professor Munch at Rome in 1861. They extend from the year 1270 to 1285, and the tax was collected by a person named Baiamundus. This document furnishes a copy of the sums of each parish of the diocese of Dunkeld—the largest contribution was from the parish of Dull, Perthshire.

[2] The view of this noble river, the Tay, given in the illustration, fully confirms its Gaelic most descriptive name, 'Tamh' (pronounced Tav), 'quietness,' or 'stillness,' in reference to its current. This is even more apparent above the bridge.

others were planted twenty-four hours sooner at Monzie, near Crieff, Perthshire. The two very fine trees to the left of the illustration, are directly behind the flower-garden of the Birnam Hotel, one of the handsomest country hotels in Britain.

It is impossible to close this short notice of Dunkeld without drawing attention to its being one of many strong proofs of the piety of the ancient Caledonian Pictish kings, and how favourably they contrast with the petty princes of the two tribes of the colony of Irish Scots in Argyleshire, whose chief efforts were the barbarous occupation of shedding each others blood, the only record left of them. No Christian churches endowed; nothing to evince they were anything but merely Christians in name, and who, as has been proved, after having existed near a hundred years as rulers in the district of Kintyre, allowed the population to remain in heathen ignorance, whereby arose the martyrdom of a Christian missionary; but to the liberal piety of the Pictish monarchs was due first, the gift of Iona, by King Brudhi, the metropolis of the ancient Pictish Church, and its greatest support. To King Nechtan is due the Christian institution of Abernethy,[1]

[1] Abernethy became a university, with a rector of the schools there.—See the Register Priory St Andrew, page 116.

and a Royal capital. The great King Angus M'Fergus founded and endowed St Andrews, and Dunkeld, as above explained, arose from the Christian zeal of the Pictish King Constantine I. All these are great proofs of the Christian piety of the Pictish monarchs. But of the petty barbarous kings of the Irish Scots in Argyleshire, their names come down, only known for strife and bloodshed with each other.

III. SHICHALLIEN.

From the North-East End of Loch Rannoch.

This noble mountain is situated in the valley of Rannoch, within the ancient earldom of Atholl, and Highlands of Perthshire; and though it occupies a central position in the Grampians, yet it appears insulated from the other mountains. Its Gaelic name has been already spoken of in this work, and by the native Highlanders who dwell within sight of it, it is called, ' Tichaillinn,' or 'the Maiden's Pap;' and a reference to the illustration will at once confirm how correct and applicable is this designation. Nothing could better describe its appearance. Some dogmatical Gaelic etymologists fancy they can give their far-fetched imaginations, as if alone to be received, but it is surely the native Highlanders who best know the names of their mountains. The height of Shichallien, according to General Roy, is 3281 feet above the level of the sea, whilst other authorities make it 3500 feet; but even that, we see, is considerably less than the Benagloe's already described.

Shichallien was last century selected by the then Astronomer-Royal, Dr Maskelyne, to make observations as to the power of high mountains attacting the pendulum, and which it was found considerably to affect. Loch Rannoch, which is partly represented, is about 12 miles long. It abounds in very large trout, some of the enormous weight of 20 lbs. have been caught. There are two islands at the upper or west end of the loch, one of which is artificial. In it the founder of the Clandonachy or Robertsons, named Duncan de Atholia, but in Gaelic called 'Donachadh[1] ramhar,' confined the Lord of Lorn, after a battle fought near at hand in 1338. Opposite to the foot of Shichallien is the place where King Robert Bruce and his Queen took refuge in 1306, in a small castle that then existed in a wood. There is a pool close by it, on the river, that comes out of Loch

---

[1] That is 'Duncan the stout or robust.' He acquired the whole of Rannoch, tradition says, by marriage; but his eldest son, Robert de Atholia, appears to have given up the north half of it, to remove the forfeiture of the clan in 1392, for what was called 'the raid of Angus,' by Scotch historians of that period.

Rannoch, called the Queen's Pool. There are very extensive and beautiful native pine woods on the south shore of Loch Rannoch, which for five centuries belonged to the Robertson's of Strowan. Their property extended to the boundary of Perthshire and Argyleshire, in a westerly direction, near 30 miles from Shichallien, and also went to the east of it near 20 miles. The situation whence the illustration is taken is near the place called Annat or Annatty, where there must, in remote times, have been a temple or altar, dedicated to the heathen goddess of victory of the Gael, called Annat. The distant mountain at the extreme left of the illustration is Benavrakie (Beinn-na-breac, or 'the spotted mountain'), and next it the hills overhanging the Pass of Killiecrankie. The few houses composing the village of Kinloch Rannoch is at the east end of the lake, where good accommodation is to be had; and the scenery of Rannoch well deserves a visit, though out of the line of fashionable tours. The Gaelic etymology for Rannoch is generally given as from the word 'Raineach,' or 'Ferns,' which used to grow in far greater abundance anciently, from the wet swampy nature of the land, than at the present time.

IV. BENAGLOE

From the South-West,[1] *at Bridge of Tilt.*

From the former view of Benagloe a stranger could not recognise the present one. There are only two of these mountains conspicuous, the Benlia and Benvoule. The woods that appear about the centre are at the entrance of the valley well known as Glentilt, formerly thickly inhabited by a fine race of Highlanders, but at the end of last century and beginning of the present it has been depopulated, and is now quite a desolate scene. The woods descending from the right to the left[2] and centre of the illustration, are on the margin of a romantic stream called the Fender, from the Gaelic 'Fionndur,' or 'Fingal's water.' On it are several fine cascades—the upper one of

---

[1] There are two illustrations of Benagloe from the south-west, but of course one description suits them both.

[2] There is here on the rocky sides of the Tilt, two most singular Gaelic names, the one that is on the east side for the lands, is called 'Tolldaoine' (corrupted in English into 'Toldunie) or 'the hole of the men or people;' and on the west side of the Tilt, opposite, are the lands of 'Tolldamh,' or 'the hole of the oxen.' The tradition of their origin is, that the people of the first named place had offended the Druids, who, by their magic arts caused the earth to open, but that the oxen alone came out. The early Christians also claimed the names for ploughing on Good Friday. The places still go by these names.

which is a very beautiful specimen.[1] This stream has its source between the Benlia, the nearest of the Benagloes in the illustration, and the further one, called the Benvoule. The river Garry is here represented in the foreground, being the same as goes through the Pass of Killiecrankie. It has its name from the impetuosity of its course, being called in Gaelic 'Gath-ruith' (pronounced Gā-ruee) 'the swift running,' or 'running like a dart.' It rises near twenty miles off from Loch Garry, and its first progress gives its name to a small valley called Glengarry, before it enters the vale of Atholl; there is a similar named river and glen in Inverness-shire. The small top and most remote hill represented to the left of Benvoule in the illustration, is called 'Carntorc,' or 'the wild boar's mountain,' which is about nine miles up the valley of Glentilt. The Tilt water, which gives it the name, is from the Gaelic 'Teth-allt' (pronounced Tayalt) or 'the warm stream.' Up Glentilt the scenery is very romantic, and will be found highly deserving of being visited.

It now only remains to speak of the fore-

[1] About a mile due south of this fall, there is a well which is named 'Tobar-bean-Fionn,' that is, 'the well of Fingal's wife.' The topography of this neighbourhood, in the various streams, etc., would lead to the inference that it had been a place of residence of the ancient Fingalians.

ground, which is taken (by permission) from a very interesting photograph, done by Mr Wilson, photographer, Aberdeen. The tower appearing over the wood is that of the Free Church; beyond, to the left, is a small Episcopal chapel, called after an ancient saint, Kilmaveonog in English, possibly a corruption of the Gaelic Eogan-ōg, or young Ewen. The chapel was rebuilt in the end of last century[1] on the same spot as a former one, which, in the year 1745 was burned by the Campbells of Lord Loudon's regiment. To the right, up among the woods, is the mansion-house of Lude,[2] built by the present proprietor, J. P. M'Inroy, Esq. Upon the same spot as the old one, which has been already spoken of as being on the exact site of Balnagrew (from the Gaelic, signifying the Druids' town, as before explained), and which name it had continued to bear through a long course of ages till last century. To the right of Lude, in a straight line, about

[1] By James Robertson of Lude. To show how the intolerance of former times is passing away, it may be mentioned that a belfrey was not then allowed, and even early in the present century, when General Robertson, the son and successor of the above, placed a bell and belfrey on this place of Divine worship, it was debated in the Dunkeld Presbytery whether some notice ought not be taken of it.

[2] In ancient writings corrupted into Leoad, derived from the Gaelic 'Leathad,' or 'the sloping grounds,' situated in Glenfender, three miles off.

half a mile off, is the place before mentioned, and called 'Dochann-le-las,'[1] or 'the agony of the flame of fire,' from the Druidical ordeal of fire, to discover the guilt or innocence of persons in doubtful cases; directly to the right, also adjoining to Lude (the Druids' town), is the Druids' strath, or 'Srath-gruidh,' corrupted in English into Strathgroye and Strathgroy.

V. BENLEDI.
From the South side of the River Teith.

The scenery in every direction of Benledi is highly picturesque. It is surrounded by lakes, mountains, etc., that add much to all to be seen in its neighbourhood. The author hereof wrote the following as to Benledi, and which appears in another part of this book:—'In the southwest of Perthshire, and in the parish of Callander, there is situated a very picturesque mountain called Benledi; it has a very fine appearance, particularly when viewed from Stirling Castle; also from the south side of the river Teith, from which position the illustration

---

[1] This place is mentioned in the Exchequer Rolls so far back as the year 1450, when Robert Duncanson of Strowan gave in his account for the king's taxes for the Earldom of Atholl, it is therein corrupted by the spelling of the Lowland scribes into 'Dauchinlelus.'—See this account in the Chamberlain Rolls, 4to edition, vol. iii., page 509.

of it is given. Loch Lubnaig is due north, and Loch Venacher due south of it. The name of Benledi is a very slight alteration from its Gaelic name, 'Beinn-le-dia, or 'the hill of God,' that is, the hill belonging to the god Bel or Baal, who thus had this mountain specially dedicated to him; and, according to the universal tradition of the country, it was here on Beltane-day that the whole population of the adjacent country assembled to worship this deity, and receive from their Druids, that is, their magi or magicians, the 'teine eigin,' or 'need fire,' or 'fire of exigency,' the heathen custom being throughout the whole neighbourhood to put out their fires and have them re-lighted from the sacred fire of the god Bel, on his day (the Beltane-[1] day), namely, the 1st May, being also considered the first day of summer, when this solemn meeting took place on the top of this mountain. Any one who has ever been at the summit of Benledi must have noticed how very different it is there to almost every other Highland hill; instead of a mere heap of bare stones or rocks, it is remarkably verdant, having been evidently cleared of stones and smoothed by the hand of man, which is fully accounted for by its Gaelic name, and which, though given undoubt—

[1] Beltane, as already shown, is from the Gaelic 'Bealtiene,' or 'Bel's fire.'

edly more than 2000 years ago, it is still the language of the Highlanders of Scotland at this hour. How distinctly therefore does this Gaelic name, Beinn-le-dia, or as in English, Benledi, prove the language of the Picts and present Gael to be identical, and nothing but this identity could have preserved the name through such an immense space of time, and that although the inhabitants have ceased to be heathen for 1300 years. Another corroboration in regard to the heathen sanctity of this mountain is, that on its north side there is a hollow called in Gaelic, ' Coire am faidh,' or, ' the prophets dell,'—this name also must be heathen, as none in Christian times could pretend to foretell future events, but it is clearly consistent with the heathen name of the mountain. The little eminence which appears in the distance to the right of the foreground of the illustration, is called in Gaelic, ' Dunmòr,' or ' the large fort,' and which is confirmed by the remains of an entrenchment, and a hill fort on its summit; where the rocky masses are seen to the right, is the well known Pass of Lenney. The enclosure in front of these is an old burial-place of the Buchannans, who formerly held large possessions in this neighbourhood. The Pass of Lenney, before named, is situated due east of Benledi; and from it, and going north, Loch

Lubnaig is soon reached, and which combines both beauty and grandeur. The chief sources of the water supply of Loch Lubnaig are from two smaller lochs, called Lochs Doin and Voil. In the Gaelic names of the waters in this district, we have two most striking instances of descriptive truth. The name of the river that flows from Loch Voil to Loch Lubnaig is in English, the Balvac, very near the exact pronunciation of the original from the Gaelic it is derived from, namely, 'Balbhachd,' or 'the silent or dumb river,' its current being very slow and tranquil; but when it issues from Loch Lubnaig, it is called 'Garbh-uisge,' or 'the rough water,' from the impetuosity of its course—these names given in the remote ages of the Pictish Gael, are still the language of the Highlanders of Scotland, proving they now speak the very same Gaelic as did the Caledonians.

VI. BEN LOMOND AND LOCH LOMOND.

From Glenfalloch.

This noble mountain and loch has been the most frequented of any other in the Highlands of Scotland during the present century. In the illustration there is presented to the reader the steep and rocky side of the summit of Ben Lomond, and which is its grandest and most distinguishing feature. The loch, and the lower end of Glenfalloch, are highly picturesque, the upper end of the loch is on both sides clothed with oak coppice, and gives much beauty to this illustration of the country of the Gael. The name of both the mountain and loch is said to be from an ancient Caledonian hero named Laomain, and now corrupted into Lomond.[1] Glenfalloch is a slight corruption from the original ancient Gaelic name 'Glean-falach,'[2] or 'the valley of concealment,' arising most probably from its being the place of assembly of the armies of the ancient Caledonian Picts, and from its hiding them from the view of their enemies, the Romans or the Britons, who latterly held part of the country bordering along Loch Lomond. The rugged mountain to the right of the illustration is called in English, Ben Vorlich; there are in Scotland two mountains of this name, the other is in Perthshire, at the south-west end of Loch Earn, they are both of the same meaning, from the Gaelic 'Bein-mhor-loch,' which signifies 'the great mountain of the loch.' The letters mh, in the original language, are pronounced the same as

[1] See Book, Dean of Lismore, English Part, note 3, page 134; Gaelic part, page 103.
[2] The Gaelic and its Saxon corruption are almost identical in pronunciation.

v; the Benvorlich of Loch Lomond is considered by many to be higher than Ben Lomond, and certainly the name given it by the primitive Gael strongly favours that view. Loch Lomond is twenty-six miles long, and at some places six miles broad; in it are fine trout, and salmon have also been known on its southern shore. The water of Falloch glides gently into the loch, and its margin is adorned with some fine old trees at the bottom of the glen.

VII. CARNGORM.

From the North Side of Loch-an-eilean.

This is from its well-known chrystals, one of the most celebrated mountains in the British empire; and the scenery here given of it, conjoined with the Loch-an-eilean[1] and ancient ruined castle, is of great beauty; but this view of it is seldom seen from its secluded situation. The boundaries of the counties of Inverness and Banff pass over the top of Carngorm, or 'the blue mountain.'[2] Aberdeenshire also closely adjoins it. This mountain is of great height, being upwards of 4000 feet above the level of the sea. There is a hollow on it, which,

---

[1] Loch-an-eilean means, the Loch of the island.

[2] All the Highland mountains have a blue appearance at a distance. This one, from its magnitude, would in this respect be more prominent than the others near it, whereby the ancient Caledonians were likely induced thus to denominate it.

although it has a southern exposure, is never without snow. Directly to the north is the valley of the Spey, called Strathspey; and on the further side of it rise the range called 'Monadh Liath,' or 'the grey mountains.' Persons desirous to examine the beauties of this neighbourhood can find eligible accommodation at Aviemore. The district of Rothiemurchus, close to it, covers a space of sixteen miles square of fine native pine woods. There is a loch near the illustration called Loch Morlich, which seems, from its far greater extent to be a corruption of Mòr-loch, or 'the large loch.' The mountain of Carngorm is part of the old Gordon estates, and belongs now to the Duke of Richmond.

Explanatory Remarks on the Map.

The Map is constructed and intended to assist the reader in being able to learn the exact spot of the different places that are mentioned in this work, and from even the most remote period, namely, that of the Romans. the site of their first camps is laid down, namely, Lindum or Ardoch, Ierna or Strageth, and Victoria at Dalginross,—all in Perthshire. They can still be identified, particularly the first, Ardoch, which is probably the most perfect Roman camp in Britain. These three date so far back as A.D. 80. The position of the great Caledonian battle of 'Mons Grampus,' in A.D. 84, is laid down, also the Roman walls, and the possessions of the Picts south of the Forth, by which name the Caledonians came to be called in A.D. 296, is marked, as also the line of that highly curious structure 'the Picts' work,' or 'Catrail.' The ancient names have been preserved, as it is considered they should bear that of the period to which the Map refers, namely, from A.D. 80 to 1020, at which last date. the country before known as the land of Alban (and is so called at this hour by the Highlanders), then began to be named by the Latin chronicle writers, Scotia and Scotland; and the same people who had previously borne the arbitrary name of Picts (of which the native Gael knew nothing in their own language as a designation), that of Scots came to be substituted for it, though this is *even now* unknown in the Highlander's language as the true name. The country of the Irish Scots, or Dalriada, as it was called, is marked, and its boundary with the Caledonian Picts clearly defined. The occupation of a part of the Isle of Mull by the Irish Scots rests on but very slight authority. As to the Island of Iona, Bede tells us,[1] ' sed donatione *Pictorum* qui illas Britanniæ *plagas incolunt* jamdudum monachis Scottorum perceperunt,' thus showing not only that Iona[2] was in the Pictish territories in the days of St Columba, but that they (the Picts)

[1] Bede lib., cap. iii.
[2] With regard to Iona being ' *unoccupied* and *unclaimed*,' till the time of Columba, in the end of the sixth century, as stated at page 436, by Dr Reeves in his edition of Adomnan, it may be justly said to be an *impossibility*. Iona has been proved herein to have been the island of the Druids, who were, according to Grant (see his book on the Gael, page 174), cultivators of the soil, as we know the monks in after times were. At page 387 of the above work by Dr Reeves, he has a note as to Fergus M'Erc and his brothers being buried at Iona. What could induce these *Christian* Scots to be buried at a very remote *desert* island ? or to go for that purpose to the territories of the *heathen* Picts, so distant from their Kintyre residence, it is evident will be a hard task to explain, by those who believe these fables.

actually possessed and inhabited the neighbouring districts of Britain in his own time, that is, in the eighth century. A testimony so direct and positive as this to the existence of a fact in his own life time, and at the very time he is writing, it is impossible, by any reasoning or criticism, to overcome."[1] The monks 'of the Scots,' mentioned in the above extract from Bede, were monks from Ireland, and not of the colony of Scots in Argyleshire. Some of the names of the firths, given by the Danes and other Norsemen, are inserted. The occupation that is represented by the Map is only a century earlier than King David I., in whose reign, however, an immense change in the designations of places, through the bishopricks, etc., founded by him took place. Several of the ancient names have been inserted on the authority of the Irish Annuals. It is hoped by the writer hereof that the Map will be found of much use to the reader.

[1] Skene's Highlanders, vol. i., page 32.

Conclusion.

IT is confidently expected and believed, that a deliberate and careful perusal of all the proofs and authorities given in the preceding pages, and which having been maturely weighed and considered, the reader will be convinced and satisfied that the following points have been fully proved and established:—

1st. That the Caledonians and Picts were the same people.

2d. That the Scots first named in A.D. 360 were natives of Ireland, and that it alone was called Scòtia at and after that period.

3d. That there was no colony or permanent settlement of Irish Scots in Argyleshire, till the sixth century, in A.D. 506.

4th. That the proper date of Christianity taking place in North Britain was the beginning of the fifth century; that Palladius being sent in A.D. 431 to any Christian Scots in Argyleshire or any part of North Britain is a fiction; and that Columba was the most successful Christian missionary, and that almost all the inhabitants of Kintyre in the end of the sixth century were heathen.

5th. That the Irish Scots or Dalriads, were conquered by Angus M'Fergus, king of the Pictish Gael, in the eighth century.

6th. That the pretended conquest by the colony of Irish Scots in Argyleshire over the Pictish kingdom and people in A.D. 843, is a fable and a deceit.

7th. That the language of the people (called Picts in A.D. 843, and afterwards Scots), that inhabited all Scotland north of the two Firths, was the Gaelic of the present Highlanders, and that the whole topography of the Highlands is also in their language, and therefore the language of the Picts was the same as the Highlanders of this day.

8th. That the national dress, poetry, etc., descended to the present Highlanders from the Picts, who are their real ancestors.

9th. That the Irish Scots or Dalriads, and their descendants, never quitted their country, but remained there, and they are properly the *only Scots* in Scotland.

10th. That the appellation of Scots was a new name applied to the Picts by foreign nations, and unknown to themselves, as it still is, to their descendants the present Highlanders.

Conclusion.

11th. That the country was not designed Scotland earlier than 1020, but is still called Alban by the Gael or Highlanders.

12th. That the accession of Kenneth Mac-Alpin to the Pictish throne was a peaceable one, and in all respects precisely the same as King James of Scotland to the throne of England.

Appendix.

APPENDIX.

THE following is a list of the Celtic kings that have reigned in the country of the Gael of Alban from A.D. 554 to 1285, after which they became extinct in the male line, and were succeeded by their nearest heirs in the female line. There were kings long prior to King Brudhi, who is the first named in this book, which is the reason of not going further back; the number attached always in all the chronicles to his name is the 48th monarch. Tradition makes Cruithne, Cruden, or Cathluan, the first monarch of the Caledonians, and that he died in A.D. 25. However that may be, or also as to his seven sons obtaining the seven provinces[1] and the tribes that inhabited each of them, we have the express authority of Tacitus[2] that in A.D. 84 the native tribes of Caledonia were united under one king, named Galdi or Galgacus.

---

[1] The notices of these seven provinces will be found in Robertson's 'Early Kings,' vol. i., pages 32, 33. Also in the Pictish Chronicles, in Appendix, vol. ii. of T. Innes' 'Critical Essay.'

[2] Tacitus 'Life of Agricola,' chapter 28.

360 Appendix.

Celtic Kings of the Gael of Alban.
A.D. 554 TO 1285.

Name.	Reign begun. A.D.	Died. A.D.	
48 Brudhi M'Melchon,	554		584
49 Gartnay MacDonald,	584		599
50 Nechtan Hy Firb,	599		620
51 Kenneth MacLachtren,	620		631
52 Gartnay MacFoith,	631		635
53 Brudhi MacFoith,	635		641
54 Talorcan MacFoith,	641		653
55 Talorcan MacEanfred,	653		657
56 Gartnay MacDonald,	657		663
57 Drost MacDonald,	663		672
58 Brudhi MacBili,	672		693
59 Gharan MacEnfisedech.	693		697
60 Brudhi MacDerili,	697		706
61 Nechtan MacDrost,	706	Resigned	724
62 Drost,	724	Expelled	726
63 Alpin,	726		728
64 Nechtan MacDerili,	728		729
65 Angus MacFergus,	729		761
66 Brudhi MacFergus,	761		763
67 Kenneth MacFeredach,	763		775
68 Alpin MacFeredach,	775		778
69 Talorcan MacAngus,	778		782
70 Drost M'Talorgan,	782		784
71 Conal MacTaidge,	784	Expelled	789
72 Constantine MacFergus,	789		820
73 Angus MacFergus,	820		834
74 Drost MacConstantine,	834		836

Appendix. 361

	Name.	Reign began.	Died.
75	Euganan MacAngus,	836	839
76	Feredach MacBargoit,	839	842
77	Brudhi MacBargoit,	842	843

UNION OF PICTS AND SCOTS.

	Name	Reign began	Died
78	Kenneth MacAlpin,	843	859
79	Donald MacAlpin,	859	863
80	Constantine II.,	863	877
81	Aodh or Hugh MacKenneth,	877	878
82	Cyric, Eocha, } Jointly,	878	896
83	Donald II.,	896	900
84	Constantine III.,	900	943
85	Malcolm I.,	943	954
86	Indulf,	954	962
87	Duff,	962	967
88	Colin,	967	971
89	Kenneth II.,	971	995
90	Constantine IV.,	995	997
91	Kenneth III.,	997	1005
92	Malcolm II., whose daughter Beatrice married Crinan, Abbot Dunkeld,	1005	1034
93	Duncan I.,	1034	1040
94	Macbeth,	1040	1058
95	Malcolm III.,	1058	1093
96	Duncan II.,	1093	1094
97	Donald III.,	1094	1097
98	Edgar,	1097	1107
99	Alexander I.,	1107	1142
100	David I.,	1124	1153
101	Malcolm IV.	1153	1165

Name.	Reign began.	Died.
102 William the Lion,	1165	1214
103 Alexander II.,	1214	1249
104 Alexander III., the last Celtic King; his granddaughter was	1249	1285
105 Margaret.	1285	1290

The Throne of Scotland contested by the descendants of the Celtic kings in the female line, and the Crown came to the eldest female's heirs.

106 John Baliol,	1292		1296
An interegnum of ten years.			
107 Robert Bruce, called Robert I.,	1306		1329
108 David II., son of the above,	1329		1370
109 Robert II., grandson of Robert Bruce,	1370		1390
110 Robert III.,	1390		1406
111 James I.,	1406		1436
112 James II.,	1436		1460
113 James III.,	1460		1488
114 James IV.,	1488		1513
115 James V.,	1513		1542
116 Mary, daughter of James V.	1542	Deposed	1567
117 James VI., son of Mary,	1567		
Do., as I. of England,	1603		1625
Union of England and Scotland.			
118 Charles I.,	1625	Beheaded	1648
119 Charles II.,	1648		1685
120 James II.,	1685	Abdicated	1688

Appendix.

	Name.	Reign began.	Died.
121	William and Mary, daughter of James II.,	1688	1702
122	Anne, second daughter of James II.,	1702	1714
123	George I.,	1714	1727
124	George II.,	1727	1760
125	George III., grandson of above,	1760	1820
126	George IV.,	1820	1830
127	William IV., brother of above,	1830	1837
128	Victoria I., niece of the above king, being now our monarch, and the 80th from the king of the Gael of Alban, whose reign began A.D. 554,	1837	

Alban Duan.

This very ancient poem has been already mentioned and commented on, and for the reasons there stated, its interpolation of Pictish kings among the petty rulers of the Dalriads, it cannot be received as correct in that respect; but it is an evidence and proof of the very highest value, that when it was composed the pretended conquest by the colony of Irish Scots over the Pictish kingdom was wholly unknown, and thereby refutes it, as such an achievement by them or their leader Kenneth M'Alpin would *never* have been suppressed by the bard who composed it, and whose whole duty was to magnify and extol the deeds of the ancestors of the kings' predecessors, *never to diminish them*.

THE GAELIC POEM,

WRITTEN CIRCITER A.D. 1057, AND

GAELIC.

A Eolcha Albain uile,
A shluagh feta, folt buidhe
Cia ceud ghabhail an eol duibh,
Ro ghabhustar Alban bhruigh.

Albanus do ghabh ria n shlogh,
Mac sein oirdhairc Isiocoin,
Brathair do Britus gan brath,
O raitir Alba eathrach.

Ro ionnarb a bhrathair Bras
Britus tar muir, n Iocht namhnas,
Ro ghabh Briotus Albain ain,
Go roinn Fiaghnach Fothudain.

Fada iar m Britus mblaith, mbil,
Ro ghabhsad clanna Neimhidh
Earglan iar ttocht as a loing,
Do Aithle togla Tuir Conaing.

Cruithnigh ros ghabhsad iar ttain,
Iar ttiachtain a h Eirinn Mhuighe,
X Righ tri fichid Righ rau
Ghabhsad dhiobh an Cruitheu chlar.

Appendix.

'A EOLCHA ALBAIN UILE,'

EDITED FROM THE CODEX STOWENSIS, NO. XLI.

TRANSLATION.

Ye learned of all Alban,
Ye wise, yellow-haired race,
Learn who first
Acquired the districts of Alban.

Albanus acquired them with his race,
The illustrious son of Isiocon,
Brother to Britus without treachery:
From him Alban of ships takes its name.

Britus expelled his intrepid brother
Over the sea, called Iocht:
Britus acquired illustrious Alban
To the territories of the Fiaghnach Fothudain.

Long after the pleasant, good Britus,
The race of Neimhidh, after they had come
From their ships, acquired Earglan,
Till after the building of the Tower Conaing

The Cruithne acquired the western region
After they had come from the plains of Erin:
Seventy noble kings of them
Acquired the Cruithen plains.

Cathluan an ced Righ dhiobh sin,
Aisneidhfiod dhaoibh go cumair,
Rob e an Righ deidhenach dhiobh
An cur calma Cusantin.

Clanna Eathach in a n diaigh,
Ghabhsad Albain iar n ardghliaidh,
Clanna Conaire na caoimh fhir,
Toghaidhe na tren Ghaoidhil.

Tri mic Erc mc Eathach ait,
Triar fuair beannacht Padraice,
Ghabhsad Albain, Ard n gus,
Loarn, Fergus, is Aonghus.

Deich m bliauna Loairn, leir bladh,
Illlaithios oirir Albain,
Tareis Loairn, Sgel go n gus,
Seacht m blianna fichiot, Fergus,

Domhangort mac Fergusa Aird
Airemh cuig m bliadhna m bioth ghairg,
A ceathair ficheat, gan troid,
Do Chomhghall, mc Domhanghairt.

Dha bhliadhna conaing, gan tar,
Tareis Chomhghaill do Ghobhrain,
Tri bliadhna fa chuig, gan roinn,
Ba ri Conall mc Comhghaill,

Ceithre bliadhno fichiod thall,
Ba ri Aedhan na n orlann.

Cathluan[1] was the first king of them,
(I relate it to you explicitly):
This was the last king of them,
The daring hero Cusantin.

The race of Eathach after them
Acquired Alban by great deeds.
The race of Conaire the mild
Elevated the strong Gaël.

The three sons of Erc son of Eathach the prosperous,
The three who obtained the blessing of Saint Patrick,
Acquired Alban, great there strength,
Lorn, Fergus, and Angus.

Ten years Lorn with complete dominion
In the kingdom of Oirir Alban [reigned].
After Lorn (keenly the tale),
Twenty-seven years Fergus.

Domangart the son of high Fergus
Numbered five years of fierce life.
Four and twenty, without strife,
Comgall the son of Domangart.

Two gentle years, without contumely,
After Comgall to Gabhran [are assigned].
Three years, and five without division,
Was King, Conall son of Comgall.

Four years and twenty besides,
Was King, Aidan of golden swords.

[1] This is by some considered to be the same as Cruithne.

Appendix.

Deich m bliadhna fo seacht, scol n gle,
If flaithios Eochaide Buidhe.

Conchad Cerr Raithe, reil bladh,
A se deg dia mhac Ferchair.
Tareis Fherchair, feghaid rainn,
Ceithre bliadhna deag Domhnall.

Tareis Dhomhnaill bhric, na mbla,
Conall Dunghal Xm bliadhna,
XIII bliadhna Domhnaill Duinn,
Tareis Dhunghail do Chonaill.

Maolduin mc Conaill na cereach
A seacht deg dho, go dlighthech.
Ferchair fogha, legha leat,
Do chaith bliadhain ar fhichid.

Dha bliadhain Eath. na neach,
Ro ba calma an Righ Righthech.
Aon bliadhain ba flaith iar ttain,
Ainchcall maith, mac Ferchair.

Seacht m bliadhna flaith Dungal dein,
Agus a ceathar do Ailpein
Tri bliadhna Muiredh. maith,
A XXX do Aodh na ardfhlaith.

A ceathair fichiot nior fhann
Do bhliadhnaibh do chaith Domhnall,
Dha bliadhain Chonaill ceim n gle,
Sa ceathair Conall eile.

Ten years and seven by fair means
In the kingdom [was] Eocha the yellow-haired.

Conad Cerr three months, a shooting star.
Sixteen after him to his son Ferchar.
After Ferchar, by dominion of swords,
Fourteen years Donald.

After Donald brec of renown,
Conall [and] Dungall ten years.
Thirteen years, Donald duin,
After Dungall and Conall.

Maolduin, son of Conall of the booties,
Seventeen [years] to him rightfully.
Ferchar of arrows (you may read)
Reigned one and twenty years.

Two years Ethach of horses,
He was daring, the royal king.
One year was Lord of the western region
Aincheall the good, son of Ferchar.

Seven years [was] Lord, Dungall the eager.
And four years to Alpin.
Three years Muiredach the good.
Thirty to Aodh the high Lord

Four and twenty, not feeble,
Of years reigned Donald,
Two years Conall, by pure descent,
And four another Conall.

Naoi m bliadhna Chusaintin cliain,
A naoi Aonghus ar Albain.
Ceithre bliadhna Aodha ain
Sa tri deg Eoghanain.

Triocha bliadhna *Cionaoth cruaidh*,
A ceathair Domhnaill Dreachruaidh.
Triocha bliadhna con a bhrigh,
Don churaidh do Chusantin.

Dha bliadhain, ba daor a dhath,
Da bhrathair do Aodh Fhionnsgothach.
Domhnall mac Cusantin chain
Ro chaith bliadhain fo cheathair.

Cusantin, ba calma a ghleic,
Ro chaith a se is da fhichiot,
Maolcoluim ceithre bliadhna.
Indolbh a hocht Ardriaghla,

Seacht m bliadhna Dubhoda Den,
Agus a ceathar Cuilen.
A seacht fichiod os gach cloinn
Don Chionaoth mc Maolcoluim.

Seachtim bliadhna Cusantin clinn,
Agus a ceathair MacDuibh.
Triocha bliadhna breacaid rainn,
Ba Ri Monaidh Maolcoluim.

Nine years Cusantin[1] the beloved,
Nine Angus over Alban [reigned]
Four years Aodh, the honourable,
And thirteen Eoganan.

Thirty years *Kenneth the hardy*,[2]
Four Donald of the ruddy countenance,
Thirty years with strength
To the hero, to Cusantin.

Two years, his success was dearly bought,
To his brother, to Aodh the white-shielded.
Donald son of Cusantin the beloved
Reigned one year under four.

Cusantin, daring was his struggle in battle,
Reigned six and twice twenty [years]
Malcolm four years,
Indulf eight in the supreme government.

Seven years Dubhoda the eager,
And four Culen,
Seven and twenty over every clan,
To Kenneth son of Malcolm.

Seven years Cusantin in direct line,
And four the son of Duff
Thirty years of chequered portions
Was King of the mountains, Malcolm

[1] These were all Pictish Monarchs.
[2] This is Kenneth M'Alpin, the fabulous conqueror or annexer of the kingdom of the Picts, it is very important to note the very different way he is described by this authority.

Se bliadhna Donncha ghloin,
A scacht bliadhna deag mac Fionnlaoich.
Tarcis MhecBeath go m blaidh,
Seacht mis ifflaithios Lughaidh.

Malcolm a nois as Ri,
Mac Donncha datha Dreach bhui.
A re noch n fidir neach
Acht an t eolach as colach.

Da Righ for chaogad, cluine,
Go mac Donncha Dreach ruire,
Do shiol Eric ardgloin a noir,
Ghabhsad Albain, a Eolaigh

Six years Duncan the pure,
Seven years and ten the son of Finlay;
After Macbeath with renown
Seven months in the kindom, Lugaidh.

Malcolm is now the King,
Son of Duncan of the yellow countenance
His duration no one knoweth
But the knowing [one] who [alone] is knowing

Two kings and fifty (listen)
To the son of Duncan of the ruddy countenance
Of the race of Erc, high, clear in gold,
Possessed Alban (ye learned).

Act of Privy Council Directing a Levy of two Regiments of Highland Soldiers, among other Scottish Levies, for Support of the King of France 1552.[1]

AT EDINBURGH 13th Dec. 1552.

THE QUHILK DAY, Forsamekle as it was devysit statute and ordanit be the quenis grace, my Lord Gouernour and Lordis of Secreit Counsall, That thair suld be reasit of the hieland pairtis of this realme within the boundis of my Lord Huntleis lieuttenendrie tua ansaingyeiss of fittmen[2] to pass with the rest of the ansaingyeis to France to the support of the maist Cristinit Kyng of France in his weiris lyk as in the Actis and Ordinancis maid thairupoun at mair lenth is contenit; and to the effect that the said fittmen may be mair abill and substantiouslie accompturit with *Jack and plait, steillbonett, sword, bucklair, new hois and new doublett of Canvouse at the lest and slevis of plait or splenttis and ane speir of sax elne lang or thairby.* It is thocht expedient that my Lord Huntlie, schireff and Lieetennent in thay bowndis suld cause the said fittmen be reasit and that he suld be commissar in they pairtis to visie, sic, considder and roll the samyn sua that throw necklegence of lawbouris thair suld be na thing left undone that may performe the reasing of the said fittmen : Thairfore Ordanis letteres to be dereck to officieris of the quenis, schireffis in that pairt, charging thame to pass and command and

---

[1] *Registrum Secreti Concilii, Acta.*

[2] Two Ensigncies of Footmen; Ensigncy meaning as many men as followed a pair of colours; *in modern language, a Regiment.*

charge all and sindric Erlis Lordis barronnis and utheris fre halderis within the bowndis of the said Erlis Leetennentrie that thay and ilk ane of thaim bring and present thair men that thai ar to be taxt and stentit to before the said Erle schireff and Commissar deput thairto at sic day and pleace as he sall appont to thaim ilk ane efferand to his awin pairt under the pane of rebellioun and putting of thaim to Our horne and eschett and inbring all thair movabill gudis to Our Soverane Ladyis wse for thair contemptioun and sae mony personis as beis rollit and absentis tham and beis fugitive, That all sic personis be denuncit rebell and putt to the horne and all thair movabill gudis eschettit as said is Withe power to the said Erle his deputtis and officiaris to serch and seik all sic personis rebellis, tak apprehend and justifie thaim to the deid and gif ony persone or personis resettis ony sic personis rollit and fugitave as said is within thair boundis and presenttis tham nocht to the said Erle and Commissar foirsaid all sic resettaris salbe siclyk denuncit rebellis and put to the horne and all thair movabill gudis eschetit for thair contemptioun.

Act of Privy Council, ordaining a levy of Highlanders to assist the Queen of England in her wars in Ireland,[1] 1602.

AT HOLYROODHOUSE, 31ST JAN. 1602.

FORSAMEKLE as the Kingis Majesteis darrest sister THE QUENE OF ENGLAND, hauing lovinglie intreated his Maiestie for the supply and levy of some Hielandmen, for the bettir repressing of the tressonabill rebellioun intertenit aganis hir within the cuntrey of IRLAND, and assisted be a nowmer of strangearis quha intendis to mak a conqueist of that land;[2] his Majestie, alsweill in regaird of the freindschip and amitie standing betwix his Majestie and his said darrest sister, as of his awin interest, richt, and appeirance[3] to that land, he voluntarilie and willinglie condiscendit to the said supplie, and hes layed the burding of the levying of thir men upoun sic of his Majesteis subjectis within the Hielandis as ar of maist power to furneis thame, viz. upoun the Duke of Lennox tua hundreth men,

[1] *Registrum Secreti Concilij, Acta.*
[2] The Lord Deputy Mountjoy was about this time waging war in Munster, with a large force of Irish rebels, under Tyrone and O'Donnell; who were assisted by a body of Spanish auxiliaries, under Don Juan D'Aguila, a brave and experienced soldier. The Spaniards had possessed themselves of the town of Kinsale, where they were besieged by Mountjoy, whose rear was threatened by Tyrone and O'Donnell, who had advanced from Ulster on hearing of the landing of the Spaniards. It seems doubtful whether this Highland levy was actually made, or if made, whether the troops ever left Scotland to join the Lord Deputy, the war being concluded very soon after this time, by the discomfiture of the Irish, and the return of the Spaniards to their own country.
[3] The King's interest, as heir apparent to Queen Elizabeth, is here meant.

the Erle of Ergyle and Laird of Glenurquhy thrie hundreth men, the Erle of Athoill one hundreth men, the Laird of M'Gregour fyftie men, the Abbot of Inchaffray, Lairdis of Lundy and Tullibairdin for Monteith and Stratherne fyftie men, the Marques of Huntley ane hundreth men, Mackintosche ane hundreth men, the Laird of Grant ane hundreth men, the Laird of Balnagowne ane hundreth men, the Lord Lovate and Laird of Foulis ane hundreth men, the Erle of Caithness ane hundreth men, the Erle of Suthirland and M'Ky ane hundred men, Glengarry ane hundreth men, the Capitane of Clanrannald tua hundreth men, M'Conill[1] duy and M'Rannald[2] ane hundreth men, M'Kenzie ane hundreth men: And, thairfoir, his Majestie gevis power and commissioun, be thir presentis, to the personis abone-specifeit, and euerie ane of thame, to levey and lift the particular nowmeris abonespecifeit layed upoun euerie ane of thame, and to appoint and name capitanes and commanderis to thame, and to caus stryke drummis, *and to use sic utheris instrumentis as ar accustumat to be usit in thay boundis and cuntreyis*[3] for levying and takeing up of men; and in cais ony within thair boundis and cuntreyis refuisses to be lifted and to entir in this service, with power to the personis respectivé abone written to preiss thame conforme to the ordour; and, being ance enrolled, to force and compell thame to conforme thameselffis to the ordour to be prescryuit and sett down to thame:[4] And to the effect that nane of the

[1] Allan Cameron of Lochiel.
[2] Allaster Macranald, or Maedonald, of Keppoch, who is frequently styled in the records 'Laird of Macranald.'
[3] An evident allusion to the Bagpipe.
[4] This compulsory mode of recruiting was by no means uncommon in Scotland, in the reigns of James VI. and his successor.

personis quha sal be employit upoun this service tak occasioun to absent thameselffis, upoun feir to be persewit and challengit upoun ony of thair bygane misdeidis, his Maiestie, with auise of his counsall, declairis be thir presentis, that thay sal nocht be callit, chargit, troublit, nor persewit for ony thair bigane attemptis quhatsumevir, and that na sic thing sal be layed to thair charge, bot that this act sal be a sufficient warrand to thame during the haill tyme of thair being in this service, and for the space of   thaireftir.

Act of Privy Council anent Wapponshawings in the Highlands[1]
1602.

AT HOLYROODHOUSE, 31ST JANUARY, 1602.

FORSAMEKLE as albeit the Kingis Majestie and his predicessouris of guid memorie, be divers actis of Parliament statute and ordanit that WAPPONSHAWINGS sould be maid over all the pairtis of this realme twyce in the yeir, and that all his Hienes subjectis sould be armit in forme and maner prescryvit in the saidis actis: Notwithstanding, as his Majestie is informit, the saidis actis hes at na tyme ressavit executioun in the HIELAND pairtis of this realme, bot hes bene altogidder neglectit and misregnairdit, quhairthrow the inhabitantis thairof ar nowther provydit nor furnisht with armour conforme to the tennour of the saidis actis, nor yit are thay trayned up and exercised

[1] *Registrum Secreti Concilii, Acta.* This curious Act is obviously connected with the preceding. It forms a strange contrast with the numerous *pacific* Acts in James' reign against 'the beiring and wearing of hagbutts and pistollettis,' etc., and the severe penalties inflicted on the contraveners of these statutes.

in the use and handling of thair armes:¹ And his Majestie being cairfull to undirstand the trew estaite of the saidis Hielandis, and in quhat forme and maner the inhabitantis thairof ar armit; his Majestie, for this effect, hes appointit a generale mustare and wapponshawing, to be maid be thame upoun the dayis following, in presence of thair masteris, cheifes, and chiftanes of Clans underwritten: That is to say, the haill inhabitantis of the Lennox and utheris Hieland boundis perteining to the Duke of Lennox, in presence of the said Duke, or sic as he sall appoint to ressave thair musteris: The inhabitantis within the haill boundis perteining to the Erllis of Ergyle, Athole, and Menteith, and within the stewartries of Stratherne and Menteith, in presence of the said Erllis of Ergyle and Athole, or thair deputis, everic ane within thair boundis; and in presence of the Abbot of Inchaffray, the Lairdis of Tullibairdin and Lundy for Menteith and Straitherne; and all to be upon the first of March nixt to come: And that the lyke mustouris be maid upoun the same day be Allaster M'Gregour of Glenstra, of his haill Clan and surename: And that the inhabitantis within the Hieland boundis perteining to the Marques of Huntley, the Erllis of Suthirland and Caithnes, and the haill men, tennentis, servandis and dependeris, and utheris of the Clans of the Laird of Grant, M'Intoshe, Balnagowne, the Lord Lovate, the Laird of Foulis, M'Ky, Glengarrie, M'Kenzie, the Capitane of Clanronnald, M'Connill duy, and M'Rannald, be reddy to mak thair mustares and wap-

¹ These assertions sound strange, after the preambles of numerous acts of Council, in regard to complaints against the Highlanders for cattle-lifting, etc., which uniformly represent the 'brokin' men of the Highlands as equipped with almost every species of armour, offensive and defensive.

ponshawingis upoun the tent day of Marche, in presence everie ane of thame of their masteris, chiefes, and chiftanes, etc. [Then follows the usual warrant to messenger-at-arms to charge all the abovenamed Chiefs] to hald thair wapponshawingis upoun the dayis abonementionat, everie ane of thame of the haill personis of their Clannis, and of sic as ar under thair obedience and commandement: And that thai enrol the names of the haill personis quha sall mak the saidis musteris with the forme and maner of thair armour, and report the same to his Majestie, as they and ilkane of thame will answer to his Majestie and councill at thair highest charge and perrill, and under the pane contenit in the act of Parliament.[1]

The following is an extremely ancient charter of one of the earliest Bishops of Dunkeld, and as it is very curious, and connected with the place of one of the illustrations, it is here given. It is a charter of confirmation by the Bishop of other charters, namely, those of King Malcolm IV., and Andrew Bishop of Caithness, of the Church of the Holy Trinity of Dunkeld to the Abbey of Dunfermline, and the confirmation would no doubt be sought for, and obtained, very soon after King Malcolm's charter was granted; therefore, though no date is expressed, we may be sure it was between 1153 and 1165, the period of that monarch's reign. This charter was copied from the original, by the author; it is among the fine collection of charters belonging to the Advocates'

[1] If this act was ever carried into effect, some of these Muster-rolls ought still to be in existence.

Library,[1] Edinburgh, and, though at least 700 years old, is easier read than many letters written yesterday:—

DATE, 1153-1165.

Universis sancte matris ecclesie filiis.—Ricardus, Dei gratia, Duncheldensis Episcopus salutem et episcopalem benedictionem. Cum ad nostrum spectabat officium, sancte religionis cultum amplificare noscant tam posteri quam presentes me concessisse et hac mea carta confirmasse Abbati de Dunfermelin et Monachis ibidem Deo servientibus donationem Regis Malcolmi et Andree Episcopi Katenensis secundum quod corum carte testantur ecclesiam sancte trinitatis de Dunchelden et omnes terras juste ad eam pertinentes liberas et quietas ab omni exactione tam ecclesiastice quam secularis, persone, salvo episcopali jure. Concedo etiam eis conversationem in episcopatu meo, et ut Divinum exerceant officium, sub ditorum suorum curam habeant animarum et ut conversantes in diocesi mea a me quod ad Christianitatem pertineret accipiant.—Testibus Matheo Archdiacono Sancte Andree—Bricio priore de Insula—Michaele clerico-magistro Matheo, et Johane fratre suo—Roberto dapifero episcopi—Radalfo capellano, Thoma presbyterro—Murdac clerico—Abraham parvo.

Charter of Confirmation by Richard, Bishop of Dunkeld.
DATE 1153—1165.

To the whole sons of Holy Mother Church. Richard by the Grace of God Bishop of Dunkeld, Health and

[1] See Book of *Original Charters* in the Advocates' Library. Charter No. 81, of Sir James Balfour's Collection, MS. Number of Library—No. 15-1-18.

Episcopal benediction. Seeing it belonged to our office to extend the rites of holy religion let posterity, as well as the present generation know, that I have granted and by this my charter confirmed to the Abbot of Dunfermelin and the monks there serving God, the Gift of King Malcolm and of Andrew Bishop of Caithness, according as their charters testify, the Church of the Holy Trinity of Dunkeld, and all lands justly belonging to it, free and quit of all exaction by any lay or clerical person, saving the Episcopal right. I also grant to them Christian communion in my Bishopric, and that they exercise the Divine office and have the care of souls of their subjects, and that when doing duty in my diocese, they receive from me what Christianity enjoins.—Before these witnesses, Mathew Archdeacon of St Andrew's, Brice, Prior of the Island (IIy), Michael clerk, Master Mathew, and John his brother, Robert steward of the Bishop, Ralph chaplain, Thomas presbyter, Murdac clerk, and little Abraham.

Index.

A small *n* following a figure signifies the reference is to a note in the number of the page.

ABERNETHY, 180, 181, 182, 183, 336 n.
Abercurnig, or Abercorn, 62, 128.
Adomnan, 3, 20, 25, 47, 55, 111, 115, 258.
Æthelward's Chronicle, 112.
Agricola, 3, 9, 10, 12, 13, 133, 230.
Aidan, or Aodh, a Pictish prince, 67.
Alban, 1, 25, 28, 39, 55, etc., etc.
Albanach, 2, etc., etc.
Alexander I., King, 238.
Alexander II., King, 184.
Alexander III., King, 108.
Alfred, King, 80.
Alpin, father of Kenneth, 83.
Ammianus, Marcellinus, 19, 20, 22.
Andrew, St, 69.
Angles, 28, 30.
Angus, Lord of the Isles, 123.
Angus, M'Erc, 38, 44.
Angus M'Fergus, King of the Picts, 7, 65, 66, 67, 68, 69, 76, 78.
Angus, King, grandson of Angus M'Fergus, 74, 75.
Antonine, Emperor, 3, 228.
Annat, 153.
Aodh, or Hugh, King, 96, 97.
Argyll, Duke of, forces, 286.
Ardoch, or Lindum, Camp, 10.
Armstrong, Dr, Gaelic Dictionary, 230, 233 n.
Artguso, 73.

Asser, Bishop of Sherborn, 86.
Athelstane, King of the Saxons, 99.
Atholl, the Maormor of, 65.
Atholl, Royal Pictish house of, 83.
Atholl, Gaelic poem of, 225.
Atholl, Duke of, 335.
Atholl, district of, 150, 152.
Attacoti, 22
Aulaf, or Olave, King of the Isles, 101 n.

BALIOL, King, 93.
Ballymote, Book of, 60.
Balnagown, Laird of, 284.
Balnagrew, now Lude, 164, 165.
Balvaird, 137 n, 156 n.
Bede, 3, 20, 21, 26, 28, 33, 36, 37, 47, 61, 126, 127, 129.
Bel, the heathen god, 163, 169, 175, 176.
Beltane-day, 168, 169, 172, 176.
Benachony, or Benhonzie, 11 n.
Benagloe's, the five, 328.
Benledi, 175, 176, 177.
Benchrombeg, forest, 321.
Blackie, John Stuart, Esq., Professor, 205.
Bethoc, or Beatrice, Princess, wife of Crinan, 108.
Blair Atholl, 154, 163.
Boece, 4, 5, 83, 116.
Bohn, publisher, London, 86, 87, 99.

Bower, Abbot of Inchcolm, 250.
Bran, King, 75.
Brechin, Bishop of, 52 n.
Britannia, 23.
Britons, or Cimbri, 5, 6, etc.
Bruce, King Robert, 93, 108, 123, 124, 338.
Bruidhi, MacMeilchon, King of the Picts, 45, 53, 54, 143.
Brudhi, MacBili, King of the Picts, 62, 63, 64.
Brudhi, son of Angus M'Fergus, 65, 66.
Brudhi, brother of Angus M'Fergus, 70.
Brudhi, MacBargoit, King, 75.
Brunanburgh, battle of, 99.
Buchan, Alexander, Earl of, 334.
Buchanan, the historian, 4, 83, 116.
Buchanan's, badge of, 287.

CADWALLA, King of West Britons, 131.
Cæsar, 230.
Caithness, the Earl of, 284.
Caithness, Andrew, Bishop of, 39, 112 n.
Campbell of Glenurchy, Sir Duncan, 271, 272.
Caledonia, and Caledonians, 1, 2, 12, 14, etc., etc.
Cambden, 26, 193, 230.
Campbell's, badges, 287 — chieftains of, 313.
Camerons, of Lochiel, 285, badge of, 287—chieftains of, 303.
Catrail, 28, 31.
Celestine, Pope, 48.
Chalmer's, 18, 21, 26, 33, 42, 46, 51, 61, 79, 144.
Chamberlayne, historian, 254.
Chisholms, badge of, 287—chieftains of, 326.
Clach, na h' Annat, 152.
Clach-Bhrath, 156.
Clach n'iobairt, 150, 152.
Clach neart, 179 n.
Clans, the Highland, short notices of, 258.
Clan Chattan, the badges of, 288—chieftains of, 310.
Clan Rannald, 202, 294, 295.

Claudian, 16, 23, 24.
Cleland, William, Lieutenant-Colonel, 250.
Clyde, Firth of, 2.
Colgan, 56 n.
Columba, 3, 26, 53, 54, 332.
Commodus, Emperor, 18.
Comrie, 10.
Conare, or Chonare, King, 40.
Conall, a Dalriad Prince, 53, 54.
Constantius, Emperor, 15.
Constantine, Emperor, 15, 27.
Constantine, King and Martyr, 55, 56.
Constantine I., King of the Picts, 70, 72, 74.
Constantine II., son of Kenneth M'Alpin, 95, 96.
Constantine III., 97, 99, 100.
Constantinople, 69.
Corbridge-on-Tyne, battle of, 98.
Corpus Christi College, Cambridge, 87.
Crinan, Abbot of Dunkeld and Abthane of Dull, 108, 333.
Cyric, or Grig, a usurper of the Crown, 96.

DALGINROSS, or Victoria, camp of, 10, 11.
Dalriada, 31, 36, 67, 102, 103, etc.
Dalriads, 3, 7, 31, 36, 63, 65, 71, 101, 102, 104, etc.
David I., King, 238.
Deiseal, or the turn sun wise, 117.
Diarmat, Abbot, 75.
Dicaledomes, 22.
Dio, 13, 14.
Domitian, Emperor, 12.
Donald MacAlpin, King, 93, 95.
Drest, 74.
Drost, 75, 333.
Drumceat, 44.
Drummond, James, first Lord Madderty, 272.
Drummond, badge of, 287.
Dull, the Lordship of in Atholl, 108.
Dull, sculptured stone, 232.
Dumbarton, 59.
Duncan de Atholia, 338.
Duncan I., King, 108.

Dunad, in Knapdale, 66.
Dunaverty, 123.
Dunbar, 89.
Dunblane, 89.
Dunkeld, 72, 73, 90, 188, 332.
Dundee, Viscount of, 329.
Dunleven, 66.
Dungal, a Dalriad Prince, 65.
Dunnichen, battle of, 63.
Dunolly, 65.
Dunvegan Castle, Isle of Skye, 153.

EARN, river of, 10.
Edinburgh, origin of the name, 130.
Edward I., King, 173.
Edwin, King, 130, 131.
Edred, a Saxon leader, 98.
Egfrid, King of Northumbria, 62.
Eigg, island of, 58 n.
Elder, John, a Highland priest, 244.
Eochy, Fionn, 94.
Eoganan, King, 75.
Espec, Walter, a Norman baron, 237.

FARQUHARSON'S force of, 285 ; badge, 288.
Fassiefern, family of, 142 n.
Fered MacBargoit, King, 75.
Feredach, a Dalriad Prince, 66.
Fergus M'Erc, 32, 33, 37, 39, 44.
Fergusons, etc., badge of, 287.
Fingal, also Fionn, or Finn, 198, 199, 205, 209 n.
Firth of Forth, 6, 9, 10, 13.
Fithil, writer of a very ancient MS., 171.
Forbes, badge of, 287.
Fordun, 4, 5, 6, 39, 49, 56 n, 83, 116.
Forteviot, or Dunfothir, 69, 70, 93, 94.
Fortreim, Pictish territory on the Forth, 97.
Frasers, badge of, 287—Chieftains, 326.

GABURAN, grandson of Fergus M'Erc, 45.
Galdi, or Galgacus, 11, 12, 258
Gala Water, 30.
Galloway, 10, 31, 48, 115, 116.

Garvald, parish of, 120.
Gildas, 3, 20, 24, 27, 33.
Giles, Dr, translation of Asser, etc., 86, 127.
Glenco men, 250.
Glengarry, 284, 285.
Gleutilt, 123 n.
Glenturret, 11 n.
Gordons, force of the, 285—badge, 287.
Gofraig, or Godfrey, King of Inchgall, 101.
Grants, the Clan, 103.
Grant on the Gael, 229, 230.
Grants, badge of, 287—Chieftains of, 323.
Gregory, Donald, Esq., 34, 35, 79, 80 n, 101 n, 104 n.
Grenach, lands of, on Loch Tummel, 161.
Gwddel Ffichti, or Guthel Phichti, the Pictish Gael, 88.

HADRIAN, Emperor, 12.
Haldane, John of Gleneagles, 269.
Halfdene, Danish King, 87.
Halkett, S., Esq., 317 n.
Harlaw, Battle of, 256.
Henry of Huntingdon, 194, 195.
Herodian, 16.
Hibernia, 2, 10, 25.
Highland Society Report on Ossian's Poems, 105, 133 n, 140, 170.
Huntly, Earl of, 245, 282.
Huntly, George, Marquis of, 276, 284.

IDA, leader of the Angles, 44, 62, 119.
Ierne, or Hibernia, 23, 24.
Ingulph's Ancient Chronicle, 99, 112.
Innerwick, Glenlyon, and Co. Haddington, 121.
Innes, C., Esq., Professor of History, 37, 80, 81 n.
Innes, T., 5, 17, 33, 39 n, 40, 43, 77, 93, 94 n.
Iona, 53, 55, 72, 166, 168, 183.
Inver-Almond, 95.
Innermeath, 14, n.
Invermay, 14, u.
Inverury, 160.

Index.

Ireland, 3, 25.
Isidore, 25, 60.

JAMES I., King of England, 77, 84, 91, 103, 105, 141.
James II., 329.
Jarrow, on the Tyne, 127.
Jarrow, Ceolfrid, Abbot of, 180.

KENNEDY, W. N., Esq., 29, 30.
Kenneth M'Alpin, King, 76, 77, 79, 80, 86, 88, 92, 103, 105, 108, 110, 116, 117, 138, 140, 141.
Kentigern, 56, 57.
Killiecrankie, Pass of, 253, 328.
Kilchousland in Kintyre, 58 n.
Kilrymont, or St Andrews, 60.
Kinneil, 125.
Kintyre, 56, 57, 58, 77.
Kintyre, Tribe of, 64.

LAMONT, Badge of, 288—the chieftains of, 310.
Leader river, 30.
Lewis, Gaelic poem of, 227.
Liathfail, Pictish Coronation Stone, 173.
Lid, or Liddle water, 30.
Linne, Loch, 76.
Lismore, Book of the Dean, 22 n, 54 n, 60 n, 105, 141.
Logan's Scottish Gael, 61, 187, 228 n.
Lollius Urbicus, 13, 126.
Lord of the Isles, Alexander, 242.
Lorn, M'Erc, 38, 44.
Lorn, Tribe of, 64, 66.
Lorn, District of 65, 68.
Lovat, Simon, 8th Lord, 276.
Lovat, Lord, 284.
Lude, formerly Balnagrew, 164, 165, or the Druids' town, 177 n.

MACBETH, King, 111.
Macdonald, Lord, 295.
Magnus, King of Norway, 237.
Mair, or Major, 6, 241, 242.
Maitland's History, 111.
Malcolm Ceanmore, 237.
Malcolm II., King, 108.
Malcolm IV., King, 238.

Marianus of Ratisbon, 111.
Meatæ, 13 n, 14.
Melrose, 80.
Mentz, 111.
Meyrick, Dr, 238.
M'Alpine's Gaelic Dictionary, 181.
M'Allaster's, badge of, 287.
M'Aulay's, badge of, 287.
M'Bean's, badge of, 288.
M'Donald's, badge of, 287—chieftains of, 291.
M'Dougal, Lord of Lorn, 124.
M'Dougal of Dunolly, 293, 296.
M'Dougal's, badge of, 287—chieftains of, 293.
M'Farlane's, badge of, 287—chieftains of, 318.
M'Fie, or Clanduffie's, their chieftains, 305.
Murdoch M'Fie of Colonsay, 280.
M'Gregor's, the clan, 103, 104 n.
M'Gregor's, badge of, 287—chieftains of, 321.
M'Inroy, J. P., Esq., of Lude, 342.
M'Intosh, badge of, 288—chieftains of, 300, 301.
M'Intyre, the Rev. D., Kincardine, 205.
Mackay's, badge of, 287—chieftains of, 325.
M'Kenzie, the Rev. K., Borrowstonness, 124.
M'Kenzie's, badge of, 288—chieftians of, 298.
M'Kinnon's, badge of, 287—chieftains of, 306.
M'Laren's, 266.
M'Laggan, the Rev. Mr, Blair Atholl, 164.
M'Lauchlan, Archibald, of that Ilk, 280.
M'Lauchlan, the Rev. Dr Thomas, 20 n, 21 n, 38, 40 n, 43, 45 n, 48, 50 n, 82 n, 109, 114 n, 136 n, 138, 142 n, 146 n, 178, 189 n, 190, 191 n, 204, 207, 334 n.
M'Lean's, badge of, 288—chieftains of, 297.
M'Leod of Lewis, Roderick, 278.
M'Leod of Lewis, Torquil, 278.
M'Leod's, badge of, 288—chieftains of, 301.

Index. 389

M'Millan, Alexander, his cross, 239, 240.
M'Millan's, chiefs of, 319.
M'Nab's, badge of, 287—chieftains of, 306.
M'Naughtan's, badge of, 288—chieftains of, 316.
M'Neill's, badge of, 288—chieftains of, 304.
M'Pherson's, badge of, 288—chieftains of, 300, 301.
M'Pherson, translator of Ossian's Poems, 105, 202, 203.
M'Quarrie's, badge of, 287—chieftains of, 304.
M'Queen's, badge of, 288.
Menzies, James, of that ilk, or of Weem, 272.
Menzies of Culdares, 335.
Menzies, badge of, 288—chieftains of, 326.
Mochuda, 55.
Mod, or the court of justice, 161.
Mons Grampius, battle of, 12.
Moray, Sir William, of Abercairney, 247.
Moray Firth, 14, 147.
Morton, Earl of, 245.
Monzie, near Crieff, 336.
Muckross, 69, 315 n.
Munch, Professor, 335 n.
Munro's, badge of, 288—chieftains of, 319.
Murcus, Pope, 171.
Muredach, a king of the Dalriads, 66.
Murray, Sir John of Tullibardine, 271.
Murray, Sir William, of Abercairney, 247.
Muthil, Perthshire, 159.

NAPIER, MARK, Esq., 330.
Napier, Sir Archibald, of Merchiston, 269.
Nairne House, Perthshire, 159.
Nechtan, King of the Picts, 69, 180, 181, 183.
Neithe, Celtic god of the waters, 182.
Nennius, 3, 7, 85, 126, 127.
Ninian, 46, 47, 52, 62.

OBAN, 65.
Oceanus, 24.
O'Donnovan, Dr, 32, 41 n.
Ocha, Battle of, 33.
O'Flaherty, 44 n, 171.
Ogilvie, Patrick, of Inchmartin, 274.
Orcades, or Orkneys, 62, 64.
Origen, 154.
Orosius, 22, 24.
Oscar, 198, 200, 205.
Ossian, 148, 149, 151, 198, 199, 201, 202, 203, 205, 212.
Oswy, King of Northumbria, 63.

PALLADIUS, 48, 50, 51, 57.
Penda, King of Mercia, 131.
Perthshire, 12.
Petrie, Mr, an Irish writer, 174.
Picts, 2, 6, 15, etc., etc., etc.
Picts' Work, 28.
Pinkerton, 4, 5, 6, 17, 68 n, 78.
Prosper, 50.

QUEEN MARY, 331 n.

RAE, Lord, Daughter's lament, 255.
Reginald, a Danish Commander, 98.
Reeves, Dr, 20, 21 n, 24 n, 26, 33, 37, 42, 44, 45, 54, 55, 56, 58 n, 66 n, 91 n, 177 n, 309 n, 351.
Regulus, St, 69.
Reginald, King of the Isles, 294, 296.
Reuda, 34, 36.
Riley, H. T., Esq., 99.
Ritson, 16, 24, 108 n, 193.
Robert II., King, 163 n, 296.
Robert III., King, 240.
Robertson, E. William, Esq., 16, 25, 44 n, 51, 61, 63 n, 75 n, 82, 83, 88 n, 93 n, 96 n, 98 n, 99 n, 101 n, 107 n, 109 n, 194, 334 n.
Robertson, John, of Lude, 164.
Robertson, James, of Lude, 342.
Robertson, General, 342.
Robertson, Donald, of Strowan, 273.
Robertson's, badges of, 288—chieftains of, 311.
Ross's, badge of, 298 — chieftains of, 317.
Rose's, badge of.

SACHERVELL, WILLIAM, Esq., 251.

Saxon chronicle, 28, 87.
Saxons, arrival of, 28.
Schichallien, 189, 337.
Scone Palace, 159.
Scots, 2, 6, etc., etc.
Scythia, 24.
Severus, Emperor, 14.
Skene, W. F., Esq., 5 n, 18, 22, 35 n, 47 n, 54, 68 n, 69 n, 80 n, 81 n, 84 n, 88 n, 100 n, 105 n, 133 n, 143, 144 n.
Smith, the Rev. Dr, Campbeltown, 167.
Somerled, founder of the Macdonald's, 291.
Solway Firth, 12, 13, 192.
Stewart, Sir James, of Ballechin, 274.
Stewart, General, of Garth, 204 n.
Stewarts, of Appin and Garth, 326.
Stirling, Sir James, of Keir, 271.
Stone, Jerome, collector of Gaelic poetry, 218, 219, 221 n.
Stråigeth, or Ierna, camp of, 10.
Strathclyde Britons, 64, etc.
Strathearn, 10, 12, 97.
Strathgroy, 163.
Strathallan, William, Viscount of, 272.
Strathord, Perthshire, 159.
Strathspey, 104.
St Andrew, 69.
St Andrews, 5, 115.
St Paul, 109.
Strowan, the barony of, 162.
Sutherland, Christina, 204.
Sutherland's, badge of, 288—chieftains, 326.
Symachus, Pope, 32.

Tacitus, 3, 9, 10, 11, 12, 230, 236, 258.

Talorgan, brother to King Angus M'Fergus, 66.
Talorgan, Maormar of Atholl, 66.
Tay, 10, 191, 192.
Taylor, the Rev. Isaac, 186 n, 192, 332.
Taylor, John, king's poet, 246.
Tees, river, 101.
Tethys, 23.
Theodosius, 23.
Tigernach, his Annals, 40, etc., etc.
Thomas, Captain R.N., 227 n.
Thorstein, the Danish leader, 96.
Tobar na h' Annat, or, Annat's well, 154.
Toraic, or Torry island of, 65.
Trebellius, 12.
Trumwin, Bishop of Abercorn, 62.
Tuathal the Primate, 73, 333.
Tullach-Alman, or, Almond, near Perth, 62.
Tulliebelton, 168.
Tyne, river of, 13.

Uplius, Marcellus, 13.
Urquhart's, badge of, 289.
Ussher, Archbishop, 34, 154.

Valens, Emperor, 23.
Valentia, 23, 47.
Victor, Pope, 49.
Victoria, camp of, 11.
Virgil, 24.

Wade, Marshal, 328.
Wearmouth on Tyne, 127.
Whitby, 63.
Whithern, 62.
William the Lion, King, 85.
Wilson, Mr, photographer, Aberdeen, 342.
Wynton, historian, 240.

www.ingramcontent.com/pod-product-compliance
Lightning Source LLC
Chambersburg PA
CBHW030600300426
44111CB00009B/1050